Emotionally Focused Therapy with African American Couples

Emotionally Focused Therapy with African American Couples: Love Heals is an essential guide that integrates emotionally focused therapy (EFT) with cultural humility. It provides a pathbreaking, evidence-based model of couples work that reinforces the bond between partners in the face of race-based distress.

Guillory explores and brings a deep understanding of the legacy of racial trauma and the cultural strengths of African American couples by using real-life case studies. The chapters in the book focus on several key clinical issues in the field, such as communication problems, anxiety, infidelity, depression, and porn. Each case study is enhanced by a consultation with EFT master therapist Sue Johnson.

The book is an essential text for students and mental health professionals looking to provide culturally competent therapeutic interventions. It will also appeal to psychologists, mental health workers, social workers, marriage and family therapists, and religious leaders.

Paul T. Guillory, PhD, is Associate Professor in the Psychology Department at the University of California, Berkeley, USA. He is a certified supervisor and therapist of emotionally focused therapy. He is also a former chairperson of the Northern California Community of Emotionally Focused Therapy.

"This outstanding book provides therapists practicing EFT with African American couples with a deeper understanding of the cultural strengths as well as the legacy of racial trauma these couples may bring to therapy. Both experienced and new clinicians searching for ways to increase their cultural competency will be inspired by the vivid case examples as well as the discussions with Dr. Sue Johnson. This text will make a wonderful contribution to courses addressing couple and family therapy as well as diversity training in all mental health disciplines. It is a trailblazing book, and it will have a major impact on our field."

—**Nancy Boyd-Franklin, Ph.D., Distinguished Professor, Rutgers University; author of *Black Families in Therapy: Understanding the African American Experience***

"The challenges of clinicians providing culturally informed therapeutic interventions to their clients has been made a little easier today by Guillory's text. A blending of the theoretical with the pragmatic, a meshing of the thinking with the authenticity of African-centered emotional connectedness and interdependence, and a synthesizing of the historical intergenerational trauma with the contemporary challenges of Black life in America into this EFT model make this volume a must have resource for mental health providers."

—**Thomas A. Parham, Ph.D., Distinguished Psychologist, Association of Black Psychologists; Fellow, APA**

"This unique clinical volume is essential reading for therapists seeking to provide effective couple therapy to African American clients! Guillory offers a compelling challenge and illustrates a powerful path forward. The challenge is to become culturally humble by learning about the bonds of African American love in hostile environments. The path forward is to integrate a cultural lens into the empirically validated Emotionally Focused Therapy (EFT) model."

—**Lorrie Brubacher, M.Ed., EFT therapist, supervisor, and trainer; author of *Stepping into Emotionally Focused Couple Therapy: Key Ingredients of Change* (2018, Routledge)**

Emotionally Focused Therapy with African American Couples

Love Heals

Paul T. Guillory

NEW YORK AND LONDON

First published 2022
by Routledge
605 Third Avenue, New York, NY 10158

and by Routledge
2 Park Square, Milton Park, Abingdon, Oxon, OX14 4RN

Routledge is an imprint of the Taylor & Francis Group, an informa business

© 2022 Paul T. Guillory

The right of Paul T. Guillory to be identified as author of this work has been asserted by him in accordance with sections 77 and 78 of the Copyright, Designs and Patents Act 1988.

All rights reserved. No part of this book may be reprinted or reproduced or utilised in any form or by any electronic, mechanical, or other means, now known or hereafter invented, including photocopying and recording, or in any information storage or retrieval system, without permission in writing from the publishers.

Trademark notice: Product or corporate names may be trademarks or registered trademarks, and are used only for identification and explanation without intent to infringe.

Library of Congress Cataloging-in-Publication Data

A catalog record for this book has been requested

ISBN: 978-0-367-37572-0 (hbk)
ISBN: 978-0-367-37573-7 (pbk)
ISBN: 978-0-429-35512-7 (ebk)

DOI: 10.4324/9780429355127

Typeset in Times New Roman
by Apex CoVantage, LLC

Contents

Foreword vii
Acknowledgments ix
About the Contributors xi

1 **Introduction** 1
2 **Stress and Threats to African American Romantic Relationships** 15
3 **Cultural Humility and Couples Therapy** 29
4 **Love, Attachment Theory, and Emotionally Focused Couples Therapy** 57
5 **Case Study: EFT Stage One Work With Trust as Central Issue** 74
Paul T. Guillory and Case Discussion with Sue Johnson
6 **Case Study: EFT De-Escalation With Interracial Couple With Chronic Pain** 96
Paul T. Guillory and Case Discussion with Sue Johnson
7 **Case Study: EFT With One Spouse With Serious Depression** 118
Ayanna Abrams with Paul T. Guillory and Case Discussion with Sue Johnson
8 **Case Study: EFT Withdrawer Re-Engagement** 140
Yamonte Cooper with Paul T. Guillory and Case Discussion with Sue Johnson
9 **Case Study: EFT Pursuer Softening** 161
Denise Jones-Kazan with Paul T. Guillory and Case Discussion with Sue Johnson

**10 Summary: Emotionally Focused Couples
Therapy With Cultural Humility**   184

Appendix Attachment and Culture/Race-Related
Interview Questions   204
References   206
Index   213

Foreword

Ella Baker, who said that if we give them light, people will find their own way, possessed a gift for listening and—all the more striking—an understanding that her presence and attention could empower self-worth and a demand for dignity within the Black community, which faced dehumanizing racism and oppression. These abilities proved essential in her work in the formation of the U.S. civil rights movement and her unrelenting leadership of lifting others. Baker recognized that connecting to one's experience provided a starting point for change and transformation. In her words: "Oppressed people, whatever their level of formal education, have the ability to understand and interpret the world around them, to see the world for what it is, and to transform it" (Parker, 2020). In this way, her work anticipates the work of an EFT therapist to listen, to see what is, and to transform through the resilience and attachment resources in our client's world.

In *Emotionally Focused Therapy with African American Couples*, Dr. Paul T. Guillory has written a textbook that is rich with clinical vignettes, interventions, and expert consultations. This book takes us into the consulting room of EFT couples therapists who are strengthening bonds of love, healing relational wounds, and caring for the intergenerational impact of trauma. In the EFT tradition, Dr. Guillory and his EFT colleagues share with us vivid examples of EFT therapy in action. The integration of historically primed negative microaggressions into interventions creates new ground. This work is inspiring, and it informs us all about the unique experiences of African Americans and their strengths along with how to enhance and guide couples toward the resources of security and vulnerability.

Synthesizing cultural humility with an EFT viewpoint, Guillory's approach engages a cultural lens to inform the EFT process and increase the therapist's awareness and attunement to the impact of racial stress, trauma, and threats to love that shape the experience and sharing of emotion. Dr. Guillory's revisiting the narratives of slave stories with an attachment lens is invaluable lesson for us all that helps us to see both the trauma and the love bond that existed and endured among enslaved human beings. There is a wonderful challenge that runs through this volume for all therapists who work with African American couples: to appreciate both the race-based history that has impacted African American couples and the power of their love to heal their relationships and themselves.

In Emotionally Focused Therapy (EFT) the therapist works to harness the power of emotion to transform relationships, and this begins with present experience. EFT locates the emotional realities of our clients and their efforts to grow in love and agency through relationships they rely on most. Following attachment science, the EFT therapist guides partners toward greater safety, vulnerability, and belonging. For many, this journey toward healing and growth is shaped by a world that has proven unsafe, unsure, and unpredictable. Nor has it provided the basic foundation of safety necessary to build bonds of belonging and generational resources of security. Many Black couples know this struggle by heart. They know it also from history, including the impact on them of racially based violence and stress, intergenerational trauma, and systemic racism that affects their relationships and sense of self. This book is a must-read that integrates these issues into therapy. The challenge Guillory suggests is that one must ask how a therapist with little awareness of this history or the hardships it brings might see clearly the negative impact of racism on the attachment bonds of Black couples seeking their help. Moreover, how might therapists use the broader and personal history of African American couples to both see and develop confidence and competence as a clinical resource for promoting and enhancing love?

Attachment science shows us that, as a human family, we are all wired for connection and share common needs to be seen, valued, and supported by others. As an EFT community, we stand against all forms of racism and discrimination and stand in support of the Black community's desire to build safety and loving bonds. In our efforts as EFT therapists to foster secure relationships, heal trauma, and inspire growth for all in our communities, our commitment is to share our expertise and knowledge in the service of healing racial trauma, helping people value differences, and enabling them to also embrace our common humanity all the more among those facing systematic oppression. Dr. Guillory and his colleagues provide both an example and guidance in our work as an EFT community.

The International Centre of Excellence in Emotionally Focused Therapy (ICEEFT) is dedicated to developing secure, resilient individuals and successful trusting relationships between partners and within families across the globe. We are indebted to Dr. Guillory and his EFT colleagues for their wisdom and example in treating Black couples and those partners who generously shared their lives. This text shines a new light on the transforming impact of EFT for Black couples and in doing so guides therapists to better see, honor, and empower those who seek change, healing, and growth.

On behalf of the ICEEFT Board and Community
Drs. Susan Johnson and James Furrow

Acknowledgments

I offer my deepest thanks to the following:

The physicians and nurses around the world who have been working so hard over the last year during this pandemic with COVID-19, risking their lives to save their patients. And a special thanks to the health care providers at Kaiser Permanente Oakland Medical Center who literally saved my life from pneumonia a year before the pandemic—God willing, may I never again have to use a ventilator to breathe.

My twin sister, Patricia, who has held my hand from the beginning and who reminds me to give thanks and praise to God as well as to honor and give appreciation to our ancestors and family.

My sweetheart, Tracy, who shares my commitment to the healing power of black love, and has been my best friend and loving partner. She has been a continual source of inspiration, encouragement, and support. Tracy reviewed every word of this manuscript and challenged me to think through my ideas.

My daughter, Jasmine, a beacon of light and a bestselling author who continues to give me the gift of love.

My daughter, Sasha, who reminds me that love is an action and that love is the light at the end of any tunnel.

Sue Johnson, who immersed herself in a discussion about the lack of Black therapists in EFT and was open to and curious about attracting and engaging Black therapists to learn the EFT model. That ongoing discussion led to the writing of this manuscript. During the clinical work of this manuscript she also encouraged me to think about the unique impact of race in therapy and to strive toward a high standard of work. Of course, she also supported this volume, reviewing videotapes and transcripts, as well as her own contributions.

Denise Jones-Kazan, LCSW; Yamonte Cooper, EdD.; and Ayanna Abrams, PsyD., who agreed to contribute, to meet bimonthly, to present cases to each other, and to write a chapter in this manuscript. Collectively they were and remain an amazing gift to me and this effort. It should be noted that I had originally thought of having a more ethnically diverse therapists and therapists diverse in sexual orientation; I was not successful. Perhaps this can happen with another group of EFT therapists.

The Northern California Community of Emotionally Focused Therapists, who have provided a home base to learn EFT. In particular, I am grateful to Sam Jinich, Edmund Brown, Julie Hawks, Michelle Gannon, and Lorrie Brubacher.

Finally, all the Black people that I have had the pleasure of working with throughout my career. I have learned so much from my work with you. I am forever indebted; thank you. A special thanks goes to all the couples in this volume for allowing this group of clinicians to work with them and to share their therapy stories. It is our collective EFT community's hope that your work will benefit other couples of color and help to training therapists to be more effective with Black couples. I cannot thank you enough.

Extract Acknowledgments:

"The Snail and His Wife"- Peter Noble, from *Every Tongue Got to Confess* by Zora Neale Hurston. Copyright © 2001 by Vivian Hurston Bowden, Clifford J. Hurston, Jr., Edgar Hurston, Sr., Winifred Hurston Clark, Lois Hurston Gaston, Lucy Anne Hurston, and Barbara Hurston Lewis. Used by permission of HarperCollins Publishers.

"The Negro Speaks of Rivers," Copyright 1926 by Alfred A. Knopf, Inc. and renewed 1954 by Langston Hughes; from *Selected Poems* by Langston Hughes. Used by permission of Alfred A. Knopf, an imprint of the Knopf Doubleday Publishing Group, a division of Penguin Random House LLC. All rights reserved.

About the Contributors

Ayanna Abrams, PsyD, is a licensed clinical psychologist in Georgia. She is the founder of Ascension Behavioral Health and co-founder of "Not So Strong," an initiative to improve the mental health and relationships functioning of Black women though use of vulnerable storytelling. Dr. Abrams specialties include working with college-aged populations and graduate students, entrepreneur mental health, and couples counseling. She has extensive clinical experience working with people of color, specifically Black couples. Dr. Abrams also provides consultation and training for organizations, schools, churches, and hospitals. She has been featured in *The New York Times*, *Essence* magazine, and *Allure* magazine, as well as the websites MindBodyGreen, AfroPunk, Therapy for Black Girls, and Silence the Shame.

Yamonte Cooper, EdD, is Professor of Counseling at El Camino College and an adjunct professor of clinical psychology at Antioch University. He is certified as both a supervisor and therapist in EFT. Dr. Cooper is a licensed professional clinical counselor, a national certified counselor, a certified Gottman Therapist, and certified sex therapist. Dr. Cooper specializes in working with couples, trauma, sexual dysfunction, gender, and sexual identity, as well as depression and anxiety. He is author of the upcoming book *Racial Trauma and African American Men*, published by Routledge. He is a Fulbright Scholar and international educator.

Paul T. Guillory, PhD, is an associate professor at the University of California, Berkeley, in the Clinical Science Program of the Psychology Department. He has taught courses on Emotionally Focused Therapies at U.C. Berkeley. He is certified supervisor and therapist of Emotionally Focused Therapy and currently an EFT trainer-in-training. He is the former chairperson of the Northern California Community of Emotionally Focused Therapy. Dr. Guillory was the psychological consultant to the Oakland Raiders professional football team and the National Football League for 14 years. He has also been a consultant to the Sacramento Kings professional basketball team and is a selected provider for the National Basketball Players Association. Dr. Guillory served as director of the Center for Family Counseling in Oakland, CA, for ten years. He has been in private practice in Oakland, CA for over 30 years.

Sue Johnson, EdD, is the leading developer of EFT. She is Professor Emeritus of Clinical Psychology at the University of Ottawa, Ontario, Canada; Distinguished Research Professor in the Marriage and Family Therapy Program at Alliant International University in San Diego; and Director of the International Centre for Excellence in Emotionally Focused Therapy. Dr. Johnson has been appointed to the Order of Canada, one of the country's highest civilian honors. She is a recipient of the Family Psychologist of the Year Award from Division 43 of the American Psychological Association and of the Outstanding Contribution to Marriage and Family Therapy Award from the American Association for Marriage and Family Therapy, among other awards. Dr. Johnson is the author of acclaimed books for professionals, including *Emotionally Focused Therapy for Couples, Emotionally Focused Couple Therapy with Trauma Survivors*, and *Attachment Theory Sense*.

Denise Jones-Kazan, LCSW, is a psychotherapist in private practice in Oakland, CA. She has been a licensed clinical social worker since 1993. She is a certified EFT therapist and has been a board member for the Northern California Community of EFT therapists. She was the lead clinician for an intensive day treatment program for 18 years, where she worked with couples, families, and adolescents. She served on the board of directors of Family Paths, a nonprofit organization serving children and families in Oakland, CA. She has advanced training in EMDR.

1 Introduction

This is a book about couples therapy with African Americans using an attachment lens. Emotionally Focused Therapy (EFT) is an attachment-based therapy founded by Sue Johnson. While there is a cruel and harsh history of slavery, anti-Black laws, and discrimination in the American experience; there are also the stories of attachment-based bonding among Black people—human bonding even in the face of fear, rape, beatings, loss, and sure death. Centuries ago, Africans relied on their oral tradition to tell stories, and those folktales were often stories about survival of the collective tribal community. African bonding would include Bowlby's notion of attachment between dyads and with the tribal community, ancestral relations, and the presence of spirit; all these bonding relationships engaged Africans in comforting, surviving, or dying together. I suggest that many folktales like the following Africans-in-transition folktale written by the author were lost:

> Nyjahl thought to himself that he had practiced these moves so many times in training that he was confident as he first steadied his fear and then skillfully side-stepped his charging foe with his knees slightly bent. Stepping around his foe, and with all the speed and strength he could muster, he thrust his weapon forward into his target. But he was jarred awake by the pain of his chains binding his hands, feet, and neck. "I must stop dreaming," he admonished himself. "I must be in the present to see the possibilities." He was lying on his side on the hard wooden floor that reeked of urine and feces. There was no light. Most of the time, the darkness was absolute. It was unbearably hot and wet where he was confined, and breathing was difficult in the thick, vile air. But breathe he must—this was central to all his training since he was a small boy; the warrior must breathe to live and breathe to stay present! He was fighting doubt, as his body felt weak. While nothing had quite prepared him to be in his present situation, chained in the belly of this floating dungeon crossing the Atlantic Ocean, it was now his turn to face "the Beast" and call on the spirits and generations of training. "Welcome the stench," he told himself, "and stay in the moment." It was then that he noticed her—the cracks in the wood above him offered just enough of a sliver of light to see.

DOI: 10.4324/9780429355127-1

Sobonfu had been hearing the stories about the people hunters since she was a little girl. In her work as an assistant planner for the king, Dahomey, she had come to know that the old stories about the stolen people were true. There really *were* hunters of people!! While the king had been actively engaging with nearby and distant communities for typical business, he also increasingly was concerned about their mutual protection. Sobonfu's work was now largely guided by the ideas that war was being created for no apparent reason and that local communities had to be more engaged with one another. Because the larger communities often spoke different languages and had different customs, ambassadors were needed. While it was unusual for females to travel in these matters, Sobonfu had particularly unique language skills, as did her brother, but she was calmer and less likely to cause a misunderstanding. Together with a small group of ambassadors, Nyjahl and Sobonfu both had been on a mission to engage their neighbors. They were attacked so quickly that it was all a blur at this point. The long march that followed Sobonfu's capture was a blur, too. For some odd reason, it did not occur to her until the dungeon doors slammed shut behind her that she now too was stolen.

Sobonfu was only aware of her anxiety. It was an anxiety that exposed her whole body to trembles, an anxiety that disrupted all thought. It was as if her anxiety was a demon/spirit that had taken over her body. This unshakable fear had taken her to the edge of sanity and the abyss of madness. Sobonfu prayed as she had never prayed before, and she called on all holy spirits to protect and return her home. After being returned to the miserable pit from the strangely stark sunshine above, she shifted onto her right side. At that moment she heard his voice. At first, it was hard for her to focus, and she couldn't make sense of what he was saying, but something about the tone and calmness touched her. With the sound of his voice she was being drawn out of some deep dream-like nightmare. While his dialect was not her own, she understood. "Don't be afraid," "I know you!" "I've seen you at my village." Despite the dark and the difficulty of seeing anything, she could force herself to focus and make out his face and then his eyes, because they were stacked only inches apart. Nyjahl just kept saying "I know you" until he would be shouting. Finally he could see she was focused on him. And somehow, in this moment, in this place, Sobonfu found someone familiar and found her voice and her calm.

With this fable that I wrote, I am suggesting that the "Beast" the newly arrived Africans faced in the "new world" was beyond what they could have foreseen: slaves in forced labor camps far from their homeland and their families. Yet each and every African faced this horrific situation in a uniquely human way, together—again and again.

As Nyjhal and Sobonfu are below deck of the *Hannibal* bound for American shores, they and the 700 others on the vessel thought of themselves in some nightmarish predicament (half of them would die in the darkness below); while on deck, the sailors were just a tiny apart of the very profitable transatlantic trade system of profits that would be enjoyed by American and European communities. As these separate stories of slaves and their captors unfold over time, Nyjhal and Sobonfu are sold at auctions and became two human engines for the slave labor camps in the United States. As time unfolds, slave laws are created to brutally enforce their bondage, restrict their movements, and control all aspects of their lives. The Civil War would be fought, Reconstruction would be attempted and fail, and Black laws/codes would be enshrined in the South and enforced throughout the United States. These anti-Black laws, more familiarly called Jim Crow laws, again restricted all aspects of Black lives, including education, health, employment, voting, and drinking water availability. Meanwhile, Nyjhal and Sobonfu and the others on the *Hannibal* would continue to view themselves as Africans and carry with them their stories of spirit, family, customs, folklore, music, and tribal communities. Their African psychology of "we-ness" psychology would eventually be blended into the survival of the "Black tribe" as they became Americanized African slaves.

The Lost Stories of African Americans

While the institution of slavery was the "original" sin of the United States, the deeper psychological traumas that it would unleash in the United States were just as assaultive and violent. That is, the American folktales and psychological justification for greed, cultural arrogance and violence were as damaging to Blacks as slavery itself. In this regard, it is the stories of the slavers that mainly survived, continually repackaged and retold over time. As a painful result, Africans/Black Americans became synonymous with the situations forced on them—that is, captured to be slaves and then stamped as if they were created by God for such treatment; barred from any academic learning and then judged/demeaned as having inferior intelligence; post-slavery, denied employment opportunities but their joblessness would come to be viewed as confirmation of their shiftless and lazy nature; forced to live in highly restricted housing, and thus poor and high-crime areas would be proof of their ghetto character; and finally, their "non-Whiteness" would be synonymous with ugliness.

In contrast, the slave labor camps became known as plantations (where currently tours are still given of the magnificent White Southern houses and grounds, devoid of the evidence of the slave camps), and the Civil War would be cast by some as "The War of Northern Aggression" and later "The Lost Cause"—both American folktales promoting a heroic attempt to protect the "Southern way of life" (where historical reenactments of battles and monuments to Southern warriors fighting to maintain slavery continue to promote the Confederate cause). The harsh treatment of Blacks became consistent with White people's safety, fears, and values (Blackmon, 2008; Alexander, 2010).

Meanwhile, the stories of the captive Africans were mainly lost. The Africans would arrive continually, slave ship after ship, totaling 36,000 ships to American shores from 1619 to 1863 (Hannah-Jones, 2019). While most Africans were originally captured in West Africa during the transatlantic slave trade, there were many tribal communities among the captives with their own language and customs. Their human stories were effectively silenced. Who told their individual or collective stories of day-to-day living, heroism, and love? According to Ibram X. Kendi in his book *Stamped From the Beginning: The Definitive History of Racist Ideas in America*, two main theories of African people emerged out of Europeans explorers of the African continent in the 16th century. The first was that the heat had caused intimate relationship between men and beasts and that had produced a savage, inferior human/beast. The other theory was biblical and held that enslaved Africans were God-made as "revealed" in the confabulated Bible stories of the mark of Cain or Ham, that is to say, the curse of Blackness (stamped to be slaves). Thus, Africans were stamped by God to be naturally inferior, hypersexual, childlike, greedy, sneaky, and demon-natured.

These theories produced stories, plays, and books about Africans in Europe and the Americas that were presented in theaters and in storytelling that depicted the African/Black race as a beast of burden, savage by nature, and hypersexual (Blackface continues this tradition as ritualized activity seems to be a rite of passage on college campuses). These theories also held that Africans were to be feared because of their beastly savage nature and that Blacks were created by God as inferior in all aspects of humanity, created to be the lowest of servants, and thus had to be controlled and managed. These theories laid a foundation for justifying both White superiority and Black inferiority, and thus slavery, Black laws, discrimination, and racism. These stereotypes, created over 700 years ago, also found "scientific" confirmation in the "racist science" that persisted well into the 20th century.

Stereotypes Enhanced by Academic Theories

According to Robert Guthrie, there have been four major perspectives of pseudoscientific beliefs that have promoted racist stereotypes within the academic field of psychology. He suggests that theses perspectives became the basis of academic attempts to conduct research concerning African Americans. Essentially these perspectives, while they differ in some aspects of their theories, have the following idea in common: "human differences resulted from causes within people rather than environmental forces in society" (Guthrie, 1991). As a result, Americanized Africans barely out of slavery were compared to White Americans. The four perspectives include Darwin's notion of the survival of the fittest, which maintained that the best, brightest, and strongest would dominate others and the environment (Whites' superior intelligence, competency, and power). Sir Francis Galton's, *Eugenics in the United States* makes the case for the idea that human beings inherit superior genes for greatness and genius (thus Whites were destined by "genes" to be superior and beautiful and Blacks inferior and ugly—the order of life). William McDougall developed the notion of inborn and unlearned instincts that produced predictable social behavior (of course, for Africans that meant laziness, savage nature, childlike, hypersexual). Finally, Mendelian genetics suggested that genetic traits came to the individual in large units rather than through a blending of qualities. These large units were seen as composed of both physical traits, psychological qualities, and behavioral tendencies (and thus, bad/dangerous human traits came with Black skin and great/desirable traits came with White skin).

G. Stanley Hall, one of the founders of the American Psychological Association and its first president, integrated all these racist perspectives when he declared:

> No two races in history, taken as a whole, differ so much in their traits, both physical and psychic as the Caucasian and the African. The color of the skin and the crookedness of the hair are only the outward signs of the many far deeper differences, including cranial and thoracic capacity, proportions of the body, nervous system, glands, and secretions, vita sexualis, food, temperament, disposition, character, longevity, instincts, customs, emotional traits, and diseases.
>
> (Guthrie, 1991)

These pseudoscientific theories continued to be used to justify restrictive laws and enforcement of laws against African Americans and to justify the assault on the sense of self of African American people and physical assaults on their bodies. In fact, these race-based stories continued the stereotypes, folklore, and stories of the original Portuguese slavers. These stereotypes, forged in cultural arrogance, greed, and cruelty, became the foundation of racial discrimination in the United States. African Americans have countered these stereotypes and have been forced to react to them. In this relentless battle, there have been collective wins, wounds, and losses. But this is not the main story of African Americans. This part of the story is about African Americans coping with White assaultive behavior, oppression, and race-based barriers, and the impact of race-based trauma.

According to Nikole Hannah-Jones ("The 1619 Project"), the Supreme Court of the United States built this "racist science" into the law in its 1857 Dred Scott decision, "ruling that black people, whether enslaved or free, came from a 'slave' race. This made them inferior to White people and, therefore, incompatible with American democracy" (Hannah-Jones, 2019). Hannah-Jones and her colleagues conducted a comprehensive review of United States Slavery ("The 1619 Project") and its continuing legacy in American life:

> Out of slavery—and the anti-black racism it required—grew nearly everything that has truly made America exceptional: its economic might, its industrial power, its electoral system, diet and popular music, the inequities of its public health and education, its astonishing penchant for violence, its, income inequality, the example it sets for the world as a land of freedom and equality, its slang, its legal system and endemic racial fears and hatreds that continue to plague it to this day.
>
> (Hannah-Jones, 2019)

Re-viewing of African American Love and Marriage

The main stories of the silenced Africans, Americanized Africans, and African Americans would have surely been oral accounts of personal survival and the backbreaking work of building the United States. Certainly, those stories are full of traumatized human experiences attempting to make sense of their horrific predicament (loss of loved ones, chains, torment, rape, and struggle) and stories of bonding with other Africans. The historical violence is so real, present, and painful that one would have to be blind and morally corrupt to ignore it.

Yet cruelty is not the only story. The attachment stories are different. That is, Africans were captured with other Africans, were tortured with other Africans, were sold with other Africans, worked with other Africans, and lived and survived with other Africans, Americanized Africans, and African Americans (Noble, 1991). And as fully functioning human beings, they also fell in love with other Africans, engaged with other Africans, and responded to each other. Their stories would be the stories of attachment bonds (often held in spirit and mind), and perhaps would require a "re-viewing" through an attachment lens to fully reveal their hopes, spirit, desires, dreams, and loving relationships. In this regard, an attachment perspective, "we-ness," originally forged in West African culture, was adapted to American slavery and made part of American culture by African Americans. A handful of those stories will be reported here.

The stories of African American love, relationship bonding, and marriage have received scant attention in professional literature. The recent data about Black marriages is cause for concern; that is, African American divorce rates have been significantly increasing, and Black men and women are choosing in large numbers not to marry.

The literature for African Americans in psychotherapy is sparse, and yet in increasing numbers African Americans are participating in psychotherapy (relationships are also discussed in individual therapy) and in marriage counseling. While there are many threats to love and intimacy for African American couples, both historical and current, that suggest challenges to marriage (Helm & Carlson, 2013), African American couples continue to form romantic relationship, marry, and benefit from marriage bonds (Blackman, Clayton, Glenn, Malone-Colon, & Roberts, 2005). According to Blackman et al. (2005), these include economic benefits, social and familial support, and psychological well-being. Black children and adolescents particularly benefit from having married parents. A national Gallup poll (Saad, 2006) suggested that African Americans were more likely to endorse marriage as an important and positive goal. Gallup projected that 50% percent of African Americans say it is important to marry when they have a child, and 66% indicated that marriage is important when they plan to spend their lives together. Both these positions were higher percentages than in the White sample (Saad, 2006).

According to Bryant et al. (2010), marriage has a number of benefits for African American men and women. Married African Americans report significantly higher levels of global happiness when compared to non-married African

Americans, and psychological disorders are lower for married African Americans compared to those who are divorced, separated, and widowed. Finally, for African American women, marital happiness outranks work satisfactions as a predictor of global happiness. African American couples also appear to define marital happiness similar to the way European Americans couples define it: emotional responsive, supportive partner, infrequent destructive conflict, and sexual satisfaction (Oggins, Veroff, & Leber, 1993).

There has been some suggestion that major change in American society has significant impact on the institution of marriage in the United States—and for African American couples, in particular. Raley, Sweeney, and Wondra (2015) explored the growing racial and ethnic divide in United States marriage patterns and argued that there are broad changes in Americans society, in general, about family arrangements that make marriage more optional. Changes include attitudes about divorce, acceptance of premarital sex, and delaying marriage until after finishing college. In this regard, Black Americans seem to be harbingers of these social changes regarding marriage. These authors suggest that as marriage has become less imperative, and changes in the economy have empowered women as a group, socioeconomic standing has become significant in marital decisions.

Nevertheless, a significant number of Black women compared to White women are likely to never marry and to divorce if they do marry. Importantly, the authors suggest that none of the theories that have commonly been suggested for these differences fully account for racial and ethnic differences in marriages. While these theories have some value, they are insufficient to account for differences in marriages: deficit of marriageable Black men, unemployment or low earnings of Black men, or differences in educational experiences between Black men and women. While the theories remain untested, they do suggest that factors that related to the accumulation of wealth; that is, some combination of employment, earnings, and stand-alone wealth along with economic disadvantage (segregated schools and housing) have a negative impact on Black marriages.

The major economic movements that were to develop middle-class wealth in the United States from 1930 to 1970 were closed to African Americans. They were systematically prevented from participating in the New Deal after the Great Depression (employment initiatives), the national GI Bill or state-sponsored GI Bills after World War II (housing and education financing), and all the government-backed housing loans (that is, African Americans could not get government loans, banks wouldn't lend to them, and real estate agents would not sell houses to African Americans in White communities). These discriminatory practices were enormously powerful and created fundamental racial disparities in all aspects of well-being. This discrimination affected the wealth and education of African Americans, both in their view of self and in their views of significant others.

Ibram X. Kendi (2016, 2019) suggests that while 1964 marked the historic passage of the Civil Rights Act, it was mistakenly thought to have been the end of racism in America. In fact, he suggests that Civil Rights Act was merely designed to end Jim Crow/Black laws. According to Kendi, the poisonous political and social story about the Civil Rights Act was that America had defeated racism. As a result, racial disparity in wealth, income, education, housing, and employment that was largely based on 400 years of statutory, legal discrimination was largely ignored. America was now claimed to be "color blind" and racism-free. These racial disparities, however, were in 1964 still problems and continue to be problems for African Americans today—directly resulting from slavery and the Jim Crow/Black laws.

For example, in her book *The New Jim Crow*, Michelle Alexander (2010) documents the impact of mass incarceration of African American men and their male family members in the latter part of the 20th century. She documents how aggressive law enforcement and harsh penalties resulted in second-class citizenship and lack of ability to be employed for African American men. Of course, this was not new in African American history. Douglas Blackmon had previously documented in his book *Slavery by Another Name* that Jim Crow laws in the early 20th century created new Black-only laws. For example, "mischief" and "insulting gestures" would send tens of thousands of African American men to prison where they were forced to work in virtual slave camps with high death rates (dangerous mines and manufacturing) at private Southern businesses. These racial policies are directly associated with wealth disparities and relationship distress.

These wealth, income, employment, and educational disparities have a profound impact on Black marriages and families. In this regard, the old stereotypes were repackaged, but once again, they were linked to Black inferiority and character flaws. The Black family was to blame for creating a culture of deficits; characterologically, Black women were too strong, sexual, and domineering, and Black men were too criminal, weak, and lazy. Both the "shadow" of slavery and the "shadow" of Black laws/codes and current discrimination have resulted in invisible wounds of racism, internalized devaluations, assaults on sense of self, and the sense of being voiceless (Hardy & Awosan, 2019).

It should not be a surprise that after the 1970s, as African Americans were slowly integrated into the mainstream of American society, interpersonal cross-cultural experiences led to personal comparisons to majority culture men and women and their marriages. In this regard, White couples have more middle-class and working-class advantages of wealth, income, educational, and employment opportunities than African Americans within every social class. American culture, however, had been "primed" to believe and understand that these disparities were about African Americans' personal deficits—intrapsychic deficiency and competency failures along with family dysfunction and by extension, couple failings.

As couples therapists, we need to know something about this history. It has informed American political debate, policing practices, and our psychology.

These racist stereotypes that depict African American men and women as untrustworthy, dangerous, and not measuring up may be active thoughts and perceptions about self and the other. The current impact of discrimination is also potentially adding stress to the relationships of couples. This book is also about recognizing that racist ideas are ubiquitous in American life. As couples therapists, we need to be able to name this "racist priming" and its effect on the view of self and the influence on African American disconnections and love. This book is a story about African American couple therapy using Emotionally Focused Therapy. This also is a book about attempts to apply a new conception of love inspired by attachment theory to couples therapy.

An Attachment Story by Frederick Douglass

> My mother was hired out to a Mr. Stewart, who lived about twelve miles from my home. She made her journeys to see me in the night, travelling the whole distance on foot, after the performance of her day's work. She was a field hand, and a whipping is the penalty of not being in the field at sunrise, unless a slave has special permission from his or her master to the contrary—a permission which they seldom get, and one that that gives to him that gives it the proud name of being a kind master. The night and the distance were both obstacles to her visits. I do not recollect ever seeing my mother by the light of day. She was with me in the night. She would lie down with me, and get me to sleep, but long before I waked she was gone. One night I was too hungry to sleep. The friendless hungry boy, in his extreme need and when he did not dare to look for succor . . . found himself in the strong, protecting arms of a mother: a mother who was, at the moment more than a match for all his enemies. I will never forget . . . that night I learned the fact that I was not only a child, but somebody's child. The "sweet cake" my mother gave me was in the shape of a heart, with a rich, dark ring glazed upon the edge of it, I was victorious, proud; and in the morning she was gone.
>
> (*Slave Narrative,* Andrews & Gates, 2000)

SUMMARY

Damaging Definitions of Race

This overview suggests that due to the money-making imperatives of the transatlantic slave labor trade, there was a fundamental need to create and maintain a definition of race. This definition would foster the total disregard of human and religious considerations. Always embedded in the slave labor trade was a profound cultural arrogance, greed, and cruelty perpetuated by Whites. As a result, the African people were promoted as a class of "beast"—an animal species somewhere closer to ape than human. In effect, "The African Slave" and later the "Africanized" American, became the defining animal/human species suitable for manual labor, endowed only with primitive mental functioning and requiring extremely harsh management. Most importantly for the story of this book, "The Africanized American Slave" was not mentally capable of human love. As a result, this is a story of more than 400 years of enormous attachment traumas. Of course, the definition was/is an arrogant and cruel myth, but also one with culturally defining positions that have had staying power. The Blacks who survived the Middle Passage, slave labor camps, Jim Crow anti-Black laws, and the great migration did so by the grace of God and the largely untold stories of their attachment bonds.

Threats to Effective Black Couples Therapy

Attachment theory has given the field of psychology a profound way to view human development and love relationships. Attachment is a developmental model and building block of internal growth and external competency. It also provides a unique lens with which to view human bonding and even social, political, and economic history. American slavery perverted social relationships between the "slave masters' class" and the "African American forced labor class." The bonds between slave masters and African Americans were fundamentally unhealthy, cruel, assaultive, and exploitive, and were based on the definition of Blackness presented earlier. It is clear from Frederick Douglass's attachment story (excerpted earlier) that the "kind master" is an oxymoron. The structure of American society and governmental laws and policies were built around class privilege for Whites and supported in order to maintain that social and economic privilege while delegitimizing and demeaning Black agency of any type. The social and interpersonal impact of racism often entails invisible and sensitive realities.

Structural Inequities as Threats

Of course, Black slavery has been abolished, and the Black code/laws of the Jim Crow era have been rescinded, but in many ways the structural elements that supported a class of White masters/CEOs/owners/middle class and a lower class of Black people remain. Discrimination, structural and personal, is the foundation of this hierarchy. The historical impact is dynamic and continues currently, if we listen to the stories of racial discrimination of African Americans. Research consistently reveals that past and current structural discrimination has led to sustained inequalities in education, housing, health, employment, and wealth (see Chapter 2). These structural inequalities have created conditions for a higher baseline of stress, traumatically stressful experiences, and health-related disorders among African Americans.

As Joy DeGruy, PhD, suggests, the concept of racial traumatic stress as "Post-Traumatic Slave Syndrome" crystalizes the mental impact on African Americans. There should also be concepts of "post-traumatic Jim Crow syndrome," and "post-traumatic civil rights movement," and "post-traumatic post-civil rights movement". Each of these syndromes might capture racial distress caused by race-based assaults on the agency and quality of life for African Americans. These stressors have created threats to survival, self-worth, competency, and views of self as lovable. Black romantic love relationships have been and continue to be negatively impacted by these social and structural inequities, government policies, higher stress-related cumulative mental duress in each generation along with physical disorders. This has led to greater baseline stress that African Americans couples carry in their bodies, priming them for internalized racist appraisals when vulnerable and a race-based distress-cue unique to African Americans that acts as a social alarm system for racial danger passed on from generations of racial assaults (see Chapters 2 and 10).

Challenges to Couples Therapy

The process of African American couples therapy occurs within this challenging context of American society. Of course, no amount of couples therapy can solve these social, political, medical, and economic pathologies. Couples therapists can, however, understand and operate with the awareness that these cultural phenomena exist and can practice in such a way as to enhance the lives of Black couples who seek their help. How can this "lived" experience of Black Americans be integrated into therapists' work? Is it even necessary to address these issues in couples therapy? What if Black couples enter therapy with stories about their current relationships, and they also enter with the conscious or unconscious race-based stories of their own, as well as those of their parents and grandparents? Do therapists of all races also enter the therapeutic context with the mental "legacy of slavery" (and the other legacies noted earlier)?

Fundamentally, the concept of Blackness promoted by the legacy of the slave trade and adopted worldwide as the way to view Black people represents centuries of implicit racial bias. This racial attitude has a well-established American set of appraisals of cause and effect, views of competency, perceptions of criminality, sense of truths, and concepts of beauty. Is such implicit bias damaging to the therapy process (see Chapter 3)? Should therapists who would work with Black couples consider investing time and effort to understanding the concepts associated with this legacy of slavery and their own racial identity (see Helms' theory of racial identity in Chapter 2)? Should we challenge the notion of the "good enough as he or she is therapist?" That is, is the idea of just being a "good person" or "seeing the person, not race," or even simply assuming that because they are Black therapists they are good enough? Is it good enough to understand the ideas of anti-racism, or should we understand the issues beyond that? When we take in the full measure of discrimination's impact, does that mean we should seek creative ways to integrate the racial-stress impact, Black culture, and evidence-based models into couples therapy?

Emotionally Focused Couples Therapy

I suggest that with some modifications, integrating cultural humility into African American couples therapy via Emotionally Focused Couples Therapy can be effective. Cultural humility is defined here as an interpersonal stance oriented to understanding the broader historical issues of African Americans and the unique experiences of African American client(s) in therapy. This requires an understanding of the racial identity of the therapists and clients, along with a curiosity about the "lived experiences" and impact of race in the clients' lives. It involves a centering of the "lived experiences" of African Americans with respect to their attachments and their life stories from a non-superior, non-judgmental perspective of their cultural background.

While EFT was not developed with the cultural perspective of Black couples in mind, its interventions and methods are adaptable and consistent with the concept of cultural humility. EFT is founded on attachment theory and promotes and encourages emotional safety in relationships. EFT is an experiential therapy that reflects on emotional experiences, reveals patterns of interactions, and promotes the loving ideas of belonging and becoming (see Chapter 4). The essence of EFT is to promote emotional engagement and intimacy to enhance co-affect regulation, cope with emotional vulnerability, and increase the sense of worthiness of love and competency. The goal of EFT is to promote a working model of love that includes accessibility, responsiveness, and emotional engagement (see Chapter 4). The foundation of this book is that while race is not a genetic phenomenon as promoted by White pseudo-science, it is a real social one. It is a social reality with life and death consequences, and thus, with survival threats and implications. Based on that reality, EFT therapists need to modify aspects of therapy while maintaining their essential EFT attitudes, interventions, and moves (see Chapter 3 and Chapters 5 through 10).

Book Outline

Chapter 2 reviews the relevant literature about unique stressors associated with being African American. These stressors include the extra stress of daily living such as external racial assaults and microaggressions and their impact on psychological and physical health. Internalized racism, race distress cues, and racial identity development are injuries to, and adaptive consequences of, African American life.

Chapter 3 offers a review of relevant literature regarding cultural considerations in therapy. An EFT consultation case is revisited with cultural humility considered.

Chapter 4 is an overview of Emotionally Focused Couples Therapy; attachment theory; the EFT working model of love, accessibility, responsiveness, and emotional engagement; and their relevance for Black couples.

Chapters 5 through 9 provide clinical examples of actual cases. Each chapter offers a "deep dive" into Black EFT therapists integrating an evidence-based method of couples therapy, EFT, with cultural humility.

Stage-One EFT Couples Therapy

De-Escalation

Chapters 5 and 6 are examples of the stage-one de-escalation phase of EFT work. In chapter 5, a Black couple struggles with their negative cycle that can become highly escalated in very racially destructive ways. Both partners' histories seem to foster an allergic reaction to vulnerable feelings. Paul T. Guillory, PhD, is the Certified EFT therapist and supervisor and an EFT trainer-in-training.

Chapter 6 presents an interracial couple experiencing enormous stress due to the medical condition of the Black male partner; both partners have childhood trauma histories. The COVID-19 pandemic adds an additional layer of fear to their cycle of disconnection and conflicts. Paul T. Guillory, PhD.

Chapter 7 provides an example of couples work with a depressed husband and an anxiously attached wife. Their sexual intimacy is challenged by his depression and overwhelming sense of responsibility and by her religious beliefs. As their couples therapy advances, they have an intimate conversation about their sex life. Ayanna Abrams, PhD, is an EFT pre-certification therapist.

Stage-Two EFT Couples Therapy

Withdrawer Re-Engagement

Chapters 8 and 9 are examples of stage-two EFT couples therapy. Chapter 8 presents a withdrawer re-engagement. Both partners have trauma histories and family histories significantly impacted by racial economic and social inequalities. The withdrawer discusses his fears about building a family legacy. Yamonte Cooper, EdD, is the EFT Certified Therapist and Supervisor.

Pursuer Softening

Lastly, Chapter 9 offers an example of pursuer softening. The intense negative cycle is very confusing for a deeply introverted withdrawer and a highly anxious critical pursuer. Both partners make significant gains in getting in touch with their feelings and expressing them to each other. Denise Jones-Kazan, LCSW is the EFT Certified Therapist.

Summary and Recommendations

Finally, Chapter 10 offers a summary, including the implications of the literature and suggestions for utilizing EFT with Black couples.

2 Stress and Threats to African American Romantic Relationships

The attachment story of Mary A. Bell:

> I so often think of de hard times my parents had in their slave days, more than I feel my own hard times, because my father was not allowed to come to see my mother but two nights a week. Dat was Wednesday and Saturday. So often he came home all bloody from beatings his old nigger overseer would give him. My mother would take those bloody clothes off of him, bathe de sore places and grease them good and wash hand iron his clothes, so he could go back clean... (her father never stopped trying to escape).... I married at de age of twenty-one and was de mother of seven children, but only have two living. My son's full name is William A. Bell. He is enlisted in de army in the Philippine Islands. I love army men, my father, husband, and son were all army men. I love a man who will fight for his rights, and any person that wants to be something.
>
> (*Voices From Slavery,* Yetman, 2000)

This brief excerpt from Mary A. Bell's slave narrative is a reflection of an 85-year-old African American woman talking to an interviewer about her life during slavery. Her admiration for her father's repeated attempts to escape, her mother's loving care, and her mother's focus on his survival; that is, getting him ready for the mandatory work in the fields the next morning. Mary Bell's narrative is rich with attachment love and admiration along with racial threats to her family's survival.

This is one example of the richness of slave narratives that chronicle African American life during slavery. There were a number of historical projects conducted during the 1930s to interview ex-slaves about their life experiences as slaves. While the focus of the slave narratives was to document the lives of slaves, the main focus was to provide accounts of their backbreaking work and the cruelty they faced, not attachment bonds. In this regard, while the attachment stories are embedded in the accounts, they are easily missed, but they actually jump off the page when one uses an attachment lens. Of course, there had been both autobiographies and ex-slaves' reports prior to and immediately after the Civil War. During the "Jim Crow" era, however, there were major attempts by Southern academic writers to recast slavery into a kinder, benevolent, and

DOI: 10.4324/9780429355127-2

merciful light, but of course this was done from an exceedingly White supremist perspective (Phillips, 1928).

Coping with enormous stressful circumstances and situations has been the hallmark of the African American experience historically and currently. The slave stories, the stories of African Americans living as second-class citizen under Jim Crow/Black codes, and current-day racism and discrimination involve uniquely stressful situations. As Lazarus and Folkman (1984) have suggested, the experience of stress is a unique experience of each individual, and thus there is diversity of experiences of the same stressful event. Lazarus defined the stressful experience as a perceived stressful event and the person's cognitive appraisal as to whether the event is a challenge/threat or a manageable event they have the ability to cope with. Coping is defined as either the practical or social/psychological resources that a person can bring to bear to respond to the stressful experience. There are essentially two cognitive appraisals: the first is the initial signal appraisal, which is significantly influenced by the emotions triggered by the stressful event (this is the alarm reaction), and the second is a cognitive reappraisal, which involves some measure of reflection of the coping options available. In this regard, slavery was a stressfully traumatizing circumstance, Jim Crow/Black codes were stressfully traumatizing circumstances, and current-day racism and discrimination can sometimes be a traumatizing and often stressful experience. While the range of African American coping strategies (with situations that could not be changed) is beyond the scope of this book, I am arguing in this book is that loving relationships have been a significant coping option through the centuries.

The Special Race-Based Stress of African American Couples

External Stressors and Injuries

Fundamentally, racial trauma, and/or race-based stress, is violence targeted at the self-worth and physical safety of African Americans. Race-based trauma is a psychological injury resulting from this assault on Black couples' positive view of self and significant other (Alvarez, Liang, & Neville, 2016; Comas-Diaz, Hall, Neville, & Kazak, 2019). Carter (2007) suggested that racism is not simply an internal attitude of White people; it is similar to assaultive behavior that causes emotional injuries in targeted people of color. According to Carter, racial trauma results from some action/behavior/event targeting a person of color and causing psychological pain to their sense of self. The event occurs suddenly, without warning, and is experienced as uncontrollable.

Recently there has been a growing body of research about the impact of racial discrimination on the well-being and mental health of African Americans. Racial discrimination has been linked to traumatic stress, PTSD symptoms, depression, generalized anxiety disorder, hypertension, strokes, heart disease, substance abuse, sleep/fatigue problems, and relationship aggression (Comas-Diaz et al., 2019; Nadal, 2018; Sibrava et al., 2019; Hunter, & Schmidt, 2010; Fuller-Rowell et al., 2017; Hill et al., 2017; Chou, Asnaani, & Hofmann, 2012; Pieterse, Neville, Todd, & Carter, 2019; Dolezsar, McGrath, Herzig, & Miller, 2014; Thomas, Bardwell, Ancoli-Israel, & Dimsdale, 2006). In couple relationships, racism-based stress, is thought to amplify felt tension and conflicts between African American couples (Bryant, Wickrama, Bolland, Bryant, Cutrona, & Stanik, 2010; Lavner, Barton, Bryant, & Beach, 2018; Kogan, Yu, & Brown, 2016; Kelly & Floyd, 2001; Boyd-Franklin, Kelly, & Durham, 2008). This research suggests that the physical, emotional, mental health, and relationship cost to African Americans is high (Alvarez, Liang, & Neville, 2016).

African Americans experience a lifetime of exposure to these race-based events that can be interpersonal (direct experiences) or structural (indirect experiences). These events have included racial harassment (hostility; physical attacks; teasing; belittling; ridiculing; mocking; joking, including stereotyping); racial discrimination (avoidance of interactions, rules, regulations, or costs that impact education, housing, and employment); and discriminatory harassment (aversive hostility, procedures, and practices that exclude, neglect, or deny opportunities (Carter, 2007; Aponte & Wohl, 2000). The primary reactions to race-based trauma comprising interpersonal events include intrusive memories, emotional arousal, and avoidance behavior. The core reactions to structural race-based stress can also lead to trauma-like symptoms promoting depression and anxiety. The impact of external race-based stress/trauma on African American couples has not been investigated, yet it is reasonable to suggest that it represents a major threat to intimacy in African American couples (Helm & Carlson, 2013).

Race-based stress adds an additional burden to the experience of Black Americans. All couples cope with the stressors of daily living and the unique developmental stressor each partner experiences from their individual background. These combined stressors amplify the potential for conflict in African American couples (Boyd-Franklin et al., 2008). Race-related stress appears to influence the "felt intensity" of stressful experiences. As racism has become interwoven into American culture, it has had a developmental influence on Black families systemically and in Black individuals intra-psychically. In this regard, racist-based events challenge the internal working model of self and other originally developed in the family. Thus, African American internalized working models of interpersonal fairness, responsiveness, and predictability have to adapt to the harsh American reality of racism. (Gramham, West, Martinez, & Roemer, 2016; Aponte & Wohl, 2000; Carter, 2007).

Internal Stressors and Injuries

Internalized racism is a by-product of race-based trauma that threatens one's working model of self and others of the same race (Speight, 2007; Pyke, 2010). Gramham et al. (2016) showed that internalized racism mediated the relationship between the impact of racist events and anxious arousal and stress-related symptoms. That is, the greater the internalized racism, the greater the felt anxiety and distress associated with race-based stress. In addition, Gramham et al. reported that when Black women endorsed strong beliefs in internalized negative racial stereotypes, their partners reported limited relationship trust. According to Kelly and Floyd, when African American men strongly endorsed Afrocentricity and internalized negative racial stereotypes, low levels of relationship satisfaction resulted (Kelly & Floyd, 2001). Chae, Lincoln, and Jackson (2011) reported in a large national survey of Black American life found a strong positive association between serious psychological distress and reported experiences of discrimination. High positive racial group identification, however, buffered the negative effects of moderate levels of racially perceived discrimination (Chae et al., 2011). Experiences of discrimination were positively associated with psychological aggression in African American men and women, as well as increased relationship instability in men (Lavner et al., 2018).

Pinderhughes (1982) suggested that African American couples can be understood by the influences of comingling values systems and behaviors that emerged out of the context of African American experiences: residuals of African values, American values, and values of the victim system. These came to represent profound differences in worldview and behavior. According to Pinderhughes, this diversity of values can be multilayered both within the intrapsychic experience of a person as well as in the diversity between different African American people. Residual African values are the psychology of "we-ness," that as a collective we are all in this universe/environment together. In the historic African view, spirituality is all "live force" within and between us, and we are spiritually integrated as one whole. The values include sharing, affiliation, obedience to authority, spirituality, family, and respect for the elderly and the past. Currently, this view has given rise to the Afrocentric perspective in scholarly writing about African Americans.

The victim system is a complex set of values that recognizes the oppressive history and the current racist restriction of American life with regard to wealth and education. Within this value system, the value of a collective perspective of African culture for the common good is rejected; here, the notion is survival by whatever means necessary. The basic notion here is that the system of wealth and education is rigged against African Americans, and therefore the person has to play by a different set of rules than that of the majority culture. Behaviors might include finding advantage in situations and with people and taking advantage—for self-maintenance and survival—regardless of harm caused, laws, or circumstances. American values promote individualism, independence, ownership of home, businesses, materials, mastery, and an orientation toward the future. American values also include education, hard work, and social advancement. The victim-system behaviors are alien to the traditional American middle-class perspective of engaging. Acculturation to middle-class values has largely been seen by African Americans as a fight for human status and later for civil rights. The driving notion here was showing the majority culture that many African

Americans share its worldview and were competent to participate in education, employment, and housing opportunities.

Consistent with the victim's values and behavior, Degruy (2005) coined the concept of Post-Trauma Slave Syndrome to refer to traumatic stress injuries experienced during the cruelty of slavery and the terrorizing of African American people during the Jim Crow era, which included lynching, sexual assaults, and neighborhood-destroying arson attacks. She suggest that this violence present in the history of African Americans has caused enduring challenges to African Americans in the form of negative views of self-worth, reactive expressions of anger, and the difficulty in socialization of African American children within the racist American social context. Similarly, residual effects of slavery (Wilkins, Whiting, & Watson, 2013) suggest that the intergenerational transmission of trauma, challenged self-concepts, anger, and inferiority of social status along with continual oppression contributed to psychological injuries.

The impact of the history of slavery has also been researched from a different point of view: the residual impact on White communities. Acharya, Blackwell, and Sen (2018) in their book *Deep Roots* studied the residual effects of slavery from the Southern White perspective. Their study suggests that slavery still shapes Southern politics and negative attitudes about African Americans. In this regard, their study suggests that current conservative attitudes and anti-Black ideas are more significantly associated with the large concentrations of slave labor camps in 1860 than any current political issues of the present day. In this regard, the authors suggest that an intergenerational transmission of anti-Black attitudes and cruelty took place, from grandparents to parents, and then to their children. These persistent anti-Black attitudes may account for the microaggression and discrimination experiences targeting Black people that African Americans report today.

Attachment Story of Delia Garlic

> SLAVERY DAYS WAS HELL . . . babies was snatched from deir mother's breast and sold to speculators. Chillens was separated from sisters and brothers and never saw each agains. 'Course dey cry. You think they not cry when dey was sold like cattle? I could tell you about all day, but even den you couldn't guess de awfulness of it.
>
> (*Voices from Slavery*, Yetman, 2000)

Racial Identity and Working Models of Self

Helms (1995) offered the most compelling model for the view of self, held by people of color as part of the minority culture. She suggested that people of color dynamically move through four stages of racial identity. Her model speaks to the diversity of African Americans' view of self and others. In this regard, there is diversity within group identification and diversity of views regarding the majority culture. While the implication of this diversity will be discussed later, this diversity informs appraisal of race-based stressful events. Racial identity is defined as the awareness of self as a member of a race/ethnicity that has a uniquely minority status. It involves a dual focus on the view of self and on membership in the group. Racial identity informs the appraisal of race-based stress and the coping options available.

According to Helms, racial identity awareness involves four nonlinear stages and can be influenced by circumstances and experiences. These stages are conformity, dissonance, immersion/emersion, and internalization.

The stages involve working models of self as a person of color in relationship to others within their ethnic group and to the majority culture. While attachment styles or strategies emerge from close day-to-day interactions and engagements, racial identity emerges due to one's "minority status" and the necessary engagement and interactions from a potentially hostile majority cultural environment. Helms's stages are similar to the notion of attachment styles or strategies or a person's tendency to respond in minority and majority culture interactions. Attachment literature, however, posits that the vulnerability "cue" or moment signaling vulnerability is embedded within the interactive experience; the moment matters because attachment is central. That "moment" is as central to EFT couples therapy tracking as it was to Richard Lazarus's model of stress and coping (Lazarus & Folkman, 1984). That is, it is a race-based stress moment to be explored for coping behavior, emotions, and thoughts as well as adaptive impact.

In this respect, Helms's stage model also provides a framework for exploring the stress and coping moment-to-moment emotional, cognitive, and behavioral strategies of people of color dealing with race-based events. Race-based trauma occurs when much is at stake in the moment, including personal safety, and in cases of racial mocking in front of significant others, microaggressions from an esteemed professor/supervisor, or being ignored when attention matters. Moreover, while no literature links attachment strategies to ethnic identity stages or coping, the following is suggested based on attachment theory, stress and coping research, and race-based stress of a "minority status."

1. The conformity stage (or moment) occurs when persons of color devalue their own ethnic/racial group and emulate and value White standards and norms. In other words, they internalize negative stereotypes, project negative stereotypes to others in their ethnic/racial group, and maintain an overly positive view of Whites. At this stage, it is likely that people of color are insecurely attached due to their developmental experiences with caregivers. When faced with a race-based stressful encounter with a majority person, they are fearful of their perceived competence, power, and authority. This fear is felt as vulnerability and a danger to their safety and self-worth. They protect themselves from minority status anxiety by self-blaming and linking their distress to the larger perceived failing of their racial group. In addition, they hope to be seen as "safe" and "different" by the majority. As a group,

they anxiously avoid discussions about race matters and highly critical of self and others in their ethnic group. They feel shame about themselves and race-related matters. They are anxiously preoccupied and seek approval and safety from majority people.

2. The dissonance stage is characterized by persons of color becoming aware of their ethnic/racial identity and what it means to be a member of a group negatively defined by society. (It is a transition period fraught with mixed feelings and a conflicted view of self. There are also associations with their negatively viewed ethnic group and with values and perspectives of majority/White culture.) They are filled with self-doubt about whether or not they have value. They are conflicted about race-based events and insecure around people in their own ethnicity as well as majority people. They also tend to avoid any discussions about race. They are likely insecurely attached, with elements of avoidance, and they are anxiously preoccupied with appraising signs and symptoms of race-based matters. When confronted with a race-based, stressful event, they are likely fearfully anxious about their vulnerability (and their dread of the negative stereotypes applying to self) and the dread of perceiving a majority person as competent, powerful, and authoritative. They protect themselves from minority-status anxiety by being vigilant around majority people and preoccupied with hints of race matters in the social environment.

3. The immersion/emersion stage is described as persons who view a commitment to their ethnic/race as positive and can totally reject White standards, values, and individuals. This can involve blaming all ethnic group problems on racism. This stage likely includes people who use avoidance and dismissive strategies to manage their view of themselves and others. They manage their view of people of color and themselves as rigidly positive, and those of the majority culture as rigidly negative. This rigidity protects their view of self from minority-status anxiety and provides clear prescriptions about behavioral responses to race-based events. Individuals in this stage are more likely to overlook people of color acting badly and to dismiss majority-culture people acting well.

4. The internalization stage is described as persons of color maintaining a positive view of self and ethnic group and possessing the capacity to use internal standards to objectively define oneself and White individuals. This is a balanced, flexible, and complex view of their racial identity and that of majority people. These people have the capacity to step back emotionally from their experience of race-based events, maintaining the ability of meta-reflection (Fosha, 2003) on the situation and the people involved. This ability to take a step back emotionally and have the ability of meta-reflection is a hallmark of securely attached people (Fosha, 2003).

Research using the Helms stages as a model of racial identity focus has produced mixed results regarding romantic relationships (Kelly & Floyd, 2001, 2006). In this regard, it has largely been used as a static stage model of general behavioral tendencies. Perham (2000) extension is the concept of racial identity to a lifespan developmental task, and thus expanding the concept beyond a static categorical stage model. These stages could also be a way of understanding specific behavioral reactions to race-based situations, and thus stages could be viewed more dynamically as a way of race-based coping strategies. This dynamic view of race-based coping with behavioral tendencies might help in examining African American couples' differences in coping with race-based experiences, internalized racism, and amplified conflict and the felt sense of closeness and distance in relationships.

Strengths of African Americans Attachment Bonds

> I never see how my mammy stand such hard work. She stand up for her chillen though. De old overseer he hate my mammy, 'cause she fight him for beatin' her chillen. Why she get more whippin' for dat dn anythin' else. . . . Every night she pray for de Lord to get her and her chillen out of de place. One day she plowin' in the field. All suden like she let out big yell. Den she start signin' and a-shoutin' and a-woopin' and a-hollerin'. Den it seem she plow all de harder. Master told her "you think we put you out in the fields to just whoop and yell? No siree, we put you out there to work . . . else we get de overseer to cowhide you old black back.' My mammy just grin . . . and say "I'se been saved. De Lord done tell me I'se saved. Now I know de Lord will show me de way . . . no matter how much you all done beat me and my chillen de Lord will show me de way.
>
> (*Voices from Slavery,* Yetman, 2000)

"The 1619 Project" (2019) documents the hard and exhausting work of slaves that were driven by several factors, including normal farm market factors, the particular factors of the harvest process, leveraging assets for loans (slave numbers), and stock market vicissitudes. The combined impact of these factors would mean more harsh treatment and extremely long work days for working slaves. The account of Fannie Moore, just presented as an excerpt from *Voices from Slavery*, describes her mother's work ethic, which would be mirrored by later reports of the orientation toward hard work by Black women during the Jim Crow/Black codes era (Valk & Brown, 2011) and by Black men and women (Hill, 1972, 1993; Boyd-Franklin, 2003). Of course, slavery forced Black women to work alongside men in the fields; West African women also worked alongside African men in the fields, and their tribal communities had more of a collective view of the work roles and childcare of men and women.

Fannie Moore's mother's strong belief in the power of God to eventually save her and her children from bondage reflects the assimilation of an African understanding of spirituality and its accommodation to the Western Christian belief in Jesus Christ as savior and protector. According to Nobles (1991), the West African beliefs of spirituality were an integral part of life, work, and relationship among American slaves. According to Boyd-Franklin (2003), spirituality is deeply interwoven into African American psychology, and this accounts for the large percentage of African Americans who continue to make spirituality central in their lives.

While it is well understood that families were broken up and sometimes destroyed during slavery, what is not appreciated is the strength of the attachment bonds that remained connected between the hearts and souls of the enslaved people. Clearly, Fannie Moore's mom and many other slave mothers fought for their children, brothers, and husbands. In her case and surely in others, they risked their lives. As family members were sold off, they found ways to discover where they might have gone. As slavery ended, many searched for their loved ones. These family bonds would also extend to non-related ken as Black women mothered each other's children during and after slavery (Boyd-Franklin, 2003).

SUMMARY

STRESS AND AFRICAN AMERICANS

Stress and Adaption

Richard Lazarus (2006), reflected on his research on stress and coping, saying that he has essentially focused on adaptability—one's ability to adapt, learn, and even grow from stressful events. Americanized Black slaves adapted to the social conditions of slavery. That social context offered them no agency or protection from the consequences of White violence. Adaptability in that social arrangement meant knowing the rules, rules that only protected White people. It also meant vigilant alertness for the danger signals of White people—their emotional whims, their displeasure, their anger, and even their excitement.

The Jim Crow era (approximately 1865–1965) was also an extremely dangerous time to be Black in America. Of course, Black people adapted, focusing attention on White people and their danger signals. Stress-provoking danger signals could be any emotional expression of a White person. Even a sign of interest, attraction, and, of course, signs of meanness might trigger a fear of being sold away or assaulted. This period of American history was so dangerous and unpredictable for African Americans that it led to the greatest migration in human history not caused by war. While the North offered some relief from racial violence and possible job opportunities, there were also harsh discriminatory practices in employment, housing, and schools that continue to exist today. The health disparities currently highlighted due to COVID-19 also dramatically impact segregated African American communities and increase the visibility of the health vulnerabilities associated with racism.

Racial Danger Alarm Signal

DeGruy (2005) has suggested that we consider "Post-Traumatic Slave Syndrome" an enduring legacy of psychological injury from slavery. I am suggesting that there is another adaptive feature of American slavery and the Jim Crow anti-Black laws/codes: an alertness for, and an alarm signal warning about, White racial assaultive behavior. This racial-based alarm signal is an adaptive distress cue that emerged over generations to cope with White violence and unpredictability. The race distress cue is a stress alert that triggers an initial appraisal of danger in a social situation. Consistent with Lazarus's model of stress and coping, a subsequent reappraisal (that occurs within seconds) is an assessment of whether the event/situation is a threat or a challenge. This reappraisal is based on the coping resources available. Compared to White Americans, African Americans have not had the full range of coping responses available to them for race-based violence or events. Assertive responses for fairness traditionally have been met with hostility and aggression. As a result, the primary sources of coping have included managing the extra baseline of stress, race-based alarm triggers, helplessness, social support from other Black people, and close family relationships.

Higher Baseline Stress

Research on African Americans shows the negative impact of discrimination on nearly every aspect of their lives. Physical and mental disorders along with marital stress are some effects of discrimination on the lives of African Americans. Studies of Posttraumatic Stress Disorder (PTSD) in the African American community are particularly disturbing, as they show that this disorder has been resistant to typical interventions of psychotherapy and medication.

This stress research further suggests that African Americans have an increased baseline of stress that has led to a higher intensity of personal conflicts, and thus, a negative impact on the overall quality of African American romantic relationships. It is likely that the interplay of greater baseline stress, personal trauma histories, and the racial distress cue (activated with race-based events and discrimination bias) accounts for the intensity of disconnections in Black romantic relationships and the resistance of PTSD symptoms to standard interventions. These factors, coupled with limited coping strategies, increase the emotional burden on Black relationships to manage the negative feelings engendered by race-based events and the resulting sense of helplessness and distress.

Internalized Racism

Internalized racism is a unique psychological injury caused by racist ideas that are promoted and encouraged by social laws and government policies. It has been linked to increased anxiety, harmful self-doubt, and interpersonal distrust. Internalized racism is the felt sense of low self-worth and disturbing doubt about one's competency. It is insidious, particularly in moments of vulnerability, uncertainty, threat, or challenge. In effect, it is the infusion of 400 years of propaganda of Black inferiority into a moment of insecurity. It is the successful racial priming of negative self-appraisals and negative appraisals of other Black people. This race priming increases shame and fear internally and increases irritability and aggression interpersonally.

Racial Identity

Racial identity, as a dynamic concept, represents the intersection of race-based events, perceptions, behaviors, and racial distress cues. It is a framework for exploring the moment-to-moment emotional responses of African Americans adapting to race-based events. The static model originally developed by Cross, Parham, and Helms (1991) and expanded by Helms (1990, 1995) presents a continuum from the conformity stage to the internalization stage. Conformity is when the individual devalues Blackness and internalizes racism as the predominant self-view. On the other end of the spectrum, the internalization stage is a balanced view of race and positive view of self and others. Black racial identity is developed in social engagements with the majority culture. Of course, White racial identity is mainly developed in White communities and sometimes with limited engagements with people of color.

Interpersonal racial identity relates to the active engagement of self and others involving emotions, perceptions, and behaviors. A dynamic model of interpersonal engagement, racial identity provides a base for the view of self and perceptions of others. In this regard and similar to attachment theory, racial identity can have an emotionally secure or insecure base. The insecure base is characterized by anxiety and fear, with troubling doubts about internalized racism. Toward the middle continuum of racial identity are Black people who take a more active stance against the majority culture but with a more rigid personal definition of Blackness such as with Afrocentrism, with the victim/street system (see section "Internal Stressors and Injuries" in this chapter), or with specific beliefs about Black men or women (e.g., Strong Black Women or John Henryism). These views represent very different orientations to racial identity. The issues in the midrange are not the orientations per se but the rigidity of racial beliefs, the view of self and others, emotional engagement, and coping behaviors. On the secure end of the continuum, there is a positive view of self and other African Americans. Moreover, there is a balanced, flexible, and complex view of racial identity and majority culture. There is an ability of meta-reflection (Fosha, 2003) on race-based events and the people involved. On this end of the spectrum, flexibility and adaptability to race-based events constitute a secure base for coping.

Working Model of Stress, Racial Identity, and Attachment

The working model of racial identity and attachment theory involves distress cues with appraisals of danger and reappraisals for safety. Of course, when there is no perceived threat to attachment bonds, attachment alarm signals are not activated. Similarly, when there is no race-based threat in the interpersonal area, there are no alarm signals involving race. Anxiety can come from insecurity in one or both areas without a specific external trigger. Just as insecure attachments can generate anxiety from self-appraisals of unlovability, insecure racial identity can generate self-appraisals of low self-worth, perceived unattractiveness, and threats to competency.

Not all attachment or racial identity threats have the same depth of fear, challenge, or meaning. In this regard, the attachment and racial identity systems can operate independently or jointly. For example, "I am lovable, but compared to those White guys at work, I'm inferior." Or "I don't deserve my wife, but compared to others, I'm a competent student." Or, when they are both operating together, "I am lovable and I am a wonderful, beautiful, competent Black woman." These distinctions are important, complex, and a function of the social context of Black life. This is important because race-based events are assaultive to Black bodies, self-worth, and competency. Race-based stress events can range from milder microaggressions, such as bullying, racist jokes, demeaning comments about Black women or Black men, to the extremely harmful, involving employment and housing discrimination, under-prescribed pain medication to a Black person, being falsely arrested or detained by police, being physically attacked or tortured, resulting in murder.

Case Example

For the impacted Black person or partner in a romantic relationship, the recovery needs will vary from brief and small to enduring and larger, depending on the intensity, duration, and frequency of race-based events. In some circumstances, this places a greater burden on the couple's relationship—particularly when the race-based event involved a sense of helplessness, such that the aftermath to the injured partner is hurt fueled by intense feelings. One couple's recent experience follows.

Kathy worked for a boss she described as overtly racist. One morning, her boss said that Kathy should be "grateful" that she allowed her to work at the firm and told her to stop complaining that her salary was less than her White counterparts. Kathy was "stung," felt trapped and helpless in the moment, and uncharacteristically went quietly back to work but fumed inside the rest of the day. When she finally got home, her husband Chris reported, "She came rushing through the door and was just so angry, and she launched right into the story. I didn't know what to say, so I just listened. It just seemed so clear to me that she should just quit, but when I said that, she came at me. All that anger was directed at me. So I stopped saying anything. She worked there for a few more years before she finally quit."

This was a source of repeated distress and disconnection for this couple. Their disconnections were based on continual reminders of discrimination that evoked intense emotional reactions to racial stress and Kathy's needs to express her hurt and rage. Many situations might involve a one-time racially traumatic event that still would be processed as described below, consistent with how EFT therapists process attachment distress. In Kathy's case, however, the reminders increased her need for validation and an enormous amount of emotional support. This moment in their couples therapy suggested that we needed to revisit this race-based incident, their racial identity, and their attachment disconnection. First, conceptually it would mean unpacking a race-based emotional experience and an attachment disconnection (see Chapters 3 and 4). Second, a willingness to unpack the open emotional wound from a race-based event was important so that Kathy's experience made sense to her. As her emotions are assembled—drilling down—it was her boss' "joyful sadistic look" that impacted her. Third, it was important to focus on the distress caused by the secondary wounding of Chris as he listens to Kathy's experience. As the race-based event is unpacked, Chris is better able to emotionally engage, and is available to help with Kathy's recovery in very specific ways.

Racial Identity as a Form of Diversity

The individuals in a couple might have a similar or different racial-identity. Both could be secure, or one could be insecure and the other secure. When a couple's racial identity is different, it can cause repeated disconnections and conflicts (Smith, 2005). EFT therapists know how to assemble emotional experiences, and assembling race-based experiences requires the same curiosity and exploration of race-related matters. Racial identity involves the dynamic emotional engagement with racial events. The couple's attachment bond is challenged here by their ability to stay connected while enduring the intensity of the triggers. Empathic reflections, validating Kathy's emotional experience, and assembling her experience of the race-based threat is essential for her to feel seen and for her to be emotionally engaged with Chris. This promotes healing. Encounters/enactments also would help (see Chapter 4). The attachment connection is still essential for the healing process. I suggest that in disconnections like this, externalizing the race-based assault is an added intervention (see Chapter 10). Sometimes the events are less triggering, or involve within-couple microaggressions, yet race-based events can add enormous burdens on the couple's ability to support each other and stay connected at these consequential moments. Maintaining connection still requires accessibility, responsiveness, and emotional engagement (EFT working model of love, see Chapter 4), along with alignment/appreciation for each of their racial identities.

In the next chapter, therapists of color suggest that therapists need to explicitly name racism as the source of this couple's distress and be willing to explore the experiences of racism in these matters for both partners (see Chapters 4 and 10). Moreover, I suggest in subsequent chapters that we have to expand EFT to include these conversations in emotionally healing ways.

3 Cultural Humility and Couples Therapy

"Beale Street Blues" is a song created by composer and lyricist W.C. Handy and popularized by Louis Armstrong, among others. It is fundamentally a blues song about the love of Black men and women and a celebration of the African American community spirit. While Beale Street was the center of African American music in the early 1900s in Memphis, Tennessee, it has come to represent any spirited, thriving, and fun African American community. James Baldwin wrote the novel *If Beale Street Could Talk*, a love story about an African American couple and their families who endured despite the oppressive race-based events of the time. *Beale Street* is a bittersweet love story. Like Zora Neale Hurston and Toni Morrison, Baldwin was criticized by White male book critics when he told stories in which African American love, joy, and spirit were central.

Despite the growing awareness in psychotherapy research of the need to include ethnically diverse populations and requirements to include them in normative research trials, nearly all empirical studies of psychotherapy are normalized with White middle class populations (Bernal & Scharron-Del-Rio, 2001). As I have pointed out, African American individuals and couples have had unique experiences. And history has largely ignored their voices and experiences, actively promoting distortions, misrepresentations, and racist assaults. While there is much diversity among African Americans, it is suggested here that all Americans share a cultural-historical context that includes slave labor camps, discrimination, and racist ideas that have created inequities in wealth, income, employment, education, and threats to the attachment bonds of African Americans. This strongly suggests that implicit bias or racial stereotypes are deeply embedded within the day-to-day interactions of all Americans. This is just as true for Black couples as it is for Black, White, Asian, and Hispanic therapists who treat them. We have all been consciously or unconsciously socialized in racist ideas. Diversity training, culturally sensitive and responsive supervision, and increasing the number of Black EFT therapists are critical. Because there are so few Black EFT Certified Therapists in the United States, it is most likely that an African American couple seeking an EFT therapist (or any other model of couples therapy) is likely to see a non-Black therapist (Aponte & Wohl, 2000).

There is diversity both between African American couples and within African American couple relationships. There are differences in skin color, hair texture, size and shape, social class, language, religious practices, worldviews, gender orientation, values about marriage, psychology of money, acculturation to majority culture, political beliefs, music, dance, attitudes toward intimacy, and sexual and emotional expression. These differences can be present within one minimum-size Black family. According to Ng, who works as a physician in Chinatown in Oakland, California:

> There are 20 zillion cultures out there and there's no way [one] can know every quirk. What we can do as providers is be curious. We have to ask, and then ask again. . . . It's about caring, and out of caring, searching out what we need to know.
>
> (Aponte & Wohl, 2000)

Impact of Implicit Bias

Given the historical racist propaganda and miseducation of most Americans regarding African American life, contributions, struggles, and experiences, the literature suggests that psychotherapists could benefit from a combination of reading, attending plays, museums, and Black tours, and taking courses about African American history. That is, therapists have to be curious about ethnicity and willing to talk about culturally related nuances, ideas, meanings, and feelings. In this regard, it is important to discuss reactions to racial discrimination and racism, racial identity, and the influence of majority culture Parham (2000), Jones (1991), Sue et al. (2008). Rowe and Rowe (2013) suggest that therapists should go even further and affirm the health of African American relationships. In this regard, Black love, as writer bell hooks (2001a) suggests, is revolutionary to racism and is both wonderful, spiritual, and larger than the couple.

According to Sue et al. (2008), psychotherapists have to become aware of their own worldviews, their framework for evaluating what is normal or dysfunctional, their implicit values and assumptions about human behavior, and the biases, racist ideas, and stereotypes they have inherited within the social conditioning of the social context of the United States. Sue goes on to suggest that overall racism in the United States has evolved; however, Black and White Americans view these changes differently. In this regard, Whites associate racism with overt acts of aversive racism and hate crimes by White supremacist groups; Black Americans tend to perceive that racism is a constant reality. Aversive racism still exists, and even well-intentioned Whites continue to respond to African Americans with erroneous assumptions that Whites are superior, have the right to control situations and treat people more harshly because of race.

Blair, Judd, and Fallman (2004) suggested that racial stereotypes of African Americans come from group categorizations as well as negative biases about Afrocentric facial features, that is, negative stereotyping based on implicit bias toward Afrocentric features (dark skin, wide noses, and thick lips).

These negative attitudes and behaviors are communicated through microaggressions directed toward African Americans. Sue et al. (2008) define microaggressions as:

> brief and commonplace daily verbal, behavioral and environmental indignities, whether intentional or unintentional, that communicate hostile, derogatory, or negative racial slights and insults to the target person or group, and are expressed in three forms: micro-assaults (direct expressions of hate), micro-insults (insensitive communication that demeans a person's ethnicity), and micro-invalidations (exclude, negate or nullify the experiences of people of color).

Microaggressions in Psychotherapy

Constantine (2007) suggested that perceived racial microaggressions were negatively associated with African American clients' perceptions of the working alliance and therapists' counseling skills, along with the therapists' multicultural responsiveness. Similarly, Owen, Imel, Wampold, and Rodolfa (2014) stated that racial and ethnic minority clients in a university setting reported that microaggressions occurred frequently in therapy and were significantly negatively associated with lower-quality working alliances with their therapists. According to Katz and Hoyt (2014), the most troubling finding was the automatic and deliberate nature of anti-Black perceptions as a threat to the working alliance negatively associated with therapists' perceptions of prognosis. Similarly, Abreu (1999) found that the perception of hostility can be influenced using words associated with African Americans (expressiveness) but not semantically related to hostility. Abreu suggested that the priming effects of stereotypes had a negative impact on therapists' first impressions but not on the overall diagnostic rating.

The evidence of racial bias in healthcare should give every mental health provider pause when considering implicit racial bias. Fitzgerald and Hurst (2017) conducted a literature review of 42 peer-reviewed articles associated with negative racial bias in healthcare. They found that implicit bias influenced healthcare professionals and created a lower quality of care. Racial bias influences diagnosis, treatment decisions, and quality of care. Hoffman, Trawalter, Axt, and Oliver (2016) found that one-half of a sample of 222 White medical students and residents endorsed beliefs about biological differences between Blacks and Whites, including that Black skin is thicker than White and that Blacks can endure more pain than Whites. These racial biases continue to influence treatment recommendations and the healthcare of Black Americans.

Cultural humility, a relatively new concept, can help develop responsiveness and an engaging stance of therapists, one that embraces cultural differences and understanding. Cultural humility is defined as a readiness to hear, engage, and explore cultural-related communication in therapy or an "openness to the other." Cultural humility is also characterized by a readiness to repair cultural misunderstandings and microaggressions that occur in counseling (Hook, Owen, Davis,

Worthington, & Utsey, 2013). Hook et al. (2016) used a community sample and found that counselors perceived as high in cultural humility appeared less likely to communicate microaggressions and were more effective in repairing therapeutic disconnections when cultural ruptures occurred. The common types of racial microaggressions are denial of bias about ethnic issues and avoidance of discussion of cultural matters. Another important finding in this study was that cultural humility (readiness to engage and respond to cultural issues) was associated with lower negative impact from microaggressions.

As therapists of color have continued to write books and articles, and teach psychotherapy, they send alarms to all therapists about the unique American experiences of people of color. The following represents a summary of warnings against implicit bias and challenges to the working alliance:

- Awareness of one's own culture and formation of therapist values and worldview of other cultures. Helm and Carlson (2013), Parham (2000), Sue et al. (2008, 2019), Boyd-Franklin (2003), Pinderhughes (1989), and Hardy and Awosan (2019).
- Recognize "color-blind ideology" as not honoring one's own culture and cultural differences and historical barriers to communication across differences. Sue et al. (2019), Hardy and Awosan (2019), Pinderhughes (1989).
- Promotes personal work by the therapist around race, values, biases, personal values, judgments, and internalized stereotypes. Helm and Carlson (2013), Jones (1991), Pinderhughes (1989), Hardy and Awosan (2019).
- Some assessment of race matters in the life and family of African Americans and exploration of clients' stage of racial identity development and their worldview toward majority culture. Sue et al. (2008), Hardy and Awosan (2019), Jones (1991), Nobles (1991), Parham (2000), Aponte and Wohl (2000).

Even when the cultural alarms are offered by scholars, will mainstream theorists integrate these cultural frameworks into practice? When the experiences of African Americans have been written by White psychological theorists, just as when the history of African Americans has been written by White historians, it has been written too often for self-serving purposes. The Black people portrayed are often unrecognizable to African American therapists or historians. The alarms raised by therapists of color go unheard. As reported in *From My People* (Dance, 2002), "Things mean one thing to us and something else to white people."

Hardy and Awosan (2019) offer a comprehensive framework that therapists from diverse clinical perspectives might use to encourage discussion about race matters. They suggest that it is clinically useful to explore the potential for discussing the invisible wounds of racism. These wounds are vulnerabilities to the relentless undermining and pressure brought by inequities of power, competencies, or wealth generated by racist policies as personalized confirmation of inferiority. Hardy refers to these wounds as internalized devaluation (when I don't measure up to my partner's expectations, it's because Black men just can't), an assaulted sense of self (I just cannot count on him; I'm not good enough or Black enough for him), and voiceless-ness which is the sense that it doesn't matter whether I say anything; he/she won't listen, so I will just say yes or agree.) Hardy suggests five ways to integrate race into therapy: (1) Acknowledge the influence of racism on African American people and include race in assessment; (2) Create space for race by encouraging and attuning to race-related matters that are the contextual and intersections of race and gender; (3) Name and validate specific influences that relentless exposure to racism can have on relationships, emotions, and view of self; (4) Unmask and name racial trauma wounds; and (5) Foster emotional support and the legacy of connection and love that heal racial trauma.

Intersection of Attachment and Culture

It is unlikely that a Black couple would have questions about the generalizability of EFT for African American couples; it should, however, be a genuine concern for EFT practitioners and researchers. Even the "universality" argument (that attachments and emotions are "hard wired") of attachment theory, an important foundation of EFT theory, would be strengthened with more cross-cultural studies. As Otto and Keller (2014) suggest, Bowlby and Ainsworth were theorists and reformers. Their work focused on White middle-class mothers and children and demonstrated the critical importance of sensitive, responsive caretaking for healthy child development.

Otto and Keller (2014) suggest that the development of White middle-class children occurs within the context of Western society. These authors offered another model of attachment based on West African farming communities. It suggests that mother-bonding behavior prepares the baby/child for engaging with the farming collective. Consequently, the baby bonds with many, rather than one, caregiver; thus, mothers seem less sensitive and responsive compared to White middle-class mothers, but their babies are effectively bonded. The authors challenge the notion that secure attachment, as defined in the strange situation research, is the only socialization goal in diverse cultures. For example, in farming societies, attachment practices seemed to have multiple caregivers as a way of introducing the sense of the collective as the central unit rather than the dyad of mother and child. The collective community is more responsive to the child, even when the child continues to feel a unique bond to their mothers, and while their mother is responsive to both the collective community and their child. This West African farming culture, compared to White middle-class society, would seem to require some larger degree of frustration tolerance earlier in child development. Otto and Keller seem to suggest, however, that the West African children are as effectively attached and adjusted as White middle-class children.

Revisiting the earliest stories of African Americans' life during the harshest and most oppressive periods reveals that the struggle for personhood and civil rights were full of accounts of collective attachment experiences, such as *Slave Narratives* (Andrews & Gates, 2000), *Voices from Slavery* (Yetman, 2000), *Incidents in the Life of a Slave Girl* (Jacobs, 2012), and *Living With Jim Crow* (Valk & Brown, 2010). While slave life was restrictive, harsh, and filled with cruelty, the attachment-significant reports were diverse. This diversity is reflective in childcare, marriage, and slave communities. For example, in some camps babies were cared for by older women or older children, and also breastfed by different women. Marriage might be allowed in some camps but not allowed in others. The importance of attachment bonds was consistently reported across different living conditions, and spirituality was very strong. Of course, the freedom to engage in loving behavior could be dramatically different between slave camps. According to Bruce Levine (2012), slave labor camps varied in size and harshness. The larger camps could have over 1,000 slaves, the typical-size slave camps had 100–500 slaves, and the smaller camps had 25–100 slaves. It seems that infant mortality was generally high during slavery but likely higher in the larger slave camps where women were more harshly treated. Taken together, the kinship bonds that Nancy Boyd-Franklin (2003), Pinderhughes (2002), and Parham (2000) describe have West African roots and were adapted to the conditions of American slavery, and the Jim Crow era.

Mary Ainsworth also seemed to share the belief that more field work observations were needed to understand attachment within different cultural contexts:

> [T]hat so many attachment researchers have gone on to do research with the Strange Situation rather than looking at what happens in the home or in other natural settings . . . it marks a turning away from "field work (basic research)," and I don't think it's wise.
>
> (Ainsworth, 1995)

Whether attachment theory expands to include the impact of collective bonding may or may not make a difference regarding adult romantic love relationships. It might, however, offer clues about the changing nature of marriage and integrating children into a family not solely based on White middle-class standards.

While psychotherapy studies and attachment research need to include more diverse samples, Black couples are seeking help every day. Psychotherapy research with diverse samples might suggest more or less generalizability of EFT effectiveness. Attachment research needs both field studies to construct appropriate types of experimental designs (as the strange situation) and to explore culturally sensitive attachment models (farming collective and hybrid) (Otto & Keller, 2014). Research projects are expensive. While the APA might suggest guidelines for inclusion, it seems that most psychotherapy research ignores guidelines regarding ethnic diversity. I suggest that allocating funds specifically targeted for the inclusion of ethnically diverse populations in research would begin to incentivize these policies.

It seems reasonable for clinicians to evaluate approaches to couples therapy, given that most studies of effectiveness lack cultural diversity. In this regard, demonstrated research effectiveness with multiple studies should be prioritized. Aponte and Wohl (2000) suggest that there are some positive results for evidence-based psychotherapy with people of color. While generalization to diverse populations should be done with caution, that does not mean that effectiveness is likely to be nonexistent, given the diversity within the African American community. First, as Helms has suggested, African American ethnic identity and acculturation to majority culture is diverse. Second, there also needs to be some way to measure therapist adherence to the clinical model that has demonstrated effectiveness. Adherence could be measured by reporting of experience, certification, and supervision history. Third, it also seems reasonable to ask "Does the evidence-based model align with important aspects of the Black experience?" Finally, is there unique clinical literature that might inform couples therapists about culturally sensitive and responsive adjustments that might be helpful in therapy with Black couples?

OVERVIEW OF EMOTIONALLY FOCUSED THERAPY MODEL OF COMMUNICATION

EFT for couples is an evidence-based psychotherapy model uniquely focusing on the attachment bond in couples therapy (Johnson, 2009, 2013, 2019). While EFT effectiveness with an African American population has not been studied, there are several key attributes of EFT couples therapy uniquely suited for Black couples. First, EFT brings the science of attachment into couples work. Attachment theory revolutionized our understanding of love relationships in families and adult romantic relationships (Johnson, 2004, 2019; Hughes, 2007; Fosha, 2000). While much has been written in scholarly journals about "the African American experience," love has not been a focus. I suggest that the attachment bonds of African Americans have been the primary undocumented source of survival. Since the 1980s, extensive research has confirmed that attachment bonds are significant for child and adult development as well as adult love relationships (Main, Kaplan, & Cassidy, 1985; Cassidy & Shaver, 2008; Hughes, 2007; Fosha, 2000).

As attachment theory has gained prominence in psychology, it has provided a framework for couples therapists to understand love, attachment emotions, and love-in-distress. Attachment theory articulates a clear approach for reducing stress and promoting competent development in adult love relationships (Johnson & Whiffen, 2003). Attachment theory is essentially a "we-ness" psychology that considers what goes on inside each partner, and between them. It offers a fresh perspective on the power of close African American relationships to heal race-related stress and promote loving bonds and positive racial identity.

The African American slave narratives are full of references to marriages and attachment love. It has been suggested by African American scholars that African Americans share a history with West African communities. In this regard, African Americans share a "we-ness" psychology that is the basis of kinship ties, spirituality, and social movement experiences (Nobles, 1991). While the attachment lens in EFT is narrowly focused on the relationship dyad, and Nobles (1991), Parham et al. (2000), Pinderhughes (2002), and Helm and Wilson (2013) have suggested that African Americans share West Africans' broader worldview of the collective, EFT clinical moves lean toward the "we-ness" of emotional engagement.

In addition, in EFT couples therapy, the totality of each partner's experience matters (this also could include cultural factors), and the therapist strives to create a sense of emotional safety in each session. The consulting room must be a safe haven for both partners, a secure base for exploring threats to the relationship and difficult emotions that emerge during couple disconnection. Specific EFT tasks that promote emotional safety are relentless validation of experience, empathic emotional reflections of interactions and intentions, and empathic interpretation of the attachment dilemmas. The therapist's stance of being accepting, responsive, and engaging with both partners can create safety in relationship counseling.

The role of the therapist is always to be alongside each partner in a nonjudgmental understanding of their attachment disconnection and desires as well as their longings for loving responsiveness. The major clinical intervention moves (the tango) are designed to slowly promote safe, careful, and soft emotional interactions between partners. Promoting emotional safety in therapy is a critical prelude for the couple to create emotional safety in their relationship. The devastating impact of slavery, segregation, racial discrimination, and racial trauma has created a unique need for emotionally safe healing environments for African Americans. Racism-based stress that amplifies conflicts and distance between African American couples becomes a potential "dragon," with both partners experiencing emotional overload. This scenario is similar to couples work conducted with trauma survivors when both partners have a history of trauma.

Attachment theory also offers a map of intrapsychic and interpersonal experienced threats to the relationship bonds. Of course, perceived threats are antithetical to emotional safety and are therefore carefully unpacked for emotional meanings. That is, attachment disconnections are signals to each partner that something happened between them that is threatening to the survival of their bond. These attachment disconnections and the corresponding emotional signals become the driving forces for the behavioral protest. EFT suggests that there are two levels of attachment experience: the reactive level in which frustration, irritability, or anger is likely expressed, and a deeper, more vulnerable level in which hurt, sadness, and fear are experienced. Distressed couples' disconnections are often fraught with problematic or confusing attachment signals. When couples become stuck in patterns of disconnection/protest/conflict, their romantic relationship becomes increasingly unsafe, and a sense of insecurity develops between the partners. EFT offers a careful, fluid, and staged approach for therapists to restore, renew, and enhance a sense of safety and security within the couple.

Couples are encouraged to see the repeated negative cycle of disconnection as the "enemy" to be worked against. The attachment disconnection "cue" sparking the sense of threat is carefully and slowly explored for the reactive emotional responses and when possible, exploring the underlying emotional attachment vulnerability, meanings, and behavior. The skillful EFT therapist helps to guide couples from insecure attachment responses to safe, secure conversations. In the early phases of couples therapy, the therapist attends to the reactive patterns and feelings that are apparent and accessible. De-escalation is the first phase of therapy. In this regard, this particular EFT focus has an additional benefit among people of color for addressing racial-identity stress (see later in this chapter and Chapter 13).

Creating trust and vulnerability are challenges for therapists and couples in the context of a racially biased society. The EFT therapist must be accessible, responsive, and engaged, allowing clients to feel accepted, valued, and understood. While all psychotherapists strive for positive working alliances, the EFT therapist is also challenged to see how their African American clients' perspectives and emotional responses make sense, given their experiences, attachment history, and love needs. In this regard, the EFT therapist is uniquely challenged to be nonjudgmental and nonpathological. For African Americans, this particular clinical stance is critical because racial bias, negative stereotyping, microaggression, and racial harassment are pervasive for people of color. This accepting stance toward experience, however, is not sufficient, given the unconscious and virtually automatic racist stereotyping pervasive in American culture. The EFT therapist, like all therapists, needs to be open to, and welcoming of emotionally significant race-based experiences of African Americans and to be curious about how those experiences impact views of self and close relationships.

A primary in-session objective of the EFT therapist is to have each partner feel seen and understood. Equally important is for partners to feel that their experiences matter, including their reactive conflict emotions and deeper attachment intentions and longings. African American clients rarely bring up race during therapy, believing that White therapists will not understand it (Aponte & Wohl, 2000). Being seen involves vulnerability of all types, including attachment emotions and racial identity threats. African Americans' expressions of fear, hurt, and anger can be intense and has been historically unacceptable in American culture. Thus, the EFT therapist's clinical stance of promoting reactive and attachment emotions as acceptable and understandable is directly antithetical to many African Americans' experiences, as they are often treated with distorted perspectives, disrespect, and racial bias for expressing them. Here again, however, therapists adhering to the EFT models have to actively self-reflect and perhaps seek consultation about their understanding of historical stereotypes that primes fears and negative appraisals of Black emotional expressions.

The EFT therapist attempts to heal each partner's working model of self and other in such a way that connections are maintained and repaired and love is promoted. Both partners, with the help of the therapist, participate in increasingly emotionally safe encounters that promote emotional engagement and healing. Using attachment theory as a guide, the EFT therapist maintains an optimistic perspective that the couple can fight against their negative loop of disconnection. These attachment threats can be understood by tracking the couple's emotions, cognitions, behaviors, and perceptions. The strengths of the relationship can be hidden within the reactive complexities of the negative cycle associated with attachment insecurity. As the communication process is slowed down, emotional experiences are assembled and organized in EFT therapy; thus, emotional softening, and loving engagements become more frequent. As emotional safety grows between partners, so does their capacity for relationship self-healing.

Particular clinical consideration has been provided, adjusting the EFT approach regarding conflict when there is a history of trauma in either partner, according to Johnson (2002). In cases of trauma, while the basic structure, interventions, and clinical stance of EFT couples therapy remain, some consideration is given to the treatment literature on trauma. The trauma literature suggests specific clinical interventions regarding the very challenging view of self and other that are the emotional injuries and sequelae. Among the adjustments are naming reactive emotions that are trauma based (the emotional dragon), employing brief psycho-educational schemes about trauma, and understanding that therapy is likely slower and longer for Black couples. EFT as a practice has not focused on the impact of race-based stress and traumatic experiences on African American couples. Suggestions are emerging from cross-cultural counseling regarding assessment and interventions about these issues that could be incorporated into EFT (Sue et al., 2019; Liu et al., 2019; Comas-Diaz et al., 2019).

Attachment Story of Harriet Jacobs

> Why does the slave ever love? Why allow the tendrils of the heart to twine around objects which may at any moment be wrenched away by the hand of violence? When separations come by the hand of death, the pious soul can bow in resignation and say, 'Not my will, but thine be done, O Lord!' But when the ruthless hand of man strikes the blow, regardless of the misery he causes, it is hard to be submissive. I did not reason thus when I was a young girl. Youth will be youth. I loved, and I indulged the hope that the dark clouds around me would turn out a bright lining. I forgot that in the land of my birth the shadows are too dense for light to penetrate.
>
> *(Slave Narratives, 2000)*

Harriet Jacobs wrote her autobiography and remained hopeful regarding love. As she wrote the piece just presented, she had been denied the opportunity to marry her African American lover, because her slaver wanted to continue his sexual assault of her. She had three children by him, and eventually escaped to Canada and then to England. As she continued to write in England, she remained hopeful about marrying a man of her choosing.

TWO CASE CONSULTATIONS INCORPORATING AFRICAN AMERICAN FOUNDATIONAL LEARNING

CHALLENGES TO THE EFT COMMUNITY TO ENGAGE THE BLACK WORLDVIEW

In the next section is a short edited transcript from a videotape produced at a core skills training. EFT training tapes are offered to the EFT community as exemplar demonstrations of the EFT model, sometimes demonstrating EFT work with specific populations. This consultation flowed from an interest in integrating EFT and training of therapists to work with issues of race in couples therapy. The central problem with this proposed training tape was the demonstrated lack of any significant foundational learning about the African American experience or experience in working with Black clients in therapy. As a result, when racial trauma emerged during the session, it was not seen, understood, or addressed appropriately. This appears to be true for the treating therapist and the consultant. When that trauma appeared here, it was akin to a victim of personal trauma (sexual assault or physical violence) laying bare their most shameful and humbling appraisals of self (the aftermath of assaults) in the first session of therapy. At those critical moments, it is likely that the experienced trauma therapists would have a clinical road map to aid their walk alongside their patient in some gentle way. They would carefully capture, frame, and contain in order to avoid re-traumatizing the patient, and they would set the stage for future healing. While the consulting therapist is using EFT validating and empathic reflections (EFT interventions), he does not have a race "container" to help the wife in this consultation to organize her experiences. Sadly, their reactive negative cycle does not suggest that her husband is a safe and emotionally engaged partner, and therefore the therapists have to provide this gentle, knowledgeable responsiveness. When race-based distress cues/triggers occur to the body of an already racially traumatized Black woman, it is triggering, it sounds the alarm of *danger danger*, and there is an enormous need for anxiety reduction and emotional comfort. In effect, she is pleading *(a humble wounded form of screaming) help help*. Her process results in exhausting vigilance, insecure appraisals, and a damaged self-view.

How EFT Consultations Work

The consultant meets with the treating therapist and is informed about the couple's case. Typically, the presenting problem, negative cycle of interactions, positions of the partners in the cycle, i.e., withdrawer or pursuer, and significant themes are discussed to frame the consultation. The therapist is also likely to ask for specific help in their work with the couple. For example, the therapist may ask for help in articulating the cycle. The following bullet points were offered to the working consultant regarding the case by the treating therapist:

- Wife was depressed and wanting to leave early in couples work.
- Wife would open up, get pushback from husband and shut down.
- Husband has been falsely accused of racism on multiple occasions in college and work.
- Discussion of race has been a problem between them.

Again, while racial issues were associated with this couple's disconnections, it appeared that neither the treating therapist nor the consultant had a model for talking about race and racial differences or a map about effectively integrating race into the couples' negative cycle or facilitating different perceptions and behaviors (see Chapters 2, 3, and 10). Neither the treating therapist nor the consultant had a sense that early assessment should include discussions of race and racial identity. That such an assessment might help them understand this couple's cycle and their perceptions of self and other (see Chapters 3, 4, and 10). In this case, racial identity information prior to this consultation could have offered a critically different focus to the work.

Clarity About Processing a Race-Based Event

When EFT therapists are not knowledgeable about the history of Black Americans, racial events, racial distress cues, and racial identity, it is difficult to process distressing moments between couples with specificity (the moment of disconnection). In EFT, we process distressing moments to help understand the pattern of interactions within the person and between the partners. Further, it helps us to assemble emotions so that it makes sense to each partner. I suggest that race-based events should be processed in a similar EFT way (see Chapters 2 and 10). This granular perspective allows more opportunities for connections, and exploring blocks to accessibility, responsiveness, and emotional engagement. In short, it allows for greater healing from racial assaults and microaggressions.

Notice in the transcript that follows that while the therapist is indeed talking about race and attempting to validate and reflect this Black woman's experiences with her husband, the race-based events that impact the wife's emotions are never explored. Without revisiting the specific experiences, we don't know the emotional impact of the event, but she does say that she is anxious about her appraisals of race and distressed about talking to her husband about her experiences. Nevertheless, the consultant interjects his view of racism, seemly unrelated to the Black woman's experience, "Black people can be stopped by police." What becomes clear in this transcript and within the larger context of the session is that this interracial couple becomes disconnected when a race-based event happens, and the wife attempts to talk to her husband about her experience. It appears that his personal negative experiences with race-based events, from his White perspective, block his availability and responsiveness to his wife. The husband's reactive, race-based triggers that block his responsiveness also are not explored during this session.

Consultant: . . . and um growing up African American in this country, it's going to . . . t'll often times just lead to a lot of those things . . . and it's . . . one of the most healing this is to know that the man that you love and care about gets it or understands. . .

Wife: Yeah I think that's a big part of our relationship too because I don't . . . I don't know if the things that I see are like, delusional, like, 'cause when I bring them up I feel like I'll either . . . I'm making them up in my head or these things aren't really happening because when I bring them up to him . . . I don't think that he realizes them, so it just makes me feel like I'm seeing things . . . because he doesn't look for those things. And I don't know if I'm looking for them or if they're happening.

Consultant: Okay. But you . . . you don't always also kind of know the reasons why people are doing what they're doing. You know, I mean, we, we know that . . . that African Americans are stopped more often by the police. I mean, I know there's been studies on that kind of thing. Okay. When you get pulled over you don't know if it's because you're African American or if you really did run a red light.

This is an example of a therapist's inexperience with Black people discussing race. Notice that rather than exploring a specific, stressful race-based event, that is, being curious about an actual recent event or an impactful one in her past, the consultant supplies a general experience of African Americans. While the consultant is attempting to validate and reflect on the general experiences of Black people, the wife seems to be talking very specifically about the impact of the couple's negative pattern of interactions about race. There is a misattunement here. If we understand that African Americans carry race-based distress in their bodies like other victims of traumas, then it is more helpful to focus on her experiences. She is also talking about anxiety about her appraisals of these distressing moments, which is some indication of her insecure racial identity (see the following transcript), and some history of disconnections with her husband.

Wife: I think he goes into um . . . trying to figure out. . . . I guess like he says . . . the, uh opposite side. So he takes the other side of it to try to figure out, well what that person . . . or why that person might have done it. He goes into logic.

Husband: Yeah. 'Cause I, I've been accused of being racist a lot. Like it's, like it almost got me kicked out of school when we were, you know, married and having a baby. Um, it almost got me fired from my job. Um . . . and so . . . that I think . . . it's kind of the opposite um . . . opposite perception.

Consultant: It's a place where you guys get stuck . . . so when something does happen . . . and you, you don't always know, right? You don't always know. But when something does happen and it feels like this is because you're Black . . . it very well may be because you're Black (W nods). Okay. Okay. So if, when something happens and you share that with him . . . and you're, I'm guessing, hurting or angry or frustrated or something . . . he either kind of gets logical or he kind of takes the other side or he kind of suggests. . . (to Husband) if I'm I getting this right. . . . You don't always do this but I'm guessing there's another perspective here, right? (to Wife) What do you . . . I'm guessing that . . . how do you feel at that moment?

Wife: I feel not heard. And I feel like . . . like I said I feel like I'm seeing things. Because I've always looked up to his, like, opinion, so when he gives me you know, his perception and I'm like, well maybe he's right and I'm just seeing things. So I go into a hole of like, feeling alone I think.

Consultant: You end up feeling alone.

Wife: Because I feel like I can't convince him to see what I saw. So I just feel . . . I just feel really alone.

Consultant: You go into doubt. And . . . and you shut down and you feel very lonely. So what do you need from him in those moments? What do you want from him? 'Cause he may . . . he may get triggered and he may, kind of, have a different perspective. He's a different person . . . and it's kind of outside of his life experience, some of it. Some of it . . . you know what your experience is in this area, right? But what do you need from him?

There is a great deal of EFT therapy happening here. The consultant is attempting to articulate where the couple gets stuck and that each partner gets triggered in some general way about race. Nevertheless, it seems she has been triggered twice: by the race-based event and then her husband's challenge to her perceptions. The challenges to her appraisals lead her to greater self-doubts ("am I delusional?"). Whatever the experience was that triggered her initial race distress cue is not explored ("something happen"); the therapist reflects and then conjectures that the emotions from that event are "hurting, angry, or frustrated." These are not experiences she explores from the inside and then expresses. And the husband's triggers that call him to challenge her appraisals are not unpacked.

The husband seems to suggest that he is triggered because of his own implicit bias against perceptions of race-based events. He invites the discussion of his race-based triggers, but the consultant does not follow his lead. Nevertheless, the husband's race-based challenges are at least partially validated ("there is another perspective here" rather than "there are triggers here for you too. Can you help me understand?"). The husband's appraisals of her perceptions ("whatever happened to you, it is not about race") appear to be influenced by his White identity development and his own negative experiences of race-based events. If racial microaggressions are experienced by this Black woman, it also triggers an emotional experience for her husband.

The lack of specificity in tracking this couple's negative cycle does not allow for exploring and understanding the particular ways in which the race distress triggers are activated in their attachment distress triggers. Knowing that race is social and sometimes radioactive in bodies, along with attachment distress, would have been helpful here. EFT therapists, like firefighters, run toward the emotional radioactivity. It seems that racism is triggering and damaging to this couple's relationship, and it is not safe for them to talk about race. This negative pattern does significant damage to this young woman's self-worth, mental health, and marriage.

Here is an alternative example informed by African American foundational learning, as if we could replay this moment in the consultation:

*Alternate View:

Consultant: So for your wife, something happens *(After pausing to exploring the race-based event . . . which might lead to the following)* so you said this White woman in the store "mad mugged" you after you smiled at her. And you said to yourself that this is what happens to Black women. It bothered you inside, hurt your feelings. After all you were trying your best to be nice, to be accepted. It hurt some place deep inside, something about your core of how you think about yourself. . . . Am I getting that right? So afterwards your first thought is to talk to your husband about what happened to you. That makes a lot of sense. But when you open up to him something about his response shuts you down. Makes you doubt what you saw and experienced. *(This validates and give depth to her internal world of feelings associated with microaggressions)*. For your husband, something happens inside you, when your wife is telling you this story. When she says something about "that it happens to Black people part"? Somehow that triggers something about your own experiences of being accused of racism? Is this where you all get stuck? You don't get to tell him about your hurt, and for you it reminds you of troubling race moments too? *(Frames the race-based disconnections more clearly and husband's view of self gently coming in to focus)*. Both of you end up feeling alone. There is a great deal to process here. Okay, husband, can we slow it down and stay with what happens for you inside when she is telling you about her hurt, how difficult that moment was for her in the store? *(To begin the process of husband's view of self and others . . . and race)*. He has work to do surrounding race to calm his reactivity so that his accessibility, responsiveness, and emotional engagement can be online to help his wife heal from these harmful, stressful events.

The Clinical Challenge as to What to Do With Invisible Wounds of Internalized Racism When It Shows Up in Couples Work

Wife: Oh no. I think I know why. I just don't think I've ever . . . had a chance to bring it up or to talk about it because it's not so much about what happened to me, it's so much of the things that my grandmother installed in me because she had such a higher respect . . . because she worked for a lot of White people who had a lot of money. She was, you know, she cooked and cleaned the house . So she would come home, and you know, brag about all the things that they had, and make them seem so superior to us, so I always felt inferior . . .

to White people. So I think that's why . . . all these things come up when like, little things happen, it makes me feel small . . . so then I turn it into racism, because I feel little.

Consultant: That makes so much sense. 'Cause you've gotten messages when you were young . . . you know, feeling like okay, because I'm Black, you know, White people are . . . um, um I'm inferior but it's because I'm Black . . . and then you . . . these things, and it can be kind of, simple things, but they're not simple in their effect, right? . . . The way they impact you?. . . . And it's painful and then it's like, should I feel this pain or not? And that one's tricky because you do feel the pain.

Wife: And it makes me want acceptance. I . . . I try, you know, I think I look for acceptance in people that I feel inferior to. But it, I don't think it helps me feel accepted. . . . I just look for it a lot. . . . I was raised on thinking, you know, that they're, they're better than us.

Consultant: Yeah. They're better than us, they know better than us, they're smarter than us, look up to them, you know. Because there was no Black people that I was around that were successful or smart. That makes . . . it makes perfect sense to me. 'Cause how you got those messages and they were powerful and they were consistent. So they were deeply embedded.

Consultant: And, and at times when you've been mainly around White people, around people you respect, and have seen as being better than you or something. You have had a hard time, kind of, owning your own feelings or your own opinions or your own . . . Am I getting that right?

Wife: Yep. A lot. . . . I just ignored it. I just ignored anything that would've been . . . for the good of myself I just ignored.

Consultant: Right. And that's very hard and that's very tricky. 'Cause it really makes it harder to be deeply connected with someone . . . I mean it's harder to feel . . . in many ways, that kind of squashes love in many ways because you can't be fully open and he can't be then connecting to you, so you're not going to feel alike. And if you're kind of squashing yourself down and making, you know . . . saying whatever, what you think he wants.

Wife: Yeah and that's kind of how it was for years. Just doing, saying what he wanted.

Consultant: Right. That's hard. And painful. So one of the things that's happening I guess is that you're going to need to do a couple of things but maybe check in, how do I feel, what do I think, what do I feel? And then having the courage, 'cause it takes a lot of courage to say it . . . to this man, that you do look up to. And there's nothing wrong with looking up to him, 'cause he's the man . . . he's your husband, right? You love him.

This is a painful moment in this work, revealing a deep wound to her racial identity that has been infected with internalized racism. This so clearly demonstrates the impact of 400 years of racist ideas passed on from generation to generation. There is so much to unpack here and will likely take years to process with her to facilitate the healing process. The consultant is valiantly attempting to validate and empathically reflect her experiences but has no understanding of her internalized racism. This would be a difficult moment for any EFT therapist, and the consultant is at a training event demonstrating the EFT model. She is revealing the depths of her wounded self-perceptions and insecure race appraisals. In addition to couples work, this young woman could benefit from individual therapy and perhaps a Black women's support group.

Unfortunately, these therapists did not know enough about African American psychology to provide her with some healthy platform to assemble her racial experiences at this moment in therapy. It seems apparent from this portion of the video clip that the consultant is struggling to understand what this young Black woman is talking about when she says "respect," after saying she is "inferior" and "small" compared to White people. She is also suggesting she is vigilant about and actively seeking to achieve White acceptance. And she's very likely submitting uncomfortably to her husband's logic about race matters. Any one of these emotionally loaded racial-related words should cause a consultant, knowledgeable about African Americans, to pause, slow the conversation down, and decide to gently explore, or attempt to build a platform for, future healing.

Here is an alternative example informed by African American foundational learning, as if we could replay this moment of the consultation:

*Alternate Consultant: Let me see if I've got this right. Your grandma worked for wealthy White people who were very nice to her. They were kind and decent people, they lived in a wonderful community, and grandma felt safe there. She told you stories about what they had and how good they were. You also remember that the Black people in your community, by comparison, had fewer of the good things, and were not decent or kind people. Right? Yeah, there was this difference about wealth and good people. So for you, that difference somehow shows up as being inferior? Okay, can you help me understand when feeling inferior shows up in your life? Can you think back to your earliest experiences of it? Perhaps a specific moment or an image of a time when you experienced feeling inferior? Can you let yourself go as far back as you can remember? *(Of course, Black inferiority is a negative racial stereotype with profound implications for racial identity and demands sensitive clinical attention).*

Of course, after we explore this with the wife, we might turn to her husband and ask "What was that like for you—hearing your wife talk about her experiences of feeling inferior?"

These are the types of questions I would have asked during an earlier assessment (see Attachment and Cultural, Race-Related Interview Questions: To be fair to the consultant, the treating therapist could have done that assessment and brought that information to the consultation). Because this type of experience is included in that interview, I would have at least offered a bit of a road map for race-related matters when they show up in therapy. This helps consultants when they have to think on their feet. For example, I might have asked before or after we process "inferior" about whether she went to church with Grandma. Of course, without the assessment information (church is included there, too), I don't know if they went to church, but the literature suggests African Americans of Grandma's age likely did so. Here, I would be searching for Black people who are exceptions to her point of view (of course, there are many other positive exceptions too), not to challenge her but to plant seeds for future healing of her racial identity. This moment would not be the time to pursue that, but differences in wealth and quality of communities has a racial discriminatory past. Grandma's job, educational experience, and the segregated redlined communities are all invisible by-products of anti-Black racism. In some moments, weaving these realities into the conversation about race would provide a healthy platform for self-reflections about race and racial identity.

The consultant apparently decided to build a platform with the working model of EFT love of accessibility, responsibility, and emotional engagement (A.R.E) but there is a problem with that move. She is talking about a racial, social, intellectual, power positioning (superiority of Whites, to inferiority of Blacks). Attachment disconnection is central to this couple's problem. Unhealthy attachment is damaging to the self-worth of this woman. The damaging American definition of Blackness (see Chapter 1) has found its way into the negative cycle of this couple. As a result, it places this racially insecure, wounded Black woman within an attachment cocoon with her "superior" identity, unchallenged White husband. Moreover, reflecting that she is the one to have the "courage" to pursue him is a huge mistake. Here, the consultant might have reflected that A.R.E. is mutual, and that emotional safety facilitates emotional engagement. Their negative race-sensitive pattern, not her internal process, gets in the way of their emotional safety. Sadly, one has to conclude that this was an unhealthy attachment move that "ties the bow" between this Black woman who perceives herself as inferior, who is longing for acceptance and belonging. Her longing for acceptance is tied to her husband, whose reactive challenges are tacitly validated (apparently, there is no need for him to explore his racial identity, vulnerabilities or longings). It is exactly 100 years since White women gained the right to vote; even if this were a White couple, would we tie this unhealthy bow?

Their negative cycle continues, with each partner having triggers about race. They are not clearer about this destructive force in their relationship from this consultation, and American life continues to be full of race-based triggers. Her husband's reactivity to race is crazy-making, depressing, and potentially racially verbally assaultive *(It is suggested that their conflicts escalate when they involve race, which needs to be explored; how bad does it get? Do you say mean things to each other in those highly charged moments?)*. Her insecure racial identity and internalized racism wounds are heartbreaking. While her husband does express regrets for unspecified past unresponsiveness, his White racial identity still appears central to defining what is acceptable perceptions of race in this marriage. That is the essence of White social power, and it is damaging in this marriage. I am reminded of the warning of Nightingale, Awosan, and Stavrianopoulos (2019) that without EFT becoming knowledgeable and sensitive to African American experiences, there can be unintended harm. I can only imagine how this tape would be received by a much larger group of Black mental health professionals.

In This Regard, I Suggest the Following Two Hypothetical Sets of Questions From a Panel of Black Scholars If They Had Had an Opportunity to View This Consultation

First: "Did you consider the historical implications here? The continual legacy of slavery embedded in this case? Specifically, that Grandma follows a long line of Black women housekeepers who lived through slavery... 'House Negroes'?" Their jobs were to cook, keep house, and most essentially, to help keep White people happy, and by doing so, to ensure their own survival. That structure of racist employment continued throughout the Jim Crow era, and even today for poor Black women. Grandma was passing on survival skills to her granddaughter regarding how to survive: keep White people happy and you will be safe. My answer would be . . . yes, we have to address that part of the negative pattern, managing White people's happiness. This is something that she has to grow to understand as she also develops her own agency. Her own development of agency might help her get in touch with her own sense of competency and push back against her husband's view of her and her perspective on race matters. Her husband has to work equally hard on his White identity, and they both have to work on their marriage.

The Second Set Hypothetical Questions From a Black Mental Health Professional

"Dr. G., you suggest that the legacy of slavery is an American experience. Do you think it might be showing up in the husband's attitudes and behavior? In this regard, some Black scholars suggest that the White sense of "victimhood" explains some White people's reactions to such concepts of, and challenges to, White fragility or White privilege. Did you consider this in your conceptualization of this couple? More precisely, is there any legacy of slavery represented in the husband's responses?"

There are some notable moments in this transcript that should give us pause. First, the husband does not seem to have any observable reactions as his wife shares that she thinks of herself as inferior to him. None. To be fair, his reactions in those moments are unexplored, suggesting that the consultant was unaware of the racial significance and the particular impact on their attachment bond. Does this suggest that he, too, perceives himself as superior to his wife? Does he have feelings about how she perceives him? Of course, in the time of slavery, during the Jim Crow era and afterwards, White men have been attracted to, and fallen in love with Black women, while simultaneously maintaining their superior social privilege. And that inequality limits intimacy but likely supports a superior view of the White male identity. Some White men might find that superior privilege is normal (Helms, 1995), and they become triggered when their White identity is touched upon. The husband has to feel the impact of his privilege and fragility on his wife.

Second, the husband's reactivity to race, his race triggers, seems consistent with the White backlash against the Black protest against microaggressions and other race-based events. This white backlash also has a long American history associated with racial aggression. Once again, the husband's race-based triggers were not explored in this consultation, and there is a great deal to learn about his emotions, perspectives, and behaviors. His attitude appears, however, to be consistent with a White identity arrogance and anger reactivity (see Chapter 10). I am not suggesting that he is in any way a bad person. His reactivity to his own experiences of race-based events and perhaps his White identity have to be understood as influencing his role in the negative cycle. It seems that his reactivity is playing a role in his disconnection with his wife.

Finally, it is important to note that Black women are the most demeaned, disrespected, and mistreated women in American life (McGuire, 2010; Helm & Carlson, 2013). I suggest that American culture primes, or leans toward, microaggressions of devaluing Black women's worth in romantic relationships. These demeaning attitudes toward Black women are likely to also show up in some way within Black couple relationships, particularly when Black men have been strongly influenced by victim system/street values (see Pinderhughes, 1982; see Chapter 10). There is no substitute for foundational learning about African American life.

John Oliver Killens' . . . Black Man's Burden:

> A little boy had read numerous stories in his children's books about various life and death struggles between a man and a lion. But no matter how ferociously the lion fought, each time the man emerged victorious. This puzzled the boy, so he asked his father, "Why is it, Daddy, that in all these stories the man always beats the lion, when everybody knows that the lion is the toughest cat in all the jungle?" The father answered, "Son, those stories will always end that way until the lion learns how to write."
>
> (From My People, 400 Years of African American Folklore, 2002).

EXAMPLE TWO: INTERPLAY OF CULTURAL HUMILITY AND EFT CONSULTATION

The following is an EFT core skills live consultation similar to the earlier example in which the author was acting as a co-therapist with an EFT therapist who had worked with this Black couple for six months. The couple entered therapy with significant challenges. The husband was verbally abusive. A few weeks before this consultation, he began to own his role in the negative cycle. As the consulting session developed, it became clear that the couple was processing a series of race-based traumatic events impacting their relationship. The following brief edited transcript demonstrates advancing thorough the EFT tango moves (see Chapter 4) while processing an attachment injury and race-based distress.

Guillory: Can you hold on, Amari? I want to stay with Kamala. When you were talking, Kamala, I got so sad. It does remind me of what happens to women of color, as the country would get meaner and even violent toward Black men; they, too, would have hell to pay at home. And so it just makes me sad to think about this meanness you start to embody as it comes home to you. Yeah? And it's, it's just really sad. So when you talk about being on the edge, the terror of being at home, this is so sad. So I could feel it as you were talking that way. Can you stay with that a little bit and tell us a little bit more about what it's like being terrorized at home? Would that be okay? I know you don't know me well, but I have worked with a lot of women of color, and they, too, have gotten traumatized more in some ways. And that was happening to you. Can you say a little bit more about that? Take your time (she is crying). It's okay. *(EFT move one, to frame and explore a race-based experience focusing on the couple but also including a larger cultural lens)*

Kamala: I just don't want to make him look bad more than I have already (nervous laughter as she wipes away tears).

Guillory: It is the meanness that exists for people of color. It is the meanness out there in the world for Amari. Let me be clear. I really feel it is the meanness out in the world. And we bring that meanness home. And we embody it. Now, Amari brought it home in his particular way. That's on him, and unique to his experience, and he has to be accountable for that. But yours is real, too. *(EFT move one, shaping the race-based experience impacting each of them differently)*.

Amari: You know I care about you.

Kamala: I know.

Amari: Don't worry. Don't worry, just keep talking.

Guillory: Kamala, I heard in his words, just to remind him, "We talk this way." Oh yeah. I know that. "We talk this way." And talking this way is the meanness we bring home. We talk this way. But it's no less painful. No less painful to hear it. *(EFT move two, focusing on her emotional experience using Amari's wording that reflects harsh statements directed at her)*.

Kamala: I guess growing up, I came from a very loving home. I was never yelled at and never spanked. Everyone was always kind of polite. I felt unconditional love, and knew, too, I had to get good grades. I felt safe at home and safe with my emotions. When I came into this relationship, I knew who I was marrying. I mean, I knew I was marrying a public intellectual. Nobody knew him as a quiet guy. That was part of his attraction. He gave voice to the voiceless. He may not like this word but he was always a kind of provocateur type in the public square. He has that sort of aggressive energy. The moment we had kids, things started to turn. He would come at me, that heat and aggressiveness would come at me.

Guillory: And, our bodies feel it. (*move two, staying focused on her emotional experience in her body*). And as I heard you talking about what happened to you, I thought this is really painful. It's really sad. This is happening to you guys as a couple, but you're embodying the pain, Kamala, yeah? *(EFT move two, focus on her emotional experience)*. Can you speak to that a moment?

Kamala: So I, I knew what I was getting into, but before we had kids, we could each kind of be in our own lane, and it would never kind of affect the other. He could kind of do his thing publicly, kind of get that energy out. And so it was never directed at me . . . that sort of aggressive energy. The moment we had kids, things started to turn a little bit. I still had my career, and I still wanted to live the life we had had. I did kind of hope for, and expect a little bit more of a partnership as it relates to co-parenting, co-living, and co-financing, etc. So I think that sort of encroachment on his life and his sort of freedom loss created stress—and he turned the target, the flame throwing, from the outside to the inside. So, anytime he felt that heat from the outside, that heat was taken out literally cooled on me to cool off. (teary-eyed).

Amari: You feel that way? It's that direct?

Kamala: Yeah, but it only became direct when I was also kind of nagging at his time, nagging at his attention, nagging at his contributions.

Guillory: You started to feel the heat at home. Yeah? *(EFT move two, staying with her emotional experience. Maintaining focus on her, and using racial distress cue "heat")*.

Kamala: Yeah. So yes, I was called things that I have never been called, like words that I mean, I came from a family that I had never cursed in my life, you know. I went from that, to somebody who never cursed, to using it regularly in their lexicon and directing it at me, and using very degrading terms and words that I will not repeat here.

Guillory: They stay inside and they stay in our bodies, yeah? *(EFT move two, staying with internal experience)*.

Kamala: Yes. For sure.

Guillory: You don't need to repeat them here, I don't need to hear. But it's in there inside, can you share that? *(EFT move two, focusing on her emotional experience and respecting her loyalty)*.

Kamala: And it becomes a broken record. And I became this person that even though I could reject it intellectually . . . I could not reject it emotionally. Because at the end of the day, this is the man that I love. And I started to believe I wasn't a good mother, that I was a clusterfuck, that I was a moron and a retard and a junior varsity person, and that I was mentally potentially insane. And, you know, all the other words that are out there. I started to at least maybe not believe it 100% of the time, but at least started to question it. (distressed and teary-eyed).

Guillory: So the words were starting to have an impact on how you even thought about yourself, it was hurting so badly inside? How the man you love brought home the heat. What would it be like to turn to him now and tell him about the hurt you have felt in your body? He says you are important to him, Kamala—that he want to be accountable to you. Can you turn to him now, and tell him about those hurt feelings? *(EFT move three, initiating an encounter with brief summary that includes attachment and racial distress experience).*

Kamala: It has been painful. I know that you are a good man, and I love you. It has just been so painful, worried about what was happening to me. (softly crying)

Guillory: What's it like, Amari, to hear her talk to you about her pain? *(EFT move four, beginning to process the encounter).*

Amari: I love you, and don't want to hurt you. I do feel guilty that I was bringing home the racism I was teaching and fighting against. I have been learning to see you, and I see the hurt and pain I caused. I want us to be different. I want to be in touch with your feelings. (as he reaches to hold her)

Guillory: Kamala, what's it like for you to hear Amari say he wants to be different? He wants to know your feelings? *(EFT move four, processing the emotion).*

Kamala: It's different for him, and I believe him. He has been changing, and it feels good. (as she moves even closer toward him)

Guillory: Kamala and Amari, this is a beautiful claim of love in your relationship. This was just a moment, but it was, in some way, fighting for your loving connection, against the race-based meanness in the world. Perhaps, without truly knowing, Amari, you were bringing this home. This was just a delightful experience of seeing you all reclaim love. For you, Kamala, letting Amari know your feelings, and you, Amari, hearing her and reaching back with love. *(EFT move five, emotionally engaging the love)*

DISCUSSION OF TRANSCRIPT

The attachment story of Mary A. Bell's parents (see slave narrative, beginning of Chapter 2) comes to mind as Amari comes home from his work fighting for, and teaching about, anti-racist ideas in his profession. Their couples relationship is challenged by this interaction of attachment and culture. The cycle starts with racial hostility from the outside world. Adding the cultural lens to their discord is essential for assembling their emotional experience. In this consultation, EFT is successfully integrated with cultural humility. The race-based distress experienced at work by Amari is brought home in his body and soul. Unwittingly, as he attempts to rid himself of his internally experienced racial toxicity, he traumatizes his wife and family. While this portion of their work focuses on his wife's internalized experiences, Amari has work to do to find alternative ways of coping. In this segment, we see Kamala experiencing the toxic, negative impact of racial microaggressions on her self-worth. Culture is an integral part of this couple's experience and is fundamental, not incidental, to the emotional depth of this work. Kamala's identity as a loving, loyal, and good wife has been challenged by her husband's harsh, demeaning criticisms. Her felt link to the demeaning disrespect given to other women of color dropped her immediately into her painful emotional world. It's a world that includes her own work and sacrificing herself for the benefit of family/husband. As that struggle with her self-view was validated and linked to other women of color, she began to feel heard and that it was safe enough to continue in this segment to assemble her emotions. Using the EFT tango moves as a guide for healing race-based distress and wounds was enormously helpful. The interplay of culture and attachment is seamless, and most importantly, promotes emotional engagement and healing. Amari was able to meet Kamala in her pain and be the healer he needs to be for her.

SUMMARY

COUNSELING AND CULTURALLY HUMILITY

What Therapists Need to Know About Themselves

A consistent theme from counseling theorists and scientists of color has been that therapists need to be aware of their own culture, to reflect on their own values and worldview, and those of people of color. This appraisal might involve reviewing the diversity or similarity in their own family, friends, neighbors, and colleagues. It has been suggested that this review might reveal cultural values, preferences, and implicit biases that impact counseling of the culturally different client. Following these meta-reflections, they should learn about the history of racist ideas and discriminatory practices that have impacted African Americans. The importance of understanding issues related to counseling culturally diverse groups has grown in counseling education departments since the 1970s, yet research on effective treatments that include diverse normative groups continues to be lacking. This likely reflects both a lack of interest and a lack of diversity in research groups.

Racial Identity Development

Given historical segregation and discrimination, it is likely that most White therapists grow up, go to schools, and work in majority White communities. It is equally likely that Black therapists grow up, and at least early on, attend schools within Black communities. At a certain point, whether in high school or college, many African American therapists start attending predominantly White universities and colleges. As a result, Black therapists compared to White therapists begin having challenges to their racial identity earlier in their academic and professional development. In fact, it is entirely possible that many White therapists will never have their racial identity challenged or even consider that such a social construct exists for them. By contrast, it is highly likely that African Americans' racial identity begins to develop early in their families or on their childhood playgrounds.

Learning about or reflecting on African American or race matters is a largely a choice for most White therapists and a developmental matrix (i.e., racism, racial identity; see Chapter 2) for Black people. It is a developmental perspective depending on one's worldview. The majority culture worldview is developed in the context of neighborhoods, schools, and employment opportunities that largely function independently of minority cultures. As a result, there is no need to know or learn about cultural diversity. It has been suggested that preschoolers learn about racial bias from their families well before a youngster has any diverse cultural interactions. Most general information about Black lives is negative, and largely the academic information is incomplete and influenced by implicit bias. As a result, without a specific curiosity to immerse oneself in Black psychology, sociology, or mental health, there would seem to be only a damaging amount of misinformation about racial identity available for the average White therapist. On the White identity stage of Helms's model, this would be contact status, that is, White culture is normal, not reflected upon, and whatever privileges that flow from being White are taken for granted.

Race-Based Violence that Sparked an Awakening in 2020

Since the murder of George Floyd in 2020, there have been efforts by EFT therapists to address cultural diversity in a more coherent way. Again, for White EFT therapists, this is a choice. Anti-racist workshops and cultural diversity listening sessions have been organized to learn about the worldview of Black EFT therapists and promote anti-racist thinking. Specific workshops have included exploring White privilege and White fragility along with workshops on the racial trauma of Black men and a discussion forum with a focus on "Post-Traumatic Slave Syndrome" has been conducted. A group of Black EFT therapists from mainly the United States, Great Britain, Canada, and South Africa has formed a working group to share ideas. This seems to be a fresh start for exploration of the awareness of the EFT community and for gaining an awareness of culture in the self-of-therapist and the specific impact of one's worldview, biases, and culturally different clients. This is a beginning.

Perhaps for EFT Black therapists, however, George Floyds' murder was also an "awakening," and also a likely race distress PTSD-type reaction. This type of race distress also might have occurred with the murder of Emmett Till, Medgar Evers, Martin Luther King Jr., Trayvon Martin, Michael Brown, Tamir Rice, Philando Castile, Stephon Clark, Sandra Bland, Breonna Taylor, Ahmaud Arbery and others. Perhaps Black therapists might be paying more attention compared to White colleagues to each of these events and be vicariously impacted by the accumulation of race-based murders. Hopefully, this might lead to more assertive discussions about racial identity and effective therapy for Black couples.

WHAT BLACK SCHOLARS SUGGEST AS FOUNDATIONAL LEARNING FOR WORKING WITH AFRICAN AMERICANS COUPLES:

- That curiosity about African American experiences of race might enhance the working alliance.
- That curiosity about the African American worldview and the worldview of their parents' history might enhance the working alliance.
- A willingness to explore how discrimination might have impacted their parents' lives and their own. Show in reflections some appreciation for African American lived experiences and this might enhance case formulations.
- Taking academic or professional courses and workshops or doing independent readings about African American history helps to prepare for empathic interpersonal engagements.
- Engaging in academic or professional discussions with a diverse group about culturally different people can enhance the ability to discuss race with Black couples.
- Learning about implicit bias and Black negative stereotypes helps to get in touch with internalized racism. Reflecting on how these stereotypes have shown up in your own thinking is useful for foundational race identity development. This is helpful in case formulations, how we might talk about negative patterns of interactions, and enhance an understanding of emotional experiences.
- Develop some understanding of Black consciousness
- Develop some ethnically humble views regarding acculturation vs. cultural emersion.

- Have some understanding of the intersectionality of the Black LGBTQ experiences and the Black community.
- Develop some sense of the interplay or independent influence of racial identity, social class, street mentality, and spirituality in the Black communities.
- Have the ability to discuss your understanding of the additional threats to Black romantic relationships.
- Develop some understanding of the history of Black socialization of African American girls and boys.

What the Literature Suggests, We Should Include in Assessments of African American Couples

Some General Principles

1. Have some background and training experiences with the work suggested in the preceding section before the therapeutic encounter with Black couples.
2. Have some sense of your own values, biases, and openness to social, cultural, and social class differences.
3. Always begin with open-ended questions about race (e.g., do you identify with a racial group?).
4. Be open to exploring race and be curious about the intersections of racial identity and attachment histories.
5. Conceptualize race as a dynamic social process rather than a demographic category and assemble the emotions, meanings, and behaviors that link view of self and others.
6. Explore discrimination experiences with a curiosity for understanding the racial distress cue and for assembling the emotions, perceptions, and behaviors associated with any race-based event reported.
7. Bring cultural humility, cultural self-awareness, and racial identity to EFT (see Attachment and Cultural/Race-Related Interview Questions in Chapters 2, 10 and Appendix).

USEFUL EXPERIENTIAL

EXERCISE

Imagine yourself standing to deliver a 10-minute lecture in front of a group of 250 Black scholars knowledgeable about African American romantic relationships. Your small presentation will include an additional 10-minute question-and-answer period. This 20-minute engagement would be included in a documentary about Black romantic life. You are going to talk specifically about Black romantic relationships.

Of course, many of us have difficulty speaking in front of large groups. Hopefully, for this private exercise, we can find a way to get around that anxiety

Imagine making the group a bit smaller if that would help, or somehow finding a place inside yourself to help you remain calm. So take your time to make your imagination feel real and to stay with this moment and create the imagery of the people awaiting your presentation. Close your eyes and give yourself plenty of time to allow the creative process to work. Please don't rush, and let yourself hold the image of the room and the people in it and consider what you would say.

What Is Your Experience?

What was it like it like for you? Was it difficult to come up with an image? Was it easy or somehow troublesome seeing yourself there? Did you get some view of the audience? As you let yourself develop the imagery, what do you notice about the setting? Take a moment and reflect on what you might have seen in the faces in the audience—what do you notice? How do they seem to be engaging with you before your lecture begins? Notice what is happening to your body? What are you saying to yourself? Notice what is happening with you as you are responding to this invitation.

When you are ready, you might write down your answers to the questions below:

1. How prepared were you for engaging in this talk?
2. What are some first things you would say? What might you consider as an outline for your discussion?
3. What do you imagine are the questions you would have to address?

4 Love, Attachment Theory, and Emotionally Focused Couples Therapy

Sobonfu Some', a teacher of the Dagara people in West Africa, taught that marriage is a way of spiritually responding to life. Marriage joins two souls and worlds together and expresses their combined richness to the community.

West Africans' farming attachment model (where mothers are expected to continue working in the fields) is both similar and different than the Western attachment model (Otto & Keller, 2014). Rather than privileging the mother-child dyad where the baby reaches (cries) and the mother reacts with sensitive and responsive comforting, the West Africans' model is a collective one where the child cries and the mother and any number of other attachment figures reach to comfort. The child's experiences are responded to but not privileged to the needs of the collective family/community, which is seen as the central survival group. In this regard, all the essential elements of attachment bonds for survival and development hold true; the child's bonding experience is shared with more people, and the child is socialized to view self within and responsive to their collective group. "You are because we are, and we are because you are." Similarly, couple bonds served the collective community: family, extended family, tribal community, and spirit.

Of course, African Americans' attachment is no different than love between others. Yet given the history in the United States, African Americans' love can be seen as revolutionary (bell hooks, 2001a). The West Africans brought their concepts of attachment and love with them on the slave ships. Their attachment styles were forced to adapt to lives as Americanized African slaves. Within the slave labor camps the collective came to care for the babies, the children, the sick, the wounded, the emotionally distressed, the recently sold, and the recently arrived. "It takes a village to raise a child" was practiced as every African slave was vulnerable to disappearing, but the collective slave community remained and mourned, or was waiting to receive and comfort. As would be expected, infant mortality rates were extremely high during slavery, as women were severely challenged. The enslaved community was the collective caregivers for one another, and the collective community provided support from the harshness in the Jim Crow/Black laws period of American history.

During the great American migration between 1916 and 1970, six million African Americans left the Southern states. It was the largest and most rapid migration in human history not caused by war or starvation. While collectively

DOI: 10.4324/9780429355127-4

they fled the dangers and limitations of the South, they were also leaving their established collective attachment base. That communal base had collectively been a source of survival. In this regard, African American couples and family units, as never before, had to reestablish and recreate their collective attachment base and/or adapt to a middle-class majority culture model. Secure collective attachment may be particularly adaptive for adverse situations. This historical migration away from the cruelty and unfairness of the American South paradoxically was also a move away from the supportive family and community attachment bonds. As the Black Southern migrant came to learn, the Northern, Eastern, and Western United States were largely unwelcoming and discriminatory. In this new context African Americans' families and couples as a group had to face race-based stress from a more isolated position than ever before. Undoubtedly, the strength of African Americans' spiritual practices mediated the attachment losses with church attendance and development of a church family.

Attachment Theory

From John Bowlby and Mary Ainsworth we learn that a child's internal state of vulnerability or felt sense of security can be moderated by the accessibility, responsiveness, and emotional engagement of their primary care caregivers. Shaver and Hazan (1993) replicated these attachment results with adults, which suggest that we never outgrow the need for close and emotionally engaged love. Attachment, at its root, is a theory both about human love and survival and what strategies we use to maintain human bonds (Bowlby, 1970; Ainsworth & Bell, 1970). The basic tenets of attachment theory are:

- Seeking and maintaining proximity with social bonds and having a felt sense of security with another is a primary human need. It is a "wired-in" in human instinct that is linked to survival. Social bonding help to ensure survival. Thus, survival is more due to engaged human attachments than being "the fittest," as Darwin would have it.
- The nervous system is wired to alert us to danger, and this includes threats to our close relationships. Disconnections from our close attachment figures signal an emotional alarm, and this emotional signal evokes a behavioral protest about the felt sense of disconnection. This protest is driven by strong attachment-reactive emotions. Human beings protest in very specific and predictable ways, and these behaviors are called attachment strategies. Infants protest by crying, and these behavioral signals are calls to caregivers to respond with engaged care. Emotions and emotional signals organize and structure attachment bonds for infants and adults.
- We seek an emotional safe haven with our close love bonds; that is, we find it emotionally safe to turn toward loved ones in times of stress or distress. These people provide comfort when we are near them, help us to recover from distress, and provide emotional engagement. Such emotional safety can be provided by

one person or a network of close human connections. We learn as babies and young children, with repeated call-and-response patterns, that comfort and satisfaction come to us from these attachment figures. The growing child learns to seek out safe havens from their history of responsive care. Within safe havens, the growing child learns how to maintain emotional balance with trusted others and within themselves. Patterns of interpersonal interaction become cognitive models and automatic emotion regulation strategies and styles.

- The dependable responsiveness of others to our emotional signals help with the development of a secure base. A secure base produces an emotional groundedness from which to explore and learn about the world. A secure base is a social platform of safety that allows us to take risks and develop intellectual, physical, and social competencies. Individual development is enhanced with effective interdependence with other people. This attachment secure base is a source of recovery, exploration, and strength.
- Strong emotions are the music of love, and emotional signals help organize and structure attachment bonds. Emotions act as beacons for what we need. From cradle to grave, threats to loving attachment bonds are deeply felt intrapsychic experiences. Physical and emotional isolation from attachment figures brings about powerful emotional experiences that can traumatize human beings with a sense of vulnerability, danger, and helplessness. All couples move through moments of disconnection and closeness, with emotional reactions to these moments, which suggests that we are inescapably vulnerable to moments of distress in love relationships.
- There are predictable ways individuals respond in moments of relationship disconnection. This coping has been characterized as their general attachment strategies. These are strategies largely developed within the relationships with early caregivers over time. Securely attached people tend to have internalized a sense of emotional safety and are both ready to reach for connection with their partner or respond to the reach when it is offered. Insecurely attached partners who are anxiously attached do not feel emotionally safe to reach for connection but will seek safety with behavioral demands and seek to control their partner's responses. Partners who have an insecure avoidant attachment style also do not feel emotionally safe and tend to dismiss the need for connection, turning away from their partners. Insecurely avoidant partners can also not be available to their partners' reach for them.
- Working models of self and others are a set of expectations and beliefs about the self and others and the relationship between the self and others. The particular working model of an individual is developed from their attachment histories, attachment strategies, and relationship worldviews. The working model of self is their understanding of their own behavior and the behavior of other people—whether or not they are lovable and worthy of love, whether or not they can rely on others, whether others are available, or interested in them, or will help them in time of need.

It is the working model of self and others where the negative stories of African American men and women are potential threats to their view of self and others. Racial identity is also folded into the view of self (as racial group membership) and view of other (as similar or different racial group membership). As working models of self and others are malleable to social experiences, so too is racial identity. Racial identity is a way of making meaning about the racist stories about worth, beauty, and competency; African American have been primed in moments of disconnection and conflict to see each other with the same attachment traits (as everyone else) and also through a racial color lens of fear, lacking worth, and failures. In the racist view that African Americans are untrustworthy, African Americans have been primed to not trust each other. In the racist view that African Americans need to be treated harshly, African American couples have been primed to protest their worth and dissatisfactions, forcefully. In the worldview that the majority culture is generally hostile to African Americans, the broader attachment view of culturally different people (West African, Americanized Africans, and African American) is the following: "It takes a village to support the love of the African American couple." In a hostile world, African American couples continue to need a supportive community.

Principles of Love

The attachment lens guides both the EFT therapist's view of love and the framework of therapy. The attachment foundation of EFT guides the therapist to a more descriptive than judgmental or pathological view of human interactions. There is an overarching concern with developing emotional safety in therapy so that love will emerge. There is an overarching relentless positive view of human relationship.

Adult romantic love is an attachment bond where there are repeated call-and-response interactions. For adults the questions are "will you be there for me?" or "can I count on you?" These questions arise in moments of distress and reaches for closeness. The felt sense is that "when I call" out someone will be there for us. This can be an actual internal felt sense (with mental representation) and/or actual experience of a call-and-response.

The core of a secure base and safe haven is where that felt sense that mind, body, and spirit are in sync with another human being in an effective interdependent way: "I have someone I can count on" or "she is my ride or die, person" or "we are in this together" or "I can feel her/him with me as I go out into the world." It is a profound internal sense that my genuine self is loved by another and even at my worst, I'm lovable.

Love is not a sexualized attraction nor merely a warm feeling. Erotic physical attraction may lead to seeking relation, but there is no direct path there for secure love. Love is a set of actions that flows from feelings, enhanced by emotional safety. When accessibility, responsiveness, and emotional engagement (see the next section) are working features of the relationship, the partners have a "felt sense" that their true selves are acceptable and loved by the other. This emotional safety allows for vulnerable feelings, troubling thoughts, and worrisome experiences to be talked about. Moreover, this safety also promotes responsiveness to the same deep feelings, thoughts, and experiences of one's partner. This depth of communication can only occur when the climate of emotional safety is valued by the couple and developed with practice. Love means emotional engagement when there is a call/bid/reach to talk both about one's self, the relationship, and experiences out in the world. When we choose to love we choose to move against fear, reach toward our partners and away from social isolation and loneliness.

We can choose to create emotional safety where emotional vulnerability is accepted and celebrated. Beyond choosing to create emotional safety in the relationship, a couple has to work to make safety a positive pattern of their interactions. The move toward our partners in these deep vulnerable ways is also a move toward the accepting of our genuine self. When the partner is responsive and emotionally engaged, our genuine self can be embraced, supported, and enhanced by our partners. This mutual interdependency within close relationships is a natural state of thriving or living well. In contrast, intense loneliness and social isolation from close bonds can be deadly. Human beings have survived by positive call-and-response patterns, developing safe havens and secure bases with each other.

Working Model of EFT Attachment View of Love

"The development of love sense offers us a way forward into a different kind of world, a world in which we honor our deep desire to belong, where we have a felt sense of connection to our own soul and that of others. Secure love calms and restores balance and equilibrium."

(Johnson, 2013)

Accessibility: Accessible means being available and open to experiences of your partner, so that we are able to hear and send clear signals in the call-and-response pattern. We are present for their story, even when we have a different story about their experience. We are available even when we have our own worries and concerns about ourselves and the relationship. It is an openness to hear and quiet our internal dialogue about them, the issues, and ourselves. It is a willingness to reach across our own insecurities and relationship doubts to face our partners and listen to their experience. This often means having some awareness of our own sensitivities and protective filters so that we allow the focus to be on the other. This takes some degree of self-reflection in that our sensitivities and protective filters tend to highlight certain aspects of our partner's behavior and distort other parts. Emotional safety in the relationship helps mitigate the mutual vulnerability and risk in allowing oneself to be assessible. This can mean imperfect attempts to quiet our internal world that can be full of self-doubt and insecurity while listening and being curious about the partner's feeling and perspective. De-centering from one's own perspective, temporarily suspending our own frame of reference, and focusing on listening to our partner's strain/pain of attachment disconnections and needs is the loving gift of presence and curiosity, which helps to create emotional safety.

Responding: Responding means to hear our partner's feelings, thoughts, and experiences and react with acceptance, gentle curiosity, and warmth. These soft communications are clear signals to our partners that their fears and longing are being met with emotionally involved care and respect. So often this can be communicated with a simple touch. To the extent that emotional safety is in the relationship or valued, this can enhance attentive responding. Of course, when we have been emotionally hurt growing up, and have attachment related injuries, our internal protective filters have become alert to threats to our relationship and our own felt sense of lovability. These protective strategies either promote controlling or dismissive responses. As emotional safety increases in the relationship, more secure reflective and attentive responding occurs. Having a partner respond to our vulnerable feelings is uniquely healing. We can feel responsiveness in our heart and in our bodies. This is another major attachment behavior that facilitates development of emotional safety.

Emotional Engagement: Emotional engagement means both partners have a readiness and willingness to communicate through fear and anxiety and protective strategies that often block vulnerability. When both partners value emotional safety there is positive value to expressed vulnerability. There is a felt sense that both partners are striving, even imperfectly, to develop between them a degree of emotional safety that accepts each other's attachment importance and their vulnerability. Both are willing to face each other with their genuine self, their core identity and felt sense of security that they will be accepted and validated by their partner. Each is able to reflect on their own actions and fears while also taking into consideration their partner's background and fears. This mind to mind, body to body, spirit to spirit connection allows for the courage to risk clear attachment signals in pursuit of love and intimacy. Effective emotional engagement allows the couple to regulate each other's emotions and to provide both a safe haven and secure base for the relationship. This is mutual engagement and acceptance of vulnerability, which allows love to heal old wounds and is spiritually enriching. This is where the internal view of self and the view of the other can be malleable to change from a corrective emotional experience.

When Love Was So Good, How Does It Go So Bad?

While not the specific focus of couples therapy, the social context that generates significant threats to Black love is important to understand. African Americans and African American communities are diverse, and each partner in a relationship comes from a unique background that might include "good enough" parenting or one that included trauma or abuse. The range, frequency, and intensity of traumatic experiences that occur within families are likely similar across racial groups. Of course, this means that the families of origin of African American men and women are diverse too. It also seems true that American society is harsher on African American people. It also seems that African American families are harsher on African American children (Patton, 2017), and society as a whole is harsher on African American students, workers, litigants, and just well-meaning folks [Black while driving, Black while walking, and Black within one's own home (Alexander, 2010; Blackmon, 2008; The 1619 Project, 2019)]. It is likely that the harsh treatment of African Americans is the behavioral legacy of slavery (Blackmon, 2008). Given this research and history, it is understandable that Black couples are likely harsher in their criticisms of each other when a rigid negative pattern develops. It has also been suggested that these criticisms consciously or unconsciously are linked to damaging and demeaning historical stereotypes (Boyd-Franklin, 2003). The great migration also has inadvertently resulted in greater social isolation for African American couples from extended family and base communities. Given the general racially hostile climate in the broader majority community of the United States, there is not the same community support for Black relationships of love compared to the majority culture relationships.

Of course, all U.S. communities are not the same. The history of the African Americans, however, that has included "redlining" (racist policies that still exist that forced/directed African Americans into segregated neighborhoods: *NY Times*. 2019) and anti-Black attitudes continue to be as strong in Southern counties today as they were in 1860 (Deep roots, 2018). Moreover, African Americans consistently report high rates of discrimination within their day-to-day lives. As a result, racial stress insidiously fueled by 700 years of negative stereotypic views of African American men, women, and their relationships creates a potential conscious/unconscious sense of the risk of relationship loss and urgency for maintaining connections. Moreover, protection of a healthy sense of self and self-worth from racist ideas is a lifelong internal self-defense that goes on while engaging the social community of American life. This involves both racial identity development and active coping, which can be exhausting and at times creates unique vulnerabilities. When this coping involves healthy but strong paranoia adapting to majority culture, these internal protective skills may get in the way of healthy vulnerability in close relationship and prevent accessibility, responsiveness, and emotional engagement.

All couples face challenges to their ability to stay accessible, responsive, and emotionally engaged (everyday stressors, demands of work, extended family, and health). It seems to take distressed couples a great deal of time before they seek couples therapy (Gottman, 1994). When distressed couples enter relationship therapy, the fear of emotional disengagement has likely already led to demands, criticism, arguments, and silences that are found too often in troubled relationships, perhaps along with negative views of themselves and their partners

(Johnson, 2013). These negative views about relationship disconnections are also likely to be flavored with distress, helplessness, and despair. In this regard, they also are likely to have developed negative patterns of interactions that have been repeated over and over again with no resolution. Over time, the negative patterns become rigid interactions of repeated disconnections and conflicts. The partners' mutual protest in these exchanges are their best attempts to resolve and cope with the disconnections and distress. Nevertheless, the distressed couples' pattern of engagement can be viewed as a moment to moment or incident by incident unraveling of love (Johnson, 2013). Although the full articulation of EFT will come later, the EFT therapist attempts to intervene at the very moment of felt disconnection, to shift the unraveling love conversations to ones where there is greater potential for loving engagement.

Damaging Criticism

When love goes bad, couples may increasingly perceive deficits in each other that can lead to increased complaints or criticisms. When criticisms involve critiques on the partner's family, or how they were raised, or their flawed character, these criticisms can begin to have deeply hurtful and lingering emotional effects. The frequency and intensity of these negative comments on self-worth can also have more lasting effects on the emotional climate of the relationship. That is, the emotional safety of the relationship decreases. Criticism that involves more global references of disapproval invariably carry judgment and contempt (Gottman, 1994). Gottman view of the negative impact of criticism is shared by Johnson (2013), in that both suggest that love unravels in a series of moments involving emotional disconnections and dread. For Gottman, the unraveling involves criticisms, defensiveness, contempt, and stonewalling that lead to negative emotional flooding and despair that eventually leads to divorce. For Johnson, the process begins with moments of disconnection that are unresolved threats to the relationship that foster doubts about the relationship/partner. These doubts linger and fester with continued disconnections, failed attempts at repair, and growing despair. Similar to Gottman, Johnson states that the emotional disconnections are driven by criticism and stonewalling. Over time, disconnections form into negative patterns of interactions that are characterized by hurt feelings and misattunement. These criticisms, when intense, can lead to negative flooding of emotions that have a long, lingering effect. The lingering effect here is a decrease in emotional safety, which increases protective strategies. A negative pattern of reactive interactions occurs in which the sense of emotional threat is high, and an urgent felt need for protective strategies emerges. For the anxiously attached, demanding and controlling behaviors are likely to occur, and with a person with avoidant attachment style, dismissive and unresponsive/numbness are the frequent responses.

African Americans have been, and continue to be, subjected to the worst types of name-calling that reflects the historical abuse and demeaning assaults. This is the legacy of historical trauma. When name-calling occurs in the couple relationship that includes any references to old standard negative terms depicting African Americans, it is particularly hurtful and damaging. These raw names include those that demean Black women as ugly, promiscuous, and valueless and African American men as not enough of a man, worthless, selfish, unreliable, or disloyal. Typically, African Americans will not bring this openness about name-calling to couples therapy. This type of frank talk is not meant for public consumption. For the EFT therapist, however, who is revisiting a conflict of the couple, all of the emotionally infused words/cues that trigger will be edited out by the couple. This editing is, in fact, a clinically relevant secret. Of course, it is protective of the relationship and the therapist, but it hides the internal worries, self-doubts, fears, and flaws associated with the attachment disconnection protest and the cause of the demanding lingering impact. Culturally, African Americans have learned not to air their "dirty laundry" (Boyd-Franklin, 2003). First, EFT therapists have to create enough safety in the therapy for inviting open discussion. Secondly, therapists have to invite open discussion of race matters in the therapy (see Chapter 3) and finally, therapists have to be curious about how specific language is used in moments of disconnection and conflicts; that is, therapists have to ask questions about the trigger for reactive moves and the specific wording.

Couples also differ with regard to family of origin social class and skin color, which can trigger harsh criticisms. Therapists have to be curious about how the couple criticizes each other and the meaning they make of such criticism about their partner. The victim system values, discussed previously, support individual self-focused values but not relationship-healthy values. When victim values largely govern the worldview of one partner, they can promote an unhealthy seeking of dominance and exploitive behavior. Again, this may be a legacy of slavery/racial trauma, where Black women were particularly devalued and exploited, and Black men found some modicum of distorted power over, and felt sense of perverse competence, with Black women. Also, damaging criticism occurs when social class and/or skin color is used as code for "you're not Black enough," which can be a way of mocking and belittling. It is also damaging when family or friends are not supportive of relationship bonds and promote critical views of the relationship or are only loyal to their family member during disconnections rather than promoting self-reflection and emotional engagement with both partners. Here is where the collective community strength, or lack thereof, for a particular distressed couple is critical. The church community and kinship network can promote positive couple interactions when they offer a balanced view of relationship dynamics.

Harsh Stonewalling

Harsh withdrawal (stonewalling) blocks accessibility, responsiveness, and emotional engagement. That is, when one partner in a moment of distress about the relationship completely shuts down, healing cannot occur. If one person is closed off in such a way, there is absolutely no interpersonal engagement; it is as if the bond the couple had at one time no longer exists. While partners might withdraw from difficult interactions to settle their feelings, to avoid making the situation worse, and to obtain time away to self-reflect, stonewalling is different. There is no accessibility and even a lack of awareness of any internal feeling; more likely, there is a felt numbness toward their partner and the relationship. The withdrawer is completely cut off from their partner. The is no responding to their partner's verbal bids for discussion, there is little, if any, eye contact or response to expressed feelings of the partner. Such behavior typically has a devastating impact on the other partner and causes serious emotional alarms about the survival of the relationship along with deep suffering and loneliness. When used frequently, stonewalling can have a severely damaging impact on the stonewalling partner, the targeted partner, and the relationship.

Harsh critical pursuing also blocks accessibility, responsiveness, and emotional engagement. Such blockage can occur when the partners are singly or jointly so preoccupied with their own sense of threat that the reactive emotions drive them to protest relentlessly about their distress and the felt sense that the other is to blame for causing them pain. This is often the case when there is some history of trauma in the person's past and when there is little to no ability or willingness to self-reflect. In some cases, vulnerable feelings are so linked to being weak and weakness so linked to prior helplessness against abuse that there is a strong proactive protective inner-self along with a need to pursue proximity to the other. These intrapsychic and behavioral processes can happen intensely and simultaneously. There is little to no room for the other person in the relationship. Beyond the reactive moments where some trigger may have occurred, there still remains a perspective that the other partner's needs to both see and adopt their point of view about their wrongness and the relationship. This rigid perspective is protective of any threatening idea that the blocking partner is somehow wrong in their perspective or behavior. In these situations, the person can only tolerate their perceptions and the way they make meaning. Because they are not able to quiet their own internal experiences, they are not present for, or curious about, their partner's experiences. There is no motivation to respond to their partner's emotions and no space for emotional engagement that is not consistent with their self-protective needs.

Emotionally Focused Therapy

Emotionally Focused Therapy's foundation is the attachment lens with specific guidelines toward enhancing and promoting attachment-enriched conversation. The goal of EFT is to revise and repair the internal working models of self and other in a positive, genuine, and integrated way. There are particular noteworthy features of EFT that I will highlight later in this section. The interested reader is also encouraged to read Sue Johnson (2004, 2019, 2020) and Lorrie Brubacher (2018). Before I give a summary of those aspects, however, I would like to first link the process of loving communications, couple disconnections, and in the moment-to-moment clinical work of an EFT therapist. In this regard, the EFT therapist role is one of communication consultant.

The goal of the EFT therapist is to hear the distressed couple's story about their relationship through the attachment perspective. That is, with an understanding of accessibility, responsiveness, and engagement, along with reprocessing the moments of disconnections, the EFT therapist seeks to hear the meaning the couple makes of those distressed moments, the feelings evoked, and longing for secure bonding. The goal is to create a new pattern of interaction that includes more mutual accessibility, responsiveness, and engagement. The first phase of couple therapy involves creating emotional safety and establishing the foundation for emotional engagement by de-escalating the negative cycle of interactions. Tracking the negative cycle involves slowing down the communication process in specific ways. Among other things, this involves an assessment of attachment distress and factors that are related to emotional threats to the relationship bond. The second phase of EFT therapy is helping couples soften their communication with deeper attachment-infused conversations that form the basis of corrective emotional and loving experiences. The third phase is a consolidation of both communication process and content areas that emerged during the couples therapy.

Assessment

The couple's stated goals for therapy, and each partner's story about their reasons for being in couples therapy, are explored in the first session of therapy. In the first phase of therapy, referred to as de-escalation/stabilization, the therapist is attempting to hear from both partners with the understanding that as one partner relates their experiences and stories about relationship problems, that perspective is likely escalating the other partner's emotions. The therapist's first goal is to help create safety in the consulting room. As a result, the therapist has to attempt to balance each partner's contribution and thus help regulate the emotional intensity of these early conversations. This is likely to mean, particularly with highly escalated couples, maintaining control over the flow of conversations. The EFT therapist is often relentlessly validating and empathically reflecting each partner's reported experiences and views of their couple interactions. The negative pattern of interactions that has contributed to the couple's distress will also very likely be demonstrated in the early sessions as each partner relates their views. In this regard, the EFT therapist is attempting to slow the process of discussion down (in very specific ways); track the flow of the cycle of interaction that leads to distance, conflicts, and disconnection; and infuse the conversation with attachment meanings.

One of the first tasks the EFT therapist performs is assessing the stated goals of each partner for entering therapy and the compatibility of their agendas. For a more detailed discussion of EFT assessments, consult Johnson (2004, 2019, 2020) and Brubacher (2018). Assessing the safety for exploring attachment-related process is another initial task and an ongoing clinical consideration.

Several factors have been highlighted by both Johnson and Brubacher that are safety considerations: current partner violence, problematic substance abuse, and active affairs. There also has to be an agreement/contract as to what the couples therapy will be about. EFT therapists view themselves as "communication consultants" for the couple relationship. There are clearly times when one or both partners' agenda is to document that their partner is either crazy, wrongheaded, or needing individual help of various sorts. In the worst cases, the partner wanting documentation has not come to therapy to engage in treatment but to provide the evidence of their partner's deficiencies. From an attachment point of view, this behavior could also be seen as a protest associated with relationship threatening behavior of the perceived troubled partner. Nevertheless, this is a couples therapy agenda that would have to be negotiated for both safety and whether appropriate for EFT couples therapy.

Typically, EFT therapists have at least two sessions with both partners together and at least one session with each partner individually. The individual sessions can be helpful for exploring the degree of safety in the relationship, sensitive concerns, and whether each partner is committed to the relationship. This exploration also includes obtaining relationship histories. With people of color, it is important to bring up the matter of race for discussion early in the therapy. I use an adaptation of the "Adult Attachment Interview and Racial Identity Questionnaire" (see appendix,1). This questionnaire is conducted as a structured interview in the same manner of clinical curiosity and openness as a skilled EFT therapist explores information of attachment significance. Typically, Black couples know that they are seeing either a therapist of color or a White therapist before they come to therapy. It therefore seems of little value to ask about whether it is a concern of theirs that the therapist is of a different race.

The Black couple may or may not know how racial microaggressions impact their relationship or prefer to discuss matters of race outside of therapy. The racial identity scheme of Helms (1995), previously discussed, also suggests that some Black couples might strategically pick White therapists because they identify with majority culture and to avoid talking about race. What is important to all Black couples, however, is how race might matter in their lives and between them as a couple. Asking more systematic questions about race demonstrates that the therapist appreciates both the depth that race matters and the couples therapist's comfortableness with matters of race. Moreover, it gives the therapist a platform to discuss the implication of racist ideas in the negative pattern of their interactions (if present). Eventually, this will also create a safe platform to celebrate moments of emotional engagement of Black love.

Within the early phases of couples therapy, the EFT therapist is developing an understanding of the attachment-influenced schemes of their reoccurring call-and-response dance: the couple's negative pattern of interactions. This will include reactions of each partner when something causes a disconnecting/distancing/conflictual moment. The descriptions of their reaction will include the disconnection moment and the meaning each partner makes of the other's reaction. There is also assessment of the attachment strategies, or positions, used in response to the moment of sparked relationship distress. For example, anxiously attached pursuit (blames, yells, criticizes demands) in some particular way or avoidant attached withdrawal (defends, distances, dismissive, hides), particular to that partner's tendency. Sometimes, both partners' patterns can involve Anxious pursuing or Avoidant withdrawing.

In-Session EFT Communication Processing

The skilled EFT therapist uses a variety of the following EFT macro-moves, basic techniques, and micro-interventions to enhance communication. The particular skills used within a session is, to some degree, a work of artistic style. While clinical decisions will vary, however, the attachment focus is always a key element, whether that is focused within the internal experience of one partner or the interactions pattern between partners. The EFT tango macro-moves are five basic communication-enhancing moves that the EFT therapist uses to slow the discussion down, track the negative cycle of interactions, and enrich the therapeutic conversation with attachment focus experiences. While the tango is a series of moves toward the goals of enhancing accessibility, responsiveness, and emotional engagement, often an EFT therapist is moving slowly with the couple. Often very early in the couples work there can be a great deal of emotional reactivity and low safety between the partners, and this might mean more validation and empathic reflections within the first two tango moves. It cannot be overstated that creating emotional safety in the room is a primary task of the EFT therapist. To that end, the therapist is working hard to hold both partners' points of view and feelings. With African American couples this is an extra layer of safety added as EFT therapists might also give brief rationales for procedures. Tango moves are used in combination with micro-interventions.

Move one: Within the context of building a working alliance, and as the therapist is listening to the unfolding stories of each partner's experience and their perspectives of the relationship, the therapist in the present moment attempts either to reflect what they are hearing or witnessing about the partner's view of self (within experience) in some tentative way that seeks to understand the partners internal experience. This response of the therapist can also be reflections about the couple's interactions (interactions between them) offered in a tentative way that explains the therapist's understanding of the couple's pattern of communication. Here, the therapist is attempting to explore, in session, experiential moments for attachment signal/cue (reflecting on what they see or hear). The therapist will also revisit a recent moment of conflict or disconnection. Often later in couples therapy, such revisiting might also mean the therapist seeks to reflect on moments of connection or moments of disconnection.

Move two: As the therapist engages one partner, he/she attempts to explore emotions and gently begins the process of assembling emotional reactivity (that is, a perceived threat, in early phases of the work). This might include naming and understanding the reactive feeling associated with the signal of distress or disconnection. Slowing the process down helps the therapist explore the initial cognitive appraisal, their body responses, the meaning they make of the signal/cue (which is associated with a working model of view of self and other), and finally, the behavioral tendencies. The therapist seeks to link all aspects of emotional experiences from internal experience to external expression. In the de-escalation phase, move two might only include reactive emotions (frustration, anger, annoyance, jealousy, or disappointment) and only seeding that deeper feelings may also be involved (vulnerable feelings that include fear, hurt, loneliness, sadness). The therapist attempts to create/maintain emotional safety by relentlessly validating and providing empathic reflections while holding both partners in the conversation. In later phases of couples therapy, such attempts might still include some acknowledgment of reactive feelings, but increasingly deeper emotions associated with attachment longing and needs are now more accessible. As the couple's therapy develops, each partner is more likely to own their contribution to the negative pattern of communication. The challenge here is whether partners will allow themselves to become accessible to both their voice of protest and protection along with their softer attachment feelings (mainly fear) and longing for love/connection.

Move three: During the de-escalation phase, this third move involves a facilitated engaged encounter with the other partner about some attachment-significant feeling, perspective, or moment. Typically, such a feeling, perspective, or moment can be something that could be easily missed with the speed of the reactive cycle, as can a softer feeling about the partner or hope for the relationship previously unexpressed. During the later stages of couples work, this move three is largely involving encounters of deeper attachment and vulnerable softer feelings that also include exploration of internal working models of self and their partner. Move three represents an attempt to facilitate an accessible, responsive, and emotionally engaged conversation. In the early phases of therapy, it can be an assessment about emotional blocks in the couple relationship.

Move four: The facilitated conversation is processed with both partners so that the feelings and experience of both are expressed to each other. Each partner comes to know how it feels to tell his/her partner about feelings or perspectives and how it feels to hear the other partner's perspective. Sometimes there is a difficulty with a felt sense of safety with the direct expression of feelings or perspective with each other, and here there can be a moment's pause on these expressions until it is safe enough to proceed. In that case, a therapist might decide to shift to facilitating the fear/discomfort of expressing an experience or return to either Move one (some type of reflection) or Move two, a return to assembling feelings with perspective (a reflection about the attachment significance).

Move five: The therapist summarizes and integrates, with validation, the shift or change in communication that has taken place. This move typically will be a moment where the couple is emotionally engaged with each other, celebrating something new, a reach, or acceptance that might have occurred. Of course, if no change had taken place or somehow the conversation had gotten derailed at some earlier move, the therapist would have stayed at that move, processing there or returning to Move one with a reflection about where the derailment occurred and validating the good reasons why the derailment might have occurred. This does not reflect a regression in the work or a flaw of the EFT therapist; it is a natural flow of couples work and the therapist staying attuned and walking with partners in their attachment-related conversations.

In summary, each tango move relies on the EFT therapist building a work alliance, using EFT interventions and creating a safe haven in the therapy with attunement, acceptance, and genuineness. Such an alliance also means EFT therapists need to be proactive with matters of race and culture, including assessment questions that include racial identity, discrimination, and microaggressions. Inviting culture and cultural differences into the room promotes the working alliance and genuineness. As this is done early in the work (after a focus on what brought the couple to therapy and with assessment material), it can enhance both the exploration of emotional reactions and later in the work, explorations of the working model of self and other. The goal early in therapy is to create a collaborative agenda and working alliance for engaging the couple's relationship goals. The working alliance is established and maintained with a working sense of collaborative goals, attunement, and openness to and celebration of influence of cultural matters. The basic clinical skills include clinical practices of experiential interventions that track and reflect internal experiences and system interventions that track and reflect interpersonal interactions (Johnson, 2004, 2019; Brubacher, 2018).

The following micro-interventions are used both individually and in various combinations to promote awareness, development, expressions of emotions, and attachment significance.

Experiential Interventions

- Active listening with congruent verbal and nonverbal responses that promote accessibility, responsiveness, and emotional engagement.
- Empathic reflections that are responsive to the relationship stories and personal communications that are an attempt to be responsive to each partner's internal experiences.
- Relentless validation of the perceptions, emotions, and experiences (as the partner understands and makes meaning of their experiences). This is often done while reassuring the other partner that their experiences of the story may be different.
- Relentless empathy for the experiences of each partner and their pattern of interactions, even how they get stuck in a negative cycle of interactions.
- Evocative responding to enhance the communication of emotional experiences.
- Heightening of the emotional experiences and attachment meanings.
- Empathic conjectures that are offered as the leading edge of emotional or attachment longings or needs.

Systemic Interventions

- Tracking the pattern of couple interactions, slowing the process down to assemble emotional, behavioral, and meaning elements. Highlighting the rigid and automatic negative cycle of reactive interactions.
- Catching the Bullet, when vulnerability is met with reactive criticism, dismissive responses, or otherwise rejecting stances.
- Assessment of attachment history and reframing couple experiences with attachment framing.
- Identifying the withdrawer and pursuer and linking these positions to the negative cycle of interactions.

RISSSC Essential EFT Tools for Deepening Emotions

RISSSC is an acronym for the use of language in the session to help focus and develop emotions in the conversations. Within RISSSC: "R" is for repeating words of partners, or repeating reflections, evocative reflections, and attachment-related observations and reflections; "I" is for using client imagery when using empathic reflecting and validating experiences; "S" is a reminder to keep reflections, comments, and validations simple; "S" is for talking slowly when soft emotions are being explored; "S" is for talking softly when evoking vulnerable feelings; "C" is for using clients' words that are embedded with emotional meaning.

Stages of EFT Therapy and Focus of the Couples Work

Stage One (early work): De-escalation: much of the work here is focused on developing accessibility and responsiveness that slows the process of communication down. The negative pattern of engagement is reflected repeatedly so that the partners begins to understand their role in the negative cycle, how the reactive emotions drive the pattern, and how the negative pattern takes over their relationship. The partners' attachment history and their failed attempts to resolve their issues are processed. As emotions are assembled (in specific ways), the clearer the call-and-response pattern reveals positive attachment intentions of both partners.

Stage Two (later work): Emotional engagement of both partners is the focus of stage two work. It involves a number of change events in the therapy that soften the call-and-response pattern between partners. The work here continues to develop the accessibility and responsiveness of both partners, creating a deep emotional encounter between them in sessions. The impetus for the sessions work can come from in-session observations by the therapist, revisiting a difficult moment of the couple or reflective considerations of one or both partners. It is in this part of the stage two that emotional encounters between partners builds on the safety created in the therapy.

Within these emotional engaged encounters the love bond is strengthened.

Stage Three (consolidation of work) bring the new strength of the emotional engagement to particular areas of historical difficulties between the couple.

Zora Neale Hurston gives us in the following excerpt an example of her life-long pursuit of old-school African American wisdom and love:

Negro Folk-tales from the Gulf States: The Snail and His Wife

> *"De snail's wife got sick. She was rollin' from side to side in her bed. So she tole her husban': 'Oh Lawdy, I'm so sick. Please go get de doctor for me an' hurry up. I don't speck I'm goin' be here long.'*
> *So he said, 'all right.'*
> *So she laid there seven years rollin' an tumblin' wid misery.*
> *So after seven years she heard a scufflin' at de door. So she said:*
> *'Oh, I'm so glad. Dat's my husban' done come back wid de doctor.'*
> *So she hollered an' tole him: 'Is dat you, baby, wid de doctor.?'*
> *He say: 'Don't try to rush me. I ain't gonne yet'."*
>
> (*Every Tongue Got to Confess*, Zora Neale Hurston, 2001)

5 Case Study
EFT Stage One Work With Trust as Central Issue

Paul T. Guillory and Case Discussion with Sue Johnson

This is a case example where a fragile sense of security causes major conflicts within an African American couple, Clifton and Monique. While the husband has unique anxiety about his wife's attractiveness and his sense of self, neither seems to "truly think" the other has been unfaithful. Yet trust is difficult, and their negative cycle is strong. Their educational experiences are typical of African Americans of their age group. That is, they attended segregated schools, with no expectation of college and limited work opportunities after high school. They also lived in segregated, redlined communities in the Bay Area that included more violence (with simultaneous over-policing and low police responsiveness). Each of their parents' lives were also directly impacted by segregation and oppressive work opportunities; both mothers worked as cooks and caregivers to White families (see the book *The Help*, Stockett, 2009). While each of their mothers were sources of strength and comfort, their fathers taught them about relationship betrayal at an early age. In fairness, however, both of their fathers were also directly impacted by discrimination and the limited opportunities for bright Black men. To some extent, each of their fathers obtained some degree of self-respect from their pursuit and attention from women (see Boyd-Franklin, 2003; Pinderhughes, 2002). Both Clifton and Monique, in their own prior romantic lives, have been betrayed. When their couple friends have divorced, it involved betrayal, which has influenced their negative cycle and intimacy.

The harshness of African American history, and their own early experiences combine to influence this couple's negative cycle. Their negative pattern when stress cues are triggered can be particularly harsh, damaging, and without resolution. The demeaning language in the midst of their cycle is used to demean and hurt. Their words and tone come from stereotypical demeaning terms targeted toward African Americans. The aftermath of these disconnections can also be harsh, as they might not talk to each other for up to a month afterwards. Each one feels the sting from the negative cycle and righteously waits for the other to apologize, and each one endures the feelings of isolation. It is important to note that despite their negative cycle, this is a couple that enjoys each other. The negative pattern seems to be an albatross; sometimes on fire and otherwise quietly in background.

DOI: 10.4324/9780429355127-5

Clifton is anxiously attached, and Monique is dismissively avoidant. Both see their position in the cycle as a strength. He sees his questions (prosecuting truth/ her behavior) as source of his brightness and Black community experience, and she sees her stoic avoidance (strong and no nonsense) as source of a Black woman's strength. As a couple, they have been active in African American social groups. While they have a small group of married friends that have grown up with them, they have also experienced many Black couples that have been challenged by betrayal by both men and women. Neither one is comfortable talking about feelings, both have difficulties with encounters, and each one feels the other is unlikely to change their basic self (sensitivities and points of views) from therapy. They represent a unique set of challenges to an EFT therapist, as the couple attempts to reject both the foundations of EFT as not being consistent with Black culture and the intensity of their negative cycle. This case study is an example of largely stage one work, where the therapist is building the foundation for stage two communications.

DESCRIPTIONS OF PARTNERS

Clifton and Monique are both in their early fifties and attractive; both look much younger. They were born and raised in the San Francisco Bay Area. They met in line at a grocery store. When Clifton initially approached her, Monique made it extremely clear that she was not interested. As Clifton would later say about her, "Monique can be as mean as a snake!" Nevertheless, he politely and gently persisted, and the line in Safeway was fortunately long and slow that day. According to Monique, she felt Clifton was different from the beginning. Monique is very attractive and has gotten far more attention from men than she has ever wanted. She continues to believe that Clifton is a wonderful type of Black man: kind, full of integrity, and considerate. They have been married for 20 years. They have no children together, but each has children from prior relationships. Monique has a 23-year-old disabled son, and Clifton has two daughters, 38 years old and 25 years old.

REASONS FOR COMING TO THERAPY

Monique and Clifton came to couples therapy after an explosive argument. Monique had agreed to drive her longtime girlfriend's brother to a cookout near the Bay Area. She did not tell Clifton about driving her friend's brother, because she knew how he would react to the idea of her driving alone with a man. Clifton, forever on the alert about Monique's behavior, had plenty of questions for her when she returned from her day-long trip. He couldn't understand why she hadn't called him on the way there or on the way back. He continued to return to this point, again and again. Finally, over a period of a couple of days, she reluctantly told him about the transporting of her friend's brother. They argued for days. This intense argument ended as most of their heated arguments do by feeling miserable and hopeless and not talking to each other for nearly a month before coming to couples therapy.

EARLY THERAPY TRANSCRIPT: REVISITING A RECENT CONFLICT

Guillory: Now, let me ask Monique because I'm a little confused and maybe she can fill me in on something. I'm not clear on when the talk between you all starts to go bad? *(Tracking the negative pattern for the distress cue for Monique).*

Monique: When he tells you that he starts his communications with me softly, what he has failed to say is there is something here about what Clifton does. So let me tell you. He will get a feeling, and he will have already started "the script" he would have finished his script before he's talking to you. So by the time he talking me, it is now the story. He's already pissed, he's uncomfortable, he's unhappy. I've been on the receiving end of that anger, and this has been going on for years. As years have gone by, I have no patience for it. The truth is, it doesn't matter what I say to him because he's already got the story.

Clifton: That may be true, but that's not the whole picture. Honestly, I'm glad she said all of that. Once I have filled In the blanks (with emphasis on I HAVE to), it is in response to something Monique tells me that doesn't feel right, I'll then ask questions. When she then fills in the details and tells me what actually happened, then I say "Oh, okay," and then I'm calmed down.

Monique: But that's not you! *(Sitting upright and saying emphatically)* Relaxing *(Laughing)*. That doesn't happen.

Guillory: Okay. So can you help me with when it goes bad? I don't know if that's what you said or there is something important about how it lands on you? *(Returning the focus to the distress cue that starts the cycle).*

Monique: That's where we end up at a bad place because I am not a big fighter, or an arguer. I've never have been that. He says I fight "real" good, and he doesn't like the fact when I say he's taught me well. Okay? *(Looking at Clifton).* With that said, there is a part of my own personality that is hard. I admit that, I can be hard, but the part he's not bringing to the table is the damage he brings with his script. And when he comes with his script, it doesn't come very nicely. So it seems to me I only can respond in two ways, fight back or I try to let it go. This was one of those rare occasions where his words hit in a place that was so deep, that I couldn't let it go. I could not believe that he would say those things to me. He said horrible things to me that day. I'm still feeling very insulted *(Sounding hurt and voice cracking a bit).*

Guillory: When he starts talking to you about his script, and how he had filled it in with these horrible details, even in your voice now as you talk about it, you sound really hurt. Like that went deep inside your soul in some way and it still hurts. *(Evocative summary, and using in the moment observation to focus on her emotional experience, Move two with perhaps developing Move three, an encounter).*

Monique: Why would you even put that kind of script on me? *(Voice now shifting from hurt to anger).* Something so vile and nasty like I'm some other bitch out in the street. To me, that was an insult. Even if he's right and I should have told him about the brother, he didn't have to insult me like that. *(The intensity of her anger growing).* At first I chose not to argue with him because it was insulting, but then he got to me. And then I went after him. *(As she reflects her voice becomes more even-toned).* As I think about it now and maybe I really should have handled it differently, but at the moment, no. It was like, you're going to believe what you want to believe. I am not going to spend my energy trying to convince you over something that's so unbelievable. I should have taken his feelings in consideration, I can see that now that I've stepped back from it, but at the moment we were both upset. He's still upset and will be forever.

Guillory: *(Leaning in toward them).* What I've been trying to do, Clifton and Monique, is that these are the kinds of difficult moments that happen between couples. This moment has come up again and again. I'm trying to slow it down to see what happens to you guys in those moments *(Looking back and forth to each of them using RISSSC). (Then shifting to looking directly at her).* Monique you're resigned, is what I'm hearing, to think that Clifton is a certain way, as if, he's going to be angry about this and uncomfortable about this forever. And you're saying Monique, well, "I can't change him. This the way he is from his relationship past, and I have to accept that." I think there's potential for a different conversation between the two of you about this sensitivity of Clifton's, and maybe you all can heal from this. What happens to you when I talk this way Monique? *(Assessing our working alliance with the focus on changing the way they communicate with an attachment focus).*

Monique: His scripts have always been our problem

Clifton: Well, it gets cemented because the longer it just sits there, the more I'm going to believe what it is because I have nothing else to go on.

Guillory Okay that makes sense that you would have questions. You would be uncomfortable. And unless there is a conversation with Monique, it's going to be cemented. So there is a need for a conversation with her where maybe she doesn't feel insulted. And that's where I guess it went wrong. When you quickly filled in the blanks and if I've got it right, it was the worst script possible. Does that make sense? *(Validating and evocative reflection and tracking the cycle with a distress cue and the way his emotions assemble his perspective and conclusions).*

Clifton: Yes

Guillory: When you told her that worst script, she felt insulted like you're calling her a street bitch doing something nasty and wrong? And you said that to her, and OOH that landed really badly with her. And the way I understand this issue is that you could go there with women, even before Monique; maybe the betrayal and bad experiences with women of your past you could not trust? So you have reason to doubt? *(Reflecting the cycle and his raw spot about betrayals with validation).*

Clifton: Yes That's the short answer. You said reason to doubt. That's a little questionable because as much as Monique would never think so, I still feel like I give her the benefit of the doubt based on how I know I can be and who she is. If that makes any sense whatsoever.

Guillory: Help me understand.

Clifton: I can give her the benefit of the doubt based on how I know she is. I know she loves me. I think that she's *(Drifts off to quiet* as if reflecting). I don't want to start a fight here, okay? But I think she's on my side. . . . But . . . being blunt and not to make her uncomfortable, I think Sonya is on my side 99% of the time. I wouldn't want to be in a boat with one of her friends and we need to get rid of someone. I would want to compete with that.

Guillory: This is important, and is it how you see it, Clifton, that at critical moments Monique would choose one of her friends over you? What's that like for you, Clifton, when you put it together that way? That she would choose her friends over you?

Clifton: Yes. So what I heard was, "That's my friend and I don't care what you say. I'm going to do it anyway," or, "I'd do it again," that's the 1%. That's the part that makes me the most uncomfortable. It is probably the second worst thing that she has ever said to me.

Guillory: The second worst thing she said to you *(Deep breath with pause using RISSSC)* help me, what was the worst? *(There is at least two ways to go here; following the thread of "that's my best friend," which is associated bad moment, or going with the worst things she's called him.).*

Clifton: Just the name-calling stuff that we do sometimes. I'm guilty of it, too, and it bothers me the most. It's when we call each other bitches this and niggers that. Those are the worst, and no matter what, those are the hardest. They hit me the hardest.

Guillory: Yeah, can you help me understand how hard that hits you? Is it the kind of name-calling you guys use when you're both in the heat of the argument? But it hits hard. It hits something in your core. In your core *(pause)* that's disrespectful. *(Evocative question, tracking cycle, linking the stereotypical demeaning race-based terms to unique pain when used in romantic relationships).*

Clifton: Yeah. I'm not absolving myself of blame. Sometimes I go there first, and I know it gets to her. I know it makes me uncomfortable and I know you're going to ask me for more feelings but it goes from uncomfortable straight to angry, and ready to go back at her.

Monique: We've called each other that, but not all the time. This situation touched a nerve. I know it gets to him because like most men, it represents that you're acting like a child, or girl and it gets to their pride. And then I'll say on top of that, we all say things when we're angry. If you take every single thing to the literal point, then he has a valid point—but that's something I said, yeah, we should think about.

Guillory: So you said that when you were angry? And you want him to hear that it was said in anger because of the way he came at you? *(Tracking the hurt that was done in their negative cycle).*

Monique: Most of the stuff that I said was in reaction to him. And, unfortunately, when you get angry and say stuff. He's angry and I'm angry. . . . I know that. But sometime I fall into the same place, because I'm human, I say stuff and then you can't take it back. So that, to me, is just the way it is. . . . I've already passed that. I don't know if it's something you even want to go back over again. If you do we can. But it's a nail in that cross.

Guillory: That's important, Monique, because both of you said some things when you were angry, taken over by the negative cycle, and both were hurt by what was said. Arguments happen between all couples. African American couples can be particularly harsh with name-calling, and sometimes too careful leading into each other with our hearts. Leading with love. No we can't change people directly, Monique; we can change the way we communicate with each other. When we change the way we communicate . . . like less harsh words, name-calling and such, it helps. It helps, too, when we don't quickly create a script and then go after our partner, and, Clifton and Monique, we all want to be number one . . . chosen first in love. *(it seems clear when the "bitches" and "nigger" language shows up in their heated argument it contributes to the infliction of lasting hurt and pain. It is critical to name the harm, and injecting hope that they can change how they communicate and heal their relationship).*

Discussion of Transcript

There is much to unpack in this transcript, and it nearly completely frames the focus of this couple's therapy. This is stage one work, where the central goal is de-escalation. There are several tasks needed to achieve couple de-escalation that included creating emotional safety within the couples therapy and building a working alliance that is based on shared goals. In stage one work, the EFT therapist is relentlessly demonstrating empathy toward each partner's experiences, empathically reflecting on both their reactive emotions and attachment feelings, and tracking the negative pattern of communication (for more information about de-escalation, see Johnson [2019, 2020]). There are several distress cues that become apparent for each partner. There are distress cues revealed in the reprocessing of their difficult moment, and then there are distress cues activated in the subsequent intense conflict that emerged. The therapist is mainly being curious about their experiences, tracking the negative cycle from distress cues, assembling their emotions, and seeding brief encounters. Clearly, attachment hurt and scared feelings trigger their discord, and racialized demeaning language adds intensity to their pain. Of course, the language reflects their learning within the context of restricted U.S. communities (see "Influences of Race" later in this chapter). As typical with stage one EFT work, the therapist is validating the couple's perspectives and feelings, asking them evocative questions and reflecting on their comments. I invited discussion of their African American experiences in two significant ways; first by use of an adult attachment questionnaire that has questions about racial self-identity and culture, and then by being open to and ready to engage with, their reactions to race-related matters.

MONIQUE'S ATTACHMENT HISTORY

Monique was born in the Bay Area and has four sisters. As long as she can remember, her parents had a difficult relationship:

> I watched my mother put up with so much stuff with my father's cheating. He had another woman who lived three houses away from them. When he drank too much alcohol he would turn into a loud and angry person. My parents would have arguments and break up, and he would go live with the other woman. He would never be physically aggressive or violent, but just mean and had a "filthy mouth." He could be scary when upset, however, and she remembers she and her sisters would bring pots to their bed, just in case he got physical with their mother, but he never did.

She describes her mother as a very independent and self-reliant woman who focused her life around her girls and a few close women friends. She describes her relationship between her mother and sisters as "real tight" and "very overprotective of us." Both parents were protective of their girls regarding male relatives and friends of the family. Monique and her older sisters went to work during high school to help with the family financial situation, and they took care of their baby sister when their mother worked.

Monique's father is described as "brilliant." He wanted to go to college out of high school. Unfortunately, his parents made it clear that they would not and could not finance a college education. Disappointed, he went into the military with a goal of becoming a fighter pilot but could not get into fighter pilot school. According to Monique, her dad never seemed to get over these two disappointments. He was a good father, but as they got older that wasn't enough. After her mother thought her father's womanizing and drinking started to impact her girls, she divorced him, when Monique was in the fifth grade. Nevertheless, she came to view her mother as "weak" for staying with him for so long.

Monique was described as "hard" a young girl, and she was warned that "you'll never keep a man being that hard." Her mother raised her, however, to never have to depend on a man for anything. She reflects that her stubbornness is a trait that makes it hard sometimes for her in relationships. That is, when she gets upset with someone, she can shut down and it is very hard for her to come back to normal, "When I'm done, I'm done . . . I can just distance myself from that person, and take too long to come back. That's not healthy for me, but that's the person I am."

Romantic Relationship History

When Monique was 16 years-old she had her first boyfriend, who was a 33-year-old man. They dated for three years. While Clifton refers to him as a child molester, she recalls that the relationship was not a bad experience for her. She believes that he taught her a great deal of the world and about men. She never wanted to date men her own age, and she did not enjoy dating activities of people her age. She would marry her first husband when she was in her twenties and have one child. That relationship ended in divorce when she discovered that her husband was unfaithful. It broke her heart, and she became "bitter" about relationships. She focused on her son, work, and her sisters and girlfriends.

CLIFTON'S ATTACHMENT HISTORY

Clifton was his mother's first child, and his father's ninth. His mother was to have two daughters after him. Clifton's father was married to another woman, and was having an affair with his mother at the time of his birth. His father remained married to his wife, and ended the relationship with his mother before Clifton was born. While his father reportedly never denied his parenthood, he had minimal involvement in his life. His mom worked as a maid for two different wealthy families over her working life. His father owned four small businesses in the African American community.

His father had another family, and his father's other children rejected Clifton, and he recalls little interaction between them when he went to visit. His older half-sibling had little to no engagement and the ones he was closer in age to would annoy each other. They were not friends and "it didn't bother me a bit," he said. He would later, as an adult, pursue a relationship with most of his half-siblings.

Clifton reports that his mother was known as "big mama" in their community and was known for being generous with her cooking. She was a "neighborhood mom." He spontaneously comes to tears as he recalls that she never forced him to eat something that he didn't like and would cook him particular food when he requested it. "Mom used to make teacakes, string beans, and potatoes" after he came home from the hospital. He recalls getting treated more favorability than his sisters largely because he was sick "all the time" as a young child. At eight years old he was hospitalized with tuberculosis for several weeks. He remembers having difficulty breathing and coughing and the "long" stays in the hospital. He also had constant ear infections and many colds. His mother was always there during visiting hours and would pamper, nurture, and console him.

He describes his neighborhood as complex; it was tough because physical fights were happening all the time, and it was also a great deal of fun. While he is embarrassed by it now, he suggests it was normal for the boys to sell weed and do small burglaries at the nearby factories. He reflects that he knew it was wrong, was uncomfortable with all of it, but they all did it. He knew he was just different and thinks he was just not mean like some of the other guys. He mostly enjoyed drawing and was good at art, and that's how he would spend his time while in the hospital. He stopped the gang stuff when he was 15 after his first child was born. He also dropped out of high school and went to work to support his girlfriend and baby. He was to finish high school as an adult, and he is currently working on his college degree.

Romantic Relationship History

Clifton tears up again as he reflects on how his childhood has impacted on who he has become as an adult. He sees himself as having no patience, similar to his parents. He sees himself as pessimistic (always believing the worst-case scenario) when there is bad news, and he has anger problems. His romantic relationships started early, when he was 15 years old and nearly always has included betrayal. His first major love was his teenage girlfriend who also became the mother of his first child and his first wife. She broke his heart when he discovered that she had cheated early and often during their relationship. He went to work after his daughter was born, and he lived with his wife and daughter for a while until he discovered his wife's infidelity. He would have three other major romantic relationships before marrying his current wife; he discovered she was also unfaithful.

THERAPIST'S REFLECTIONS OF PATTERNS OF THERAPY

Protests Meet Counter Protests

The following points and counterpoints occurred over the course of Monique and Clifton's couples therapy. These point/counterpoint patterns only lead to blocks in communicating by partners: Neither partner feels heard. Embedded in these interactions are this couple's negative patterns.

Point: "It's only a question," Clifton will say, as he confronts her with the initial step in his negative "scripts," after noticing something in her behavior that triggers his distress cue *(Of course, he is asking questions as a prosecuting attorney might)*.

Counter Point: Monique counters with "I have my own questions." Monique relates a story about a texted picture of a half-naked young woman she discovered on his phone. She also gives other examples of Clifton's behavior with other women that bothered her, which she kept to herself *(As a Black woman who is strong enough might)*.

Point: Monique suggests that Clifton needs to work on his insecurities on his own because it is his problem *(He is an insecure man)*.

Counter Point: Clifton suggests that Monique is a feminist, doesn't apologize for anything, she does what she wants to do, and will never back down *(She is too hard)*.

Point/Move of Guillory: Can you turn to Monique and look her in the eye and tell her those feelings you are talking about? *(Attempting an encounter after assembling his emotions)*.

Counter Point to Guillory: Clifton. . . "Yes, I can and I will, BUT can I say this first?"

Monique: "I'm just made that way ". . . *(When asked to explore her feelings)*.

Both say: "Black people don't do that, Doc" *(When attempting an encounter)*.

Negative Pattern

Negative pattern one: Clifton anxiously pursues Monique in a prosecutorial way when he notices a change in her patterns of behavior; the pattern change is a distress cue. When they are at a social gathering, a distress cue will be her being too friendly to a man. The distress cue suggests to Clifton that something is going on, and his appraisal goes to the worst-case scenario, and he starts asking questions (sooner or later the questions get to "What's going on between you and that guy?"). For Monique, with the first question, she says to herself, "Here it comes again;" her appraisal is that an attack is coming and she's tired of it. She decides to fight back either by asserting her right as a grown woman or by attacking Clifton's insecurities. As Clifton pursues more, Monique fights back, and their pattern is consistent with attack/attack couples. These episodes tend to end with mutual withdrawal for long periods of anger, hurt, wounded, and sadness about being disconnected.

Negative pattern two: Monique notices Clifton either being overly friendly to a woman, or taking a phone call in a private way and assumes it's a woman, or taking a long time away from home on what should be a short errand. While her appraisal is that these are associated with his women friends, she wards off her feelings about it (men need attention from woman and he is a social person); Her long-standing ability to suppress her feelings and protect her vulnerability also strengthened her resolve about her need for independence and to maintain her girlfriend bonds. As Clifton notices her independence from him, that becomes a distress cue that he is not number one in Monique's life. This distress cue increases his anxiety and his alertness to signs of their disconnection. Of course, this primes him for pattern number one.

As I would attempt to have Clifton develop his reactive feelings *(The distress cues)*, about the trip with Monique's girlfriend's brother, or about Monique's "hardness," he would typically suggest it made him feel "uncomfortable." With a relentless focus to expand his "uncomfortable" feeling, he might suggest that his feeling included heavy breathing, an increased heart rate, and a shift quickly to anger as his thoughts take him to the "worst case." Assembling his attachment feelings is hard work. When I ask, "What would it be like for him to turn to Monique and talk to her about his uncomfortable feelings involving her importance to him *(This would be an attachment thread I've developed with him)*," he would typically say, "Yes, Dr., I can do that, but can I say this first?" he would repeat this pattern over again as I would listen to his subsequent narrative, and then again develop his attachment feelings within this new story, and then asking him again to turn to Monique to tell her about these attachment feelings, and that would bring forth another "Yes, I can do that, but can I say this first?" And that pattern would continue, and the encounter would involve thinly sliced emotional experiences.

Both Monique and Clifton have difficulty with my attempts to develop depth of their feelings and participation in encounters. He does not want to feel "uncomfortable," and that also is an emotionally safe word for him to use. He is not comfortable with being emotionally vulnerable, nor with the appraisal of being a weak man that is linked his view of self in the negative cycle with Monique. Monique is equally uncomfortable with exploring her softer vulnerable feelings (although they are more accessible to her compared to Clifton) because avoiding emotional vulnerability has been a successful lifelong coping strategy. It has protected her from hurt, and it is consistent with long held beliefs about self-reliance and the shortcomings of Black men. While Clifton has some discomfort with exploring his internal world (accessibility), his feelings tend to bubble up in sessions, as tears will come into his eyes. We pause on those moments (move one), explore his feelings (move two), and then gently guide to brief encounters with Monique (move three). Monique's vulnerabilities show up too spontaneously with a change in the softness in her tone of voice. We also pause on those moments (move one), assemble her feelings (move two), and encourage her to encounter Clifton with her loving feelings toward him (move three).

INFLUENCES OF RACE

Clifton's and Monique's experiences growing up are unique in many ways and similar to many African American boys and girls. The Black community gleamed from both their experiences was hard on both of them, and that hardness shows up in their negative cycle and coping strategies. Their families were led by strong, responsible, and resourceful mothers. Their relationships with their fathers were more complicated and formed the base of each of their attachment insecurity in marriage. Monique's father seemed to never fully recover from his disappointment that his parents could not afford to send him to college. Discrimination limited his job advancement. Individually, both Clifton and Monique are undereducated, and underemployed. They are well-connected to Black social clubs, and that has been a source of strength and of anxiety. In particular, Clifton is uniquely sensitive to the level of infidelity he appraises to be in the Black community. Monique's attractiveness and his appraisal of his self-worth and their social engagement create opportunities for him to be triggered.

Of course, Clifton and Monique grew up in redlined Black communities. They attended largely segregated public schools within their African American communities. These social realities lead to a concentration of property and corresponding social aggressiveness. Clifton was a kind and artistic kid who was an active member in a community of boys that valued toughness and aggression. He relied on good instincts and friends to avoid danger. Monique had a protective family that attempted to protect their attractive daughters from romantic relationships early. Even within her family Monique was seen as the "pretty one." It seems her attractiveness came with danger in segregated Black communities. She learned to reject the advances of older boys/men early on and came to both be seen as "hard" and to think about herself that way. Monique, compared to Clifton, maintained lifelong attachment bonds with her sisters and girlfriends. This sisterhood has been a vitalizing strength in her life.

I am asking them to have a different type of conversation than their point/counterpoint or their negative cycle. In that regard, I try to give a rationale for these particular therapy experiences. First, I validate that it is not something that Clifton and Monique typically do with each other, and I understand that it is not their style to say "I love you," even to his daughters. I also suggested that many African Americans grow up in families that learned not to express love in these emotional ways. As a culture, for many it was understood that a child was loved because he or she was protected and their needs were provided for. Second, expressions of love by Black people have also been influenced by the struggles in this country over generations. Black love can be difficult, the world is harsh, and we can be mean or harsh to each other. Both Clifton and Monique have experienced this pain growing up and in their relationships. Somehow, for some of us, we have lost touch with parts of our hearts. The softer parts. When Black folks have been vulnerable, the world sought to crush. So we are protective and careful. When I ask Clifton to talk directly to Monique from his heart, I do think it will benefit them. It makes for a better conversation and a particular loving and softer conversation in a marriage.

TRANSCRIPT: "YOU'RE MY PRETTY TONY"

As therapy progresses, Clifton continues to pursue his attachment need to feel uniquely special to Monique. Along the way, they agreed to not use the harsh name-calling during their arguments. Monique repeatedly reflects and suggests that she plays a role in their disconnections. As Clifton's talks about his raw spots. (that his heart is "scarred" from his romantic past and that fear influences his appraisals: "scripts"). Monique continues to meet his "uncomfortableness" and his protectiveness "buts" with increasing softness. The working alliance feels strong, and they each seem a bit more willing to follow my lead regarding interrupting their cycle, assembling feelings, and having encounters. Encounters tend to be brief moments. Clifton and Monique welcome the input about how the influences of race have impacted African American couples and their relationships.

Clifton: Again, I don't know why I just brought all this up about how we met back then. I know that Monique isn't the kind of person that's going to do those things. Now, no matter how many women are like Monique, which is no nonsense kind of person, in my head, there is always a pretty Tony. That one guy that's a little bit of the exception to the rule. I can see Monique walking through Safeway. Do a whole hour of shopping, and look at me like *(Stern mean look)* "You better not say nothing." But for pretty Tony? He might get a different look. Do you know what I mean?

Guillory: Is that your general outlook on all of us, that there is a pretty Joan for you, a pretty Cleo for me, and a pretty Tony for Monique, so that there is a way we can all somehow be taken, somebody could look so attractive, and that person could make us stray? Or is that just Monique? *(Being curious and exploring his world view).*

Clifton: Well, that's what I'm saying. That could be me. I will own that myself, right, but I do think that there is that person out there somewhere that will have the gift-of-gab, or the look, or the whatever that you kind of get out of yourself.

Guillory: And when you think about it like a pretty Tony for Monique, and her having this weakness for him, what happens to you inside? *(Evocative Question).*

Clifton: Nothing. It's just a guess. I don't even know why I brought that up, other than the Safeway thing *(How they met)*. I really am only trying to be nice to Monique, back then, so it could have been anybody.

Guillory: It could make sense that you brought it up, and I'm wondering if you thought she is only with you by some happenchance. You've had your doubts, right? Have you wondered if there is truly something about you that won her over? *(Validating, evocative reflecting, and exploring view of self).*

Clifton: Huh, no. Not me.

Guillory: So somehow it never occurred to you that you are her pretty Tony?. That for Monique, there was something about you she warmed up to and loved? Something about you that made you, her pretty Tony?

(There was a choice here. To stay with his shift away from his internal experience or go with his view of self . . . I chose to reflect on his view of self).

Monique: That's right!!! *(Nearly jumps up from her seat and says loudly)*: You got it!!! Let me explain it!

Guillory: WOW, that was a big reaction. . . . Go ahead *(Responding to her emotional engagement).*

Monique: Okay, because I know. Thank you. You read my soul *(Putting her hand over her heart)*. You almost made me want to cry because that's exactly what I've been saying *(Her eyes are wet)*. He doesn't get it.

Case Study 87

Guillory: He doesn't get it, say more *(Gesturing with hands to Clifton to wait a moment, He gets my signal. Clifton and I have worked out in therapy this signal to stop his intruding "buts")*.

Monique: Yes, there are men in any given week that have tried to say something to me. He's right that happens sometimes. I don't know why but It's just my character. . . . If I want you to say something to me, then you'll know. But if I'm not interested, please just leave me alone. I have issues around men coming at me even as a young girl, so that's why I have an attitude. That's why I've been so negative sometimes toward men. But, Clifton, he was able to get around all of that.

Guillory: Help me understand how that happens? Somehow he was different. Tell me what is it about Clifton? *(Exploring her view of Clifton)*.

Monique: He was that pretty Tony. He thinks pretty Tony is a physical thing . . . good looks or muscular man, but pretty Tony is not physical at all with me. My pretty Tony is more of a mental thing and he's in here and I can feel him *(Her tone softens as she places her hand on her heart)*.

Guillory: Wow, that is so powerful, I am wondering if you can look at him, see if you can look him in the eye and say that to him? *(Could have assembled her emotions more, but she seemed really moved to talk to him, and moved to have an encounter, move three)>*

Monique: *(She turns to him, and he looks toward her)*. That's where you got me. That's why you got me for 20 years. That's why when your friends talk, especially when we first got together, some of his friends said, "Man, you got with Monique??? How did you get her?" Okay. Because I had a reputation of being negative toward men. But that didn't matter, baby *(Saying it in a soft affectionate tone)*.

Guillory: *(Leaning in toward him with a soft tone)*. Clifton, can you take in what she's saying?

Clifton: I do.

Guillory: That it was your personality, your style. It wasn't just your looks, it was your whole package?

Monique: As crazy as it has been for all these years when we get into it with each other . . . he has always been the right one. He is the right one for me.

Clifton: Okay. Thank you. I love hearing that, but *(Here comes his typical "but" that starts the cycle; and I interrupt)*.

Guillory: Take it in good *(At his point in the therapy, I'm interrupting the cycle more assertively)*.

Clifton: So I'm taking it in.

Guillory: Can you stay with it and take it in solid?

Clifton: But see, I've been hurt these 20 years, over these matters. I mean, I agree. I hear her. I must admit it because it has been 20 years we've been together and all of that.

Guillory: Let's slow it down. Can you see how it still brings tears to her eyes right now as she is talking about you? *(Not focusing on the cycle here, but attempting to bring him back to the soft moment of Monique's affection for him, perhaps another therapist might have gone with the hurt).*

Clifton: I get all of that and she is speaking from the heart *(With a tone to put a period on this discussion, and likely to shift to his "but").*

Guillory: And it does something new inside when you feel that? When you just let yourself just feel that? (*evocative question and responding*).

Clifton: How long you're going to not let me say what I was going to say? *(We all are laughing).*

Guillory: Because I'm distracting and redirecting to your feelings because I do want you to take it in to your heart and soul and not go to your typical "BUT"! *(Just being transparent that I'm interrupting the cycle, and evocative responding with focus).*

Clifton: I have taken it in.

Guillory: This is important, and you're responding so fast to take it deep inside. I want you to sit with it, and have it go into your heart and soul what she is saying here *(Briefly noting his cycle pattern, evocative responding with maintaining emotional focus).*

Monique: He's got to trust it, Doc, and that's where he's not up to trust. And that's why we still keep coming because he don't have that trust for me, or anyone.

Guillory: Let just stay here and slow it down. I think she said it so clearly when she cried and said, "You took the words out of my mouth." And she had tears in her eyes, and she's that with all that passion we just saw, just take that in. *(Repeating the emotional cue and returning to a soft affectionate moment with Monique, with details to heighten his experience and evocative reflections).*

Clifton: I got it. I swear to God. I swear to God. I got it. *(We're laughing again).*

Guillory: What does it feel like when you take it in? What did you feel? What are you feeling in your body when take that in? *(Maintaining focus with evocative question).*

Clifton: See, I don't know how to do that, Doc.

Guillory: Well, okay, just stay with what she said and what does it feel like? *(Shifting my voice tone a bit and slicing thinner while maintaining focus with evocative question).*

Clifton: What am I feeling? I. . . *(Voice trails off to silent).*

Guillory: You've got a smile on your face. Tell me what the smile is saying about what's inside? *(Using observations to ask evocative question and maintaining focus).*

Clifton: We've been together 20 years, so I know that obviously there's something between us.

Guillory: Do you know how many people I've seen who have been together for 20 years and don't talk like Monique just talked with tears in her eyes, saying that softly and with passion? You really did let yourself take it in. It changed how you were sitting over there. And you got a dance in your eyes right now. It was like a moment between you guys, and you're still smiling *(Validating their relationship, and Monique's emotional expression of love, and his spontaneous body response)*.

Clifton: So that means I felt it. I did get it.

Guillory: There is a beauty between the two of you; that is what I'm talking about. There is a beauty in the relationship between the two of you that is what I'm talking about. And that after 20 years it can still bring tears to her eyes and softness to her voice. That's unique. I don't always see that. That's why I want you to just pause and take in the beauty of it, really. If we had a Picasso painting here, I'd like you to sit in front of and pause and just take in the beauty of it. That's what I just saw, and that's what I wanted you to do too. That was a beautiful moment between the two of you *(Deciding to tie a bow around this therapy experience without having them have a complete encounter moment, also running overtime in the session)*.

Clifton: Absolutely. I felt every bit of it.

Guillory: You did!! *(Validating his experience)*.

Clifton: I did. I felt every bit of it.

Guillory: That's all I'm asking—to slow it down and let yourself feel it in your heart.

Clifton: Let's see, where we are going now is some place where we always have jokingly come back to, right, which is that Monique wanted no part of me when I met her. But a few minutes later, she started warming up to me.

Guillory: Because you were not like every other dude. *(Clifton returns to his fear, and therapist reflects Monique's view of him)*.

Clifton: The way I read that was, "Oh. Just another pretty Tony." And then somehow I was just another dude, just another N word.

Guillory: That was her style of dealing with the world. She has a way of dealing with the world of men ever since she was a child. Not trusting men and as you approached her, you were no different because she didn't know you. But somehow your character came into view for her. She saw you. Your personality, your style, and that softened her. Maybe she started getting an inkling of a different kind of man. Would that be fair? Am I overstating? *(Monique nods affirmingly . . . as therapist is reflecting Monique's view of self and her positive view of him)*.

Monique: I've said this is in various way throughout our relationship. I think that's who I am. That's how I was raised, to love even with all of the negatives. I know where his heart is. He's the youngest man I have ever been with, he is the most consistent man that I have ever been with, and he's totally different than most men. He has a lot of the same good characteristics of my father. And yes, I love my dad very much, even though I could strangle him on most days.

Guillory: There is a lot in all of this, and we will have to come back to this issue of choosing Clifton. It is deeper than just another pretty Tony. Sometimes fears of not being good enough come from our earlier relationships and just being a Black man. We learn ways to protect ourselves when we have been hurt. This work tonight has been focused on the beautiful and special parts of your relationship. Monique's choosing you, Clifton. We'll have to come back to that, and while you have said some of these things before to Monique, Clifton, it seems you need to hear more of this from her. It was beautiful to see how emotional you become, Monique, while talking about your love for Clifton tonight. We'll come back to that too. *(Summarizing the attachment work that happened and that there is more work to be done).*

Discussion of Transcript

There were two major surprises that emerged during this session. The first was Clifton's fear/threat-based worldview of the "pretty Tony." As I attempted to assemble his long-standing fear, Clifton attempts to shut down and minimize his feelings. Evocative questioning was touching on his core sensitivities about being "good enough" for Monique and his damaged view of self. When the therapist shifted from assembling feelings to Clifton's view of self ("So somehow it never occurred to you that you are her pretty Tony?)," I was expecting to explore his view of himself, However, the second surprise occurred as Monique spontaneously reacted to that question with a fully-body emotional and loving response: "You're my pretty Tony!!!" While this transcript represents a good example of relentlessly attempting to have Clifton sit with and feel the impact of Monique's love for him, it is also without Clifton offering a great deal of verbal expression about his internal world. Monique is softening her emotional engagement, however, with him. Her softening is wonderful for both of their views of self. For her it is a strong Black woman getting in touch with her vulnerability; for him it is letting his guard down to feel his vulnerability and leaning in to love. There is a great deal of validation, evocative questions, and reflections and summaries. This transcript is also a good representation of staying with an emotional cue. Monique's tears, soft voice, and passion ("you read my heart!!") work to heighten and potentially create an encounter. With the potential for a wonderful encounter so close (that might have included Clifton talking directly to Monique about the impact of her felt love), but Clifton still needing to feel more safety in the relationship and the therapy, the session pauses on move two, assembling his emotions. Deep emotional encounters are linked to long-term emotional corrective experiences and positive couples therapy outcomes.

ACCESSIBILITY, RESPONSIVENESS, AND EMOTIONAL ENGAGEMENT

Accessibility

Clifton and Monique's cycle limits their accessibility to emotional engagement. Clifton's soft attachment feelings tend to bubble up spontaneously as he is moved by Monique's expressions of love for him. While these emotional eruptions are common for him, he seems every bit as uncomfortable with the joyful moments as he is when he is fearful/upset. Emotional experiences, other than anger, seem to suggest weakness of character to him. And he filters these "weak" emotional experiences by either blocking, shifting to anger, or a felt sense that is safe to call "uncomfortable."

Clifton's attachment history has convinced him that vulnerability is not safe. His worthiness as a man has been challenged by nearly every romantic relationship. His anxious attachment to Monique blocks his ability to see her love and loyalty. His emotional traumas fuel a strong emotional reaction toward Monique, and he has a constant cognitive alertness for noticing changes/threats in her behavioral patterns as threats to the relationship. His traumatic past creates such a large need for validation as a lovable man that he seems to miss when Monique is saying "I love you" and "you matter to me."

Monique has been described as "hard" and Clifton has jokingly said that "Monique can be mean as a snake." Like Clifton, she views vulnerability as a sign of weakness. She has a strong base of women in her world; mother, sisters, and girlfriends that have been her support base and help her self-regulate.

Her "strength" has been to protect herself from "Black-men-acting-badly" (see the section "Monique's Attachment History" earlier in the chapter) with a strong emotional control of vulnerable feeling and secure bonds with other women. This "hardness" toward Clifton's behaviors tends to quiet her vulnerable reactions toward him ("I see what he does, but I don't say anything"). Only when confronted with very threatening experiences will she protest from a position of strength, standing up for self-respect but not from a place of vulnerability. Monique's avoidant style does not help him appreciate how important he is in her heart and soul.

Responsiveness

Clifton has no idea that the "friendly" validation that he gets from his women friends challenges Monique's felt sense of emotional safety. As she effectively blocks her emotional vulnerabilities, it doesn't occur to him that Monique is blocking her raw spots, and thus she is quiet about her distress. These type of vulnerable emotional states, blocked as "weak" moments, have historical reminders of her "weak" mother's painful experiences with her father. As Clifton copes with his own raw spots with female attention, she copes by avoiding sensitive moments that at times distress her, and as a result Clifton does not have opportunities to actually directly respond to her raw spots. Increasing her expression here and his responsiveness is likely to increase her softness, which is their mutual goal. It is also likely to represent a part of her withdrawer re-engagement.

Monique suggested that Clifton's sensitivities and distrust "scripts" have been too much for her, and she has no patience and reacts now only with annoyance and anger. This is a central misalignment as she see it, and she is convinced he has to work on this vulnerable "weak" self, and that she has little to do with her responses to him. It does not occur to her that more sharing of her vulnerability would create some safety for him. Her clear signals about her love for him along with how important he is to her are likely to calm his trauma-based alarms. Clifton also has to catch himself as he moves into his cycle pattern behavior and be able communicate to Monique his vulnerability link to his past, and that he can still see her as a unique and loving person. This would represent a part of his critical pursuer softening.

Emotional Engagement

Clifton and Monique's negative cycle has been eroding their sense of safety. Their negative attack/attack cycle is preventing emotional engagement. Both see the other as the "troubled person," Clifton, with personality sensitivities, and Monique, the overly strong Black woman. Catching moment when their soft feelings emerge spontaneously has been the opportunity to create encounters that prolong and enhance their moments of emotional engagement and felt sense of closeness. Nevertheless, their blocks to vulnerability woven into their cultural experiences has made assembling deep Stage Two depth encounters challenging.

As Monique seems to bring warmth and affection to their encounters, her willingness to soften toward Clifton and readily engage in encounters is allowing the therapy to move increasingly toward withdrawer re-engagement. They have largely welcomed the therapist's cultural reflections associated with the intensity and demeaning negative cycle and the goal of opening their hearts to emotional engagements.

WHERE THE WORK IS GOING

STAGE TWO OF EFT COUPLES THERAPY

EFT has been working, with a great deal of early need for explanations of EFT interventions and moves, and culturally relevant challenges. Relationship traumas and harshness of growing up in segregated, marginalized, African American communities have made Clifton and Monique's negative cycle intense and therapy slower. Maintaining emotional safety and empathy for Clifton's relationship trauma "scars" requires a nonjudgmental stance toward those sensitivities, with a reliance on the fact that Monique's emerging softness can effectively heal. It will also require empathic reflections that Clifton's spontaneous emotional experiences are wonderful expressions of his manliness. More encounters with his raw-spots linked to his wounded view-of-self, like the "pretty Tony" transcript, need to repeatedly occur. Their stage two work would also include encounters where Monique would connect with her vulnerable feelings and a stand regarding Clifton's behavior that causes her distress. Neither of their families or cultural experiences have prepared them to face each other in these risky and vulnerable ways.

CASE DISCUSSION WITH SUE JOHNSON

Guillory: *One of the challenges in working with this couple has been their lifelong view that vulnerable feelings mean you're a "weak" person. This couple explicitly states that "Black people don't talk about feelings." What suggestions might you have for my continued work with them?*

Sue Johnson: The relatively new EFT therapists might ask, "Well, what do you feel right now?" and the person would say "Nothing," or they might ask, "What do you feel right now?" and the person would tell them a story, or change the subject, and the therapist would stop. Now the more experienced EFT therapists say, "Yes, of course, can we go back to your feelings? Could you help me? You said, Clifton, that you hurt her feelings, your impatience showed up when you raised your voice (the trigger). My sense is that it must be very hard to hear. Could we stay with that for a minute? What happens to you inside when you hear her say that hurts?" Sometimes you have to go back and do it again. You have to be willing to do it four or five times. The important thing is not to give up. The person says, "No, I don't want to go there. I'm a soldier, a professional football player, a working-class guy, or I'm a Black person." We have to validate and respect and accept that that's been adaptive for them. That's something they needed to do in their lives. I also know they have the same emotions as everyone else, they have the same attachment fears, needs, and longings as every other human being. I start with validating their need to not feel, and I have to stay there with them and just be patient and assemble the emotion gradually.

This is important, Paul, before you even get to those moments, you have such lovely empathy for this couple, and you are creating safety with empathy and your empathic reflections and validations. That sets the stage for exploring feelings and allowing for vulnerability. So in those moments in therapy where his eyes spontaneously get wet, and her voice gets soft, it is what that emotional safety has created. These moments are created from the EFT tone, the safe relationship, the acceptance, and the pull for emotional engagement. Their vulnerability comes forth in spite of emotional blocks. You may have an incredible advantage because you're African American, and in some ways, they will feel that you instinctively know their experience. As empathic as I try to be, I might still have to earn that level of trust. I will have to show curiosity about them as African Americans and unique individuals. Therapists have to be able to basically, say "Teach me about your inner world. Teach me about your blocks, your fears, your longings, and your needs." Culture is embedded in our inner worlds, and experienced therapists have to be curious about that, too. And we have to give the message to clients, "I know the relationship territory. I know this emotional territory. I will create a safe way to go there with you."

As the experienced EFT therapist focuses on emotions, I wonder if African Americans are subject to more chronic triggers that are coming at them and increasing their vulnerability and vigilance. And that isn't always true in other couples that we see, where the main stress is with their partners. With Black and interracial couples, there are discrimination and diversity issues. That could make their cycle and de-escalation a bit more poignant and multifaceted, more triggering of vulnerability, more sensitivity, and more vigilance in social environments. Paul, you do a bit of psych-ed when you talk about race with them, but it is very close to their experience. It has to be very in-the-moment, relevant, and focused on what's alive in the room. You're doing what I do, not stepping back and teaching, but putting things in a larger perspective. It's taking what's alive in the session and making it bigger, like the name-calling and the intensity of their triggered responses, and the isolating, painful impact on both of them. Love is also the territory we know something about in EFT, and we make room for it, too, in soft moments of encounter.

Guillory: *They are a very likeable couple in so many ways, and yet their negative pattern is so entrenched. It a classic case where the small disconnections build up and then big, highly escalated explosions happen. What suggestions do you have for me working with their cycle?*

Sue Johnson: This is an example of two people adapting to a racially harsh world. As you have suggested, they have grown up living in a hostile world in which attachment security is hard to attain and trust is so fragile, and it keeps them caught in a defensive posture. They are stuck with ways of dealing with their emotions that make A.R.E., which we need to form a bond, almost impossible. Nevertheless, they are together, and have found some degree of safety. She is drawn to his character, his uniqueness as a man, and he is drawn to her strength of character, too. They seem to be bonded with you, too. I think that has to do with your relentless empathy, empathic reflections, and validations. You're also catching their moments of softness in therapy, assembling their emotions around those gentle, vulnerable moments. You have to continue to do all of that. You have to continue to direct the process. Stay tuned into emotions and attachment longing. Saying something like "Can we stay here?" and assemble emotions. And staying with a flash point where something goes wrong—his impatience or her hurt feelings. This is where their negative dance begins. So we tell them we are going to stay with this flash point. She dismisses, minimizes, and rationalizes around her hurt. We want her to consider an alternative, like talking about her feelings. So we stay with her defensive strategies. We go into the defensive block. "You try to have it 'roll off;' you work hard to shut down any soft feelings because this has saved your life in other situations. It's hard to say to him, or even to yourself, that maybe he hurts your feelings. He is important to you, and you don't go there because it might end up going too far . . . to those dreadful battles." We have to validate her need to be "strong" and self-regulate her soft feelings and that she is a human being who can only do that for so long. Of course, we should also ask him, "What would it be like for you to hear about her softer side?"

6 Case Study
EFT De-Escalation With Interracial Couple With Chronic Pain

Paul T. Guillory and Case Discussion with Sue Johnson

Marquis and Anastasia's experiences are unique in many ways, and yet their experiences are an example of how when a crisis hits the United States, it affects the African American community harder than the majority population. This case study is an example of stage one, de-escalation, of EFT couples therapy. The de-escalation stage has a specific focus on the emotions driving the negative pattern of couple interactions and the gentle seeding of deeper attachment emotions. While this is an interracial couple, their coping with medical vulnerabilities, the stress with COVID-19 virus, and a pattern of disconnection and conflicts highlight the reality that race and culture play in their interactions. That is, their communication becomes harsher and more intense than earlier, and misperceptions/stereotypes are more damaging than before. The attachment traumas in each of their early lives have enhanced their individual coping strategies and a focus on helping others. However, these traumas have also created challenges for each to communicate their needs and respond to their partner's needs. Their thwarted attachment needs get expressed in an escalated rigid cycle of distress and conflict. Their central dilemma is coping with physical and emotional pain and creating mutual emotional safety and engagement. Their individual histories with traumas, race, and stress make their couples therapy particularly difficult.

Descriptions of Partners

Marquis is African American, born and raised on the East Coast; Anastasia is Caucasian, born and raised in Eastern Europe. They met through mutual friends almost immediately after he moved from the East Coast to the West Coast, and she moved from Europe to the Napa area to start a new job. When they began couples therapy, they had been married for 17 years. They have two children a, 5-year-old son and 3-year-old daughter. They both have very demanding jobs. Anastasia as a research professor and Marquis manages a construction company. Anastasia's work is demanding and stressful, and Marquis's work is physically demanding. Five years ago, Marquis was diagnosed with an autoimmune disease (AD) and reports constant pain, fatigue, and muscle weakness. Historically, in moments of couple disconnection, Anastasia pursues and Marquis withdraws from engagement. As they start therapy, however, it seems Anastasia is a burned-out pursuer, and Marquis is a critical withdrawer.

DOI: 10.4324/9780429355127-6

Reason for Coming to Therapy

Anastasia called to arrange for couples therapy after an explosive argument regarding a dispute about disciplining their son, Angelo. According to Anastasia, she and Marquis have had communication problems for ten years, but their lives are so busy that they have never taken the time to address them. Their work projects and life would take over, and they pushed their communication problems aside, only to see them explode again. She stated that they don't know how to "fight fair," and how to argue in "non-dangerous" ways—especially when their life is so overwhelming and they lose the capacity to communicate. When Anastasia said this, Marquis interjected (pointing his finger at Anastasia, with a raised tone of voice), "I don't have the capacity for someone to treat me like shit! I need to set boundaries to protect my health. I tell you that 'you're hurting me,' 'you're being aggressive,' 'you're bullying me,' 'just stop, stop, stop'." In response to Marquis's frustrated and pointed commands, Anastasia mumbled under her breath "not true' and that her experience is different. Marquis pressed on, stating that Anastasia has a history of yelling at him, throwing things at him, and walking behind him yelling as he tries to move away. Anastasia responded, saying that she has worked on these behaviors in her individual therapy years ago and that while true in the past, she doesn't behave that way now.

Processing a Recent Conflict: Second Session

The escalating event that launched the couple into therapy is conflict about how to parent their son. Marquis had placed Angelo on time-out for aggressive behavior, and Anastasia didn't think it was working. Their communication in-session about the events and at home about this matter indicates a couple in serious distress. As the story unfolded in the session, it was repeatedly punctuated with moments of intense escalation of conflict. I repeatedly requested that they slow the process down for me, because they are moving so fast and I want to understand. I repeated those comments throughout the following set of exchanges. Marquis, in particular, seems to get emotionally escalated while talking directly to me and then turns his ire directly toward Anastasia. He seems distressed, passionate, and desperate as he says:

> "Angelo is hitting me and kicking me, and she will not allow me the space to discipline my son (speaking loudly at Anastasia). I have been working all day with hands that hurt (Now looking at me and showing his hands) and I can barely move them and I'm putting my son in time-out. I am there with him and I'm trying to help him calm down" *(There is some desperation in his voice).*
>
> Anastasia interjects with a controlled low tone "Marquis is working with Angelo in a way that isn't working anymore."
>
> Marquis reacts instantly "I can't take it, this is killing me *(Increasing his volume that was already loud and turning toward his wife).* I try to discipline my son and she is in the background making comments that escalate his behavior. He is already a momma's boy, and your comments make it worse."

Anastasia responds *(Looking directly at me with some desperation in her voice)*: "I think it's punitive, I don't want to be punitive. That brings up a level of discomfort in me because I am exhausted from work and I have no ability to negotiate."

Marquis turns to me and says in an exhausted, soft tone, "My son does these aggressive behaviors hitting and kicking. I am worried that he will be the only black boy in his school and the only boy hitting and kicking. I have to be able to intervene with him or society will. I don't know how much time I have, and I want Angelo to know me and learn from me" *(Looking at me with a pleading tone in his voice for help)*.

Their typical argument ends as most have with them, with Marquis withdrawing into their bedroom with intense physical pain, and Anastasia giving up her pursuit of the conversation and focusing on the children. During the subsequent moments of disconnection, both feel miserable, alone, and abandoned. At times they give the impression of an attack-attack pattern of couple interaction. As Marquis turns to the therapist for relief, however, it reflects both his tendency to withdraw from their conflicts and his seeking safety with this African American therapist. After conducting their attachment interviews and subsequent therapy, it seems that Marquis has a typically avoidant style, and Anastasia has an anxious attachment strategy. In their couple relationship, Marquis is a critical withdrawer, and Anastasia is a burnt-out pursuer. His illness complicates their negative pattern and adds an acute distress element to their disconnection and conflicts. That is, his critical withdrawal can also give way to angry reactions when he thinks he has to fight back. Anastasia's reactions to his anger is to hear even more criticism and again a greater need to defend herself.

Marquis's Attachment History

Marquis's history is influenced by race and trauma, and these experiences have made him uniquely self-reliant, reactive to being misjudged and too often socially alone. He is the youngest of five children. His dad was one of the first Black people hired at his company. As his father advanced at work, he also worked to increase the number of African Americans hired there. Marquis was born in an African American community on the East Coast, "a horrible, horrible, horrible neighborhood . . . gangs, poverty, violence—kind of the epitome of bad on the East Coast." While his older brother and sister fit into the Black community there, he never did.

His life changed tragically at the age of four. During a winter storm, the power went out in his house, and his father went to retrieve candles from an outside shed. On his way back to the house, he had a massive stroke. While at the hospital, the family home caught fire and was completely destroyed. Over the next year, the family was homeless, moving from one friend's house to another. While his father never worked again, and initially could not talk or take care of himself, he eventually recovered many functions. Marquis fears that his AD will have just the opposite impact on his development—that he is working himself into the wheelchair that his father worked himself out of.

His father eventually became a stay-at-home dad, and his mother carried the financial load. His mother was described as "absent" in his early life; his father was always present and a source of comfort. His mother also scheduled and attended all of his dad's medical appointments and rehabilitation treatments. She had a hard time working with all White males who often made negative comments about Black people. His father was dependable (he was always available), but could become easily frustrated because of his disabilities. Marquis became unusually self-reliant at an early age as caregiver for dad, taking care of his own emotional needs as his mother worked long hours and contributing to the family income by creating paying jobs; collecting and selling wood chips from trees, or mowing lawns.

After a couple of years, the family moved to the other side of the tracks, and Marquis's school changed from being predominantly Black to being nearly all White. In the White school, as a kindergartner, he came to understand that he was Black: "I came to know that I was different." Marquis suggested that from his early experience as a kindergartner, throughout his advanced schooling, he was different "because you're the Black kid in the White community, and you're too White for the Black kids; and you're never accepted in either place." He added, "I got into a lot of fights, because kids teased me as the fat black kid." Although he was in constant conflict with kids at school, he also did very well academically and was continually recognized as a high-achieving student. These experiences contributed to a lifetime of feeling alone as a Black person, as his world became increasingly White with his educational advancement. He was constantly being careful around White people in school and later at work so as not to be seen as the aggressive big Black guy. The constant fights and violence he experienced in his community as a child also developed into an adverse negative reaction to violence and aggression.

His older brother and sister had an even more difficult time adjusting to their father's illness, the temporary homelessness, and the relocation into the White community. Both of them had difficulties in school, eventually developing serious mental illnesses and substance abuse problems. His brother committed suicide a few years ago, and his sister has had one failed suicide attempt. Marquis strongly identifies with his father's commitment to Black people, and he is committed to the advancement and training of African American workers.

Anastasia's Attachment History

Anastasia's history is influenced by attachment injury and trauma, and these experiences have influenced her to be both anxious, reactive to unfairness, and on guard for social isolation. She was born in a country that would go to war before she was ten years old. When the war happened, and the family fled the country; subsequent moving became more frequent. Before the war, both parents were professional musicians. At that time it was common for people to have two jobs, and her father, a teacher, also played in a band at night. She said, "He would come home for a couple of hours after teaching and spend time with us, and then go to his night job, not good for their marriage, and not much time with us." She added:

> When I was very, very little and for a long time, I was daddy's girl. He was my idol, I guess. Just a wonderful, loving, and supportive person who always made a big expression of his love. "You're the apple of my eye." And at the same time, he was strict and we had very well-defined curfews.

Her father was the main source of nurturance, and she "adored him." She said: "I was always focused on pleasing him. We were all focused on looking after his well-being and his emotions.
It was his narcissistic needs."

The problem was that there was another side to her father "when he felt wounded by something you had said or done, God help you." She described him as "a monster," and she was always on guard for her dad turning into the monster. "My whole experience would be kind of a product of gauging the environment for that threat."

She suggested there was no space for her mother, and even her relationship with her mother was shortchanged, as he was always interfering. She reports that her mother had a very hard life. She was "sort of orphaned" as a child, didn't really know her dad, and was an only child. As a result, Anastasia suggested that her mother developed a fearful, anxious personality, not trusting of the world. "I know my mother has always loved me, but she is not a warm person." She suggested that looking back at her childhood, it's as if her mother was never there; she was there physically, but always preoccupied and unavailable emotionally. It always seemed that her mother was comparing her to a high standard of achievement and expressing disappointment about her failures.

"The war changed everything. We were displaced, and it was mainly about survival. We all handled it in different ways. After an initial period of being held in a refugee camp, we resettled in Europe." She cries as she recounts that everyone in the family had problems, and life was about surviving day to day "I wasn't able to sleep, I was anxious about school, speaking a language that wasn't my first language and just knowing you're different." She was still expected her to do well in school, and at school she was a foreign kid and "completely alone." As an aftermath of these early experiences, she suggests that she seeks approval and she is anxious in her relationships. She suggests that she has experienced so many crises throughout her life that somehow now, a life with crisis seems normal.

On the matter of race, she suggests that she thinks about it differently than Americans because she came from a different country. Until she had her son, she maintained distance from American social meanings of race. She noticed the diversity of race in America, given her experience in Europe was uniformly White, but struggled to understand the American context of race. "Because I'm so used to not really being a part of the society, I'm very good at not taking part in it. That really changed now that we have a child. She said, "Where I came from "we shit on each other because of religious differences, not racial differences." She said that she doesn't always see the racism that Marquis has seen, but now with her son, she is more willing to learn.

Escalation of Negative Cycle With Fear of Coronavirus

As the coronavirus began to spread rapidly in the United States, and just before the shelter-in-place order by California Governor Newsom, the session that follows took place in person. Marquis wore a mask and hand gloves. The infections and anxiety around the country were growing. The early moments of this session were spent talking about the coronavirus, the couple's fears, and precautions that could be taken. Prior to the session, I had been reflecting on the need to continue to spend time on Marquis's perspective, his fear, and his role in their pattern of communication. As the session began, we all seemed on the same page regarding the threat of the COVID-19 virus. I had planned to stay with Marquis longer, if his health fears came up. As shown in the transcript, I was tracking their negative cycle and exploring their emotional cue for disconnection. As the tracking was unfolding, I was also attempting to seed an encounter between them. After working with Marquis's experiences, I shifted the conversation to Anastasia. While she started slowly, her intensity sharply increased as her reactive emotions came alive. Marquis's reaction to her intensity was to shut down with a nearly vacant look and a touch of satisfaction in his eyes that the Anastasia he had described had showed up in the office. This is an example of stage one work:

Guillory: And so you're saying, in a way to Anastasia, "I want you to concentrate on my fears, and not what I said." And, "I was very scared" maybe I wanted to get some reassurance from the conversation. *(Leaning in; using his words).* Maybe you just wanted to express your heart. And you're a bright guy. There's a way on your own or with Anastasia that you'd figure out a plan. But there's a part of you that's just scared. *(Reflecting on his emotional experience, his vulnerability, and his attachment intention).*

Marquis: Literally, scared of dying. I've seen my blood test results. I see that I have. . . . I'm literally vulnerable in all parts of my immune system and I'm susceptible to chest infections. This is a wicked contagious environment. I'm scared of people coming into my house.

Guillory: *(Nodding).* Absolutely.

Marquis: Yeah. After the babysitter came over and wanted to shake my hand, "I was like, Dude, don't go for it." Our neighbor across the street just decided to drive to L.A. from here. All those stops, all the way, all those pieces. And I'm like, "You're going from one infected zone area to another infected zone."

Guillory: What you're saying, there is a way—and if this is an example, just like we've talked about the last time, you're trying to tell Anastasia to focus on this part, "I'm scared. This is scary to me." And she, from your perspective is not hearing you. *(Empathically reflecting and referring back to the moment of disconnection, where the cycle started that was discussed earlier in the session).*

Marquis: I feel not heard and hesitant to share because then I have to be so careful and conscious of how I share. All I can say is at those times it makes me feel not welcome to share and to filter what I say.

Guillory: You're saying something very important, *(Leaning in)* the filtering part. *(Slowing the process down by reflecting on his carefulness, which is part of their cycle of disconnection).*

Marquis: Yeah. Yes. I'm always conscious. I have to, yes. Do you know how tiring that shit is?

Guillory: Yes. You've done that all your life. Constantly, constantly being careful about everything and with everybody. And I'm wondering if that is what you've done all your life. That's exhausting. And we've got to work toward your not having to do that with Anastasia. "I don't want to have to filter with her." And you want her to stay with you when you're talking about something that's as important to you as this. *(Empathically reflecting "all your life." See his history and therapist's reflections of race matters for his felt sense of being the isolated Black man in a White world with a need to being always very careful. And evocatively reflecting that he wants something different: a safe haven with his wife).*

Marquis: And I know she wants me to talk to her. It's just those times and elements that make me feel not welcome to talk. So I say "Fuck it." It's not worth the battle.

Guillory: You stop? So not to have the battle. *(Tracking cycle here; his withdrawal. Again using RISSSC simply repeating emotionally loaded phrase).*

Marquis: It's not worth it.

Guillory: It's not worth it.

Marquis: It's not worth it.

Guillory: *(Nodding).* You are saying something to Anastasia here like, "I really want you to hear about my fears? Hear about that I'm worried about my health?" This is some life-threatening stuff. The main message was, "I'm scared." *(Empathic reflections with attachment intension and need to be comforted).*

Marquis: Something happens and I say, "Hey, this bothered me. Then we get into this huge blow-up. And then we talk about how we can have better communication around that. Yet what I brought up was never addressed because it's still happening in this repetitive pattern. It always gets focused on other things. How it started. How she responded back to it, this and that. But fuck, (he turns to Anastasia) you want to hear my heart, then you've got to listen. *(His tone softens here).*

Guillory: You've got to listen. *(Matching his soft tone).* And in this case, and you're also saying *(Staying very close to his experience and reflecting attachment intentions).*

Anastasia: That I'm not perfect. *(Therapist nods to Anastasia with soft hand gesture indicating that you'll get your turn; gently blocking the cycle reactions).*

Marquis: "Listen, I want to be heard. I just want you to hear me and get back to me."

Guillory: Just bring it back to me. Yeah. Just stay with me and hear my fears. *(Reflecting his experience that his needs get dropped in their cycle and his attachment need to be heard gets dropped and his longing to be comforted by her gets lost).*

Marquis: Yeah. Because I'm being very conscious about what I say to try to see how it is being received which—it's tiring. It sucks because it's still not being heard. I can't always be clear because I get foggy brains when I'm tired.

Guillory: Yeah. And that's the AD. But there's a clear message in there. So you want her to hear. And if we revisit that, that "I just wanted to focus on that this is a really scary time for me." Yeah? *(He nods in agreement and very quietly says "yes").* And when you hear that, Anastasia, what's it like to take that in? *(Validating the impact of his illness, his emotional vulnerability, and his attachment needs; EFT move two with him and exploring the possibility of move three).*

Anastasia: It's hard. *(Deep sigh).*

Guillory: I know it's a lot, yeah? But if you think back to the moment where you guys are having this discussion, and he said, "Oh, this is just scary for me." And maybe you were picking up on his fear? *(Validating her experience, and attempting rejoining the conversation at the moment of disconnection).*

Anastasia: Of course, I was picking up on that. I mean, of course, Marquis doesn't give me credit for that, but that's okay (as she shifts her body position upright in her chair and speaks in an agitated way).

Guillory: Wait, *(Leaning forward)* what just happened for you? Is it hard to stay with him here? *(Her voice tone and body movement signals a reactive emotional experience, and the therapist goes to move one by using an observation and reflective intervention).*

Anastasia: For days and days, I have been solely focused on creating a safe and protected environment at home.

Marquis: I should've brought up a different example. I could've put more pre-qualifiers on it. I'm not trying *(Marquis is sounding very worried and almost as if he is apologizing for bringing the topic up; he is sensing her reactive emotions and having a withdrawer's alert . . . see pattern dance later in the chapter. I am also wondering if his cultural lens in operating . . . see matters of culture later in the chapter).*

Anastasia: Let me have my reaction, Marquis, please! *(She says directly to him with a stern voice).* I'm not allowed to have any negative feelings because that reflects badly on Marquis. So what that I have bad feelings? It's frustrating. *(Her pursuer's alert [see pattern dance later in the chapter] and I'm also wondering* *about her cultural lens operating too . . . see matters of culture later in the chapter).*

Guillory: Wait, wait *(Leaning in and using hand gestures to get their attention)* This is moving so fast, give me a moment here to understand. This is particularly important given the world we're currently living in with the COVID virus and the fear that comes with that. And I was saying, "Here's an example of what we were referring to from last week . . . where Marquis wants you to hear him. He's saying this is only a small example of a conversation misdirection" So, you're hearing it in a particular way. And now, Marquis is trying to be very careful and almost retreating from the conversation. *(Marquis nods). (Attempting to slow the fast-moving negative cycle down, to understand with them their negative pattern that was emerging. Validating the stress they were under as a couple, and together, we were revisiting a moment of disconnection).*

Guillory: Right? So when Marquis tries to share his heart that he's "scared of contracting the virus," something goes wrong. Somehow you hear him being critical? And then this conflict pattern, this negative dance starts? *(Evocative reflecting on their cycle and her emotional cue).*

Anastasia: Yes. We're all sensitized around the virus, we're both scared. So there's a reaction to the idea that I would bring that disease into the house. But I'm the one that has to go out.

Both Marquis and Anastasia make sharp comments toward each other: Marquis "I just should stop talking;" Anastasia "I'm not perfect."

Guillory: Hold on a bit, just slow it down *(Sitting forward in seat and using hand gestures as a way of getting their attention).*

Anastasia: But if we concentrate on what Marquis is talking about, yes. We had spent a healthy amount of time in the space of exchanging how we feel. It was preparing. And it was very supportive on both ends. It was great. Then Marquis said something which triggered me, "You would only be a carrier," but for me the virus would be more dangerous. I said, "Don't say that because you're putting it out into the field of possibilities."

Guillory: Potentially deadly. Yeah. *(Validating the realities and her fear).*

Anastasia: What I heard or maybe it didn't even come out of your mouth, but what I heard was "You're a carrier." Which of course, he didn't mean that I would infect him but I would be okay and he might die. Because that's how the universe works. I'm afraid of all of this stuff as well.

Guillory: So let me slow it down because you said something important. So what I'm hearing you say is that the idea of your being a carrier is scary. *(Empathically reflecting on her emotional experience).*

Anastasia: It's horrible.

Guillory: It's a horrible notion to have and that triggered your fear. *(Validating and highlighting her emotional cue in their disconnection).*

Anastasia: *(She nods).* Because I've been going shopping to the stores. And I've been dealing with looking at empty shelves. And I've been triggered around the whole Armageddon that I have actually lived through. I've been in a place where there's nothing in the stores, and there's no food to buy, and then we have to leave the fucking country. And I have to go to the supermarket and deal with these emotions every day. And I'm sorry that I'm not perfect (increasing her volume and turning now to look directly at Marquis) and I reacted to something (*louder*). But that was one little mistake. I'm not perfect (*increasing her volume more*) And I never will be. (*Now she is screaming.*) So if you have a problem with that Marquis you can just leave. I WILL NEVER BE PERFECT!!! (*Thrusting her finger into the air at him*).

Guillory: Hold on! Hold on!! *(Leaning in, feeling the distress, and moving close to both)* This is sort of a place and you're talking about experiences that are trauma-based, these difficult experiences you guys have had. . . *(Increasing tone of voice and validating and reflecting on their struggle with stress).*

Anastasia: *(Said with tears and a softening of emotional tone that seems to change mid-sentence to bitterness)* This is so frustrating, to be held up to this standard.

Guillory: Hold on. Stay with me. Stay with me. You're absolutely right. So this fear is very raw for both of you in different ways. This is a very raw and tender spot of going back to what it was like for you *(Talking directing to her)*. Marquis and I probably have not dealt with that kind of refugee experience. *(See later discussion of transcript for where the session goes from here).*

Anastasia: I don't want to live through that again. And I don't want my family to live through that.

Discussion of Transcript

They have described their negative cycle as when "pain meets pain." And pain does meet pain when their cycle is highly escalated. It happened in this segment when Marquis's anxiety meets Anastasia's anxiety, and there is no space for them to comfort each other. It is as if both are screaming "I'm scared," and part of their internal voice saying "Help, I want you to be there for me" is not being said or not being heard by the other. This call for the other is their attachment need for reassurance. They are overwhelmed by the stress of the moment and hear something else.

I was startled by the intensity of Anastasia's reaction. This can happens in stage one work where the negative dance is loaded with strong reactive emotions. Before her response, I was validating Marquis fears and reflecting on his unique sense of threat with the coronavirus. I was assembling Marquis's emotional experiences (move two) and had turned the conversation to Anastasia to explore her experience and to see if she might be available (accessible) for an encounter (move three) with Marquis. During stage one of EFT work, however, if we spend too much time with one partner's emotional experience, the other may become triggered by aspects of their partner's story. That happened here. Anastasia was not able/ready to quiet her own internal distress/filters because it seems she was reactive to aspects of Marquis's story. She felt criticized in some deep way. As with any potential EFT conversation; I was redirected from the work with Marquis to empathize with her reactive emotions (move one). It seems that for Anastasia, being criticized is a raw spot for her; a sensitive place with old wounds from her family and from past criticisms from Marquis. She hears that she is failing him, and that she is not good enough. I validated her feelings and reflected on how difficult the virus threat was to her sense of self and family.

As she reacted with intensity, I was struck that I was witnessing the cycle of a highly escalated couple and the potential for damaging interactions. I trusted the EFT model. I needed to slow the process down to understand the attachment process underlying the reactive cycle. I had to empathically engage with both of them to explore the reactive emotions and the underlyingly attachment vulnerable feelings. I wanted to catch the "bullet;" that is, we had been processing Marquis's fears, and the conversation about his experiences had been dropped. Now Anastasia was shifting the conversation from Marquis to talk about her fears, too. Catching the bullet here meant validating both their fears, the overwhelming stress they were under as a couple, and underling attachment feelings; here that meant her love for her family and fear of losing Marquis. As she got louder, Marquis quietly sat in fearful retreat, moving to total shutdown. I validated that their fears are real and impact them differently. I validated that Marquis's fears are justified given his health vulnerabilities. I also validated that Anastasia's fears are real. Her high-volume reactions come from all the stress in their lives, her refugee history and her sensitivity to criticism. Later in the session, however, I suggested that the intensity of her reactions is part of the cycle that has contributed to Marquis shutting down and their pattern of disconnection:

Guillory: I'm trying to suggest that we consider what happened earlier in this session was that Marquis was talking about his fears and wanted you to hear that, and somehow you heard something else, a criticism? *(Reflecting their negative cycle, his attachment reach can land on her harshly).*

Anastasia: Ultimately, what is happening, Marquis, is that you don't feel safe in your relationship with me *(Said with a tone that something is wrong with her, and only seeking confirmation).*

Guillory: Anastasia, in these moments when you're very activated, you're very upset, it seems to Marquis there is no way to be helpful. He doesn't know what to do other than withdraw. To pull himself away. *(Reflecting the cycle in a non-judgmental way).*

Marquis: I just want to feel safe and I can't talk, so all I can do is shut down.

Anastasia: Sometimes I just lose it. There are such large forces working against us, including AD, my history, and being a refugee, Marquis being a Black man, and that we live in this country. . . . I know that you pull away from me because you don't feel safe. And I've been trying to earn your trust for years, and I've been trying to earn your love for years. *(Softly crying).*

Throughout the rest of the session, I am relentlessly reflecting on and validating all the forces working against them, as Anastasia has suggested, and that together they could find ways to face them. Their fear made sense, along with their mutual need to be connected to each other in stressful and scary moments. They each have spent a lifetime coping and desperately managing life alone. I suggested the focus of the couples work was to find ways for them to develop new ways to keep them emotionally engaged. While the threat and fears are real, as an EFT therapist I promoted the hope that facing those realities together could provide some unique comfort. As an American aware of African American history, I also suggested that their strengths and ability to support each other is the way Black people have survived and that this was true for Anastasia, too.

History of the Couple's Work Over 20 Sessions

Stressful Threats to Their Connection

First, they are a couple coping with Marquis's AD, and the COVID-19 virus has intensified their fears. Second, each has a background of family trauma. Third, each has work that is stressful and emotionally draining. Fourth, they have two young children and no family support. They are culturally different and have blind spots about those differences. Finally, their negative pattern of disconnection leads them to feel alone, in despair, and longing for love. They are in stage one of EFT couples therapy.

Stage One EFT Therapy, De-Escalation

Stage one of EFT therapy has four key tasks to achieve for the de-escalation process. The overarching goal of EFT therapy is to create emotional safety within the couples therapy. This is largely done by promoting, demonstrating, and encouraging empathy. The first task is building a therapeutic alliance that is based on shared goals for therapy and maintaining that working alliance throughout the therapy. The second task is to explore with the couple their pattern of emotional communication. This essentially involves two levels of emotional depth. The first element is to understand and assemble their reactive emotions that can trap distressed couples in a rigid negative pattern of interactions. This is commonly referred to as tracking the cycle, or negative dance. The second emotional element is uncovering and highlighting their attachment-related emotions that are deeper and less apparent longing and needs that underlie couple disconnections. De-escalation occurs as the couple increasingly experiences greater safety in their relationships and can talk about their negative dance, talk about their respective roles in their disconnections, and talk about their attachment longing and needs (see Johnson, 2019, 2020).

Understanding Marquis's and Anastasia's Reactive Negative Cycle on Interactions

Triggering Emotional Cues for Marquis: physical pain and fatigue, angry tone in Anastasia voice, and aggressive behavior of their children (racial distress cue).

Internally, his physical pain and discomfort are ever-present, and sometimes his anxiety is heightened with medical appointments and the lingering aftermath of their negative cycle. This is an underlying cause of tension for him. Something about the tone in Anastasia's voice will act as a triggering cue and he says to himself, "I can't take it." His appraisal of his health and her voice tone alerts him to a sense of threat. Her tone tells him that he needs to protect himself from her reactive volatility. His view of himself in these moments is that he is on his own "I'm physically vulnerable, scared, and her intensity will kill me." And from his memory of past conflicts with Anastasia, he dreads the aftermath—"I have to be so careful, it's not safe to say what bothers me." In the aftermath, he is alone and in pain.

Anastasia's criticism of his parenting is a racial distress cue. He has pride in his parenting and appraises her criticism as offensive. She will intervene to stop his disciplining of their son, and Marquis's appraisal is that he is being diminished as a Black father. In this regard, his Black self-identity suggests to him that he has to help his son with emotional regulation and that it is central to Black boys' survival in the United States. On these occasions, he fights back intensely and then eventually withdraws.

Triggering Emotional Cues for Anastasia: Overwhelming sense of responsibility, criticism from Marquis, and Marquis's disciplining of son.

She is overwhelmed with a sense of responsibility and stress. As the stressfulness of her life increases, which includes, work, care for the children, and Marquis's health, she is running out of empathy and energy and is feeling alone. Their cycle is dreadful for her because she needs Marquis's affection for a felt sense of being lovable. His critical withdrawal leaves her hurt and without a felt sense of his love.

When she is criticized by him, it seems to trigger some long-standing alarm about not measuring up and a need to defend herself. Her raw spot surrounding criticism has been sensitized by historical trauma experiences within her family. Both parents were critical and judgmental. Anastasia's accent adds a harsh element to her voice when she is distressed.

Their Pattern Dance

Parenting has been a raw spot for their connection, and this is common in interracial couples (see the section "Reflections on Matters of Race and Culture" later in this chapter). Marquis seek to set boundaries or discipline their son, saying to himself, "Angelo's behavior is out of control." He wants Angelo to learn how to control his emotions, which has cultural roots for Marquis. Anastasia wants

Angelo to have more freedom of expression and to not be unduly hampered by parental control, which has cultural roots for her.

The more she defends her intervening and perspective on parenting, the more Marquis responds that she is redirecting the conversation away from his parenting style, a raw spot for him. She hears his response as criticism, which triggers her raw spot, and she feels the need to explain herself. This argument escalates as Marquis wants to focus on his perception of disrespect, and Anastasia wants to focus on her being misunderstood.

When their negative dance gets highly escalated, it does not occur to Marquis that his reactions to Anastasia lands on her as harshly critical, controlling, or demanding. She experiences the escalations as expressing her point of view. He experiences the escalations as threatening and punishing, and he doesn't want to make them worse. It does not occur to Anastasia that Marquis wants to have a Black father's influence on his son in those moments. The louder he says, "Stop—this is going bad," the more Anastasia wants to have her say. The intensity of the cycle is a raw spot for Marquis. It parallels for him the worst he saw as a child both in his family and in his Black community: loudness, conflicts, and potential for violence. So he withdraws to the bedroom and is miserably alone. For Anastasia, it parallels her experience within her family with not having a say and her father's large presence, and there was no space for acceptance and validation.

It seem Anastasia doesn't appreciate the impact of her emotional intensity on Marquis. Marquis does not appreciate the impact of his emotional withdrawal and criticism on Anastasia. His illnesses and his and his wife's negative pattern leave him with very little stamina to respond to Anastasia's need for affection and comfort. Marquis needs comfort, too, from the pain and anxiety of his illness, and Anastasia is running out of stamina, too.

Therapist's Reflection

Throughout the sessions, I am attempting to slow the process down and understand each one's experience, with empathy. This is difficult for two reasons: First, both Marquis and Anastasia interrupt each other as they are having their say, and each one has much to say. Both can be hard for me to interrupt when they are talking and their partner is triggered. Second, their complaints can be harsh and critical, reflecting their histories; Marquis's illness concerns; and their currently stressful lives. Each of their trauma histories, in particular, influences their reactivity. Cultural differences play a significant role, exacerbating Marquis's sense of isolation fears regarding medical treatments and his personal history of managing his emotional life alone. I empathically reflected that negotiating critical medical treatments alone as a Black man can be dangerous, and yet that is the way he has learned to cope with stress—to do it alone. We spend time processing his racial distress cue associated with being a Black man receiving medical treatments, that is, he is prescribed medications safe for White people but dangerous for Black people. I also reflect how carefully Anastasia talks about Marquis's medical treatments and how difficult it must be for her that she can't be involved with his care. Finally, I reflect how hard it was for Anastasia, having grown up in a demanding, critical family and how fearful and helpless she must have been regarding her father's explosiveness. I thought about how difficult experiencing the war and being a refugee was for her, too. These experiences contribute to her reactivity and a strong need to express herself and fight back when challenged.

Developing positive encounters can be difficult with this couple. Typically such encounters have occurred when Marquis expresses moments of physical pain and Anastasia leans in to comfort him. Anastasia can also reach out for Marquis on occasion, and he expresses joy as she does this. External stressors, their historical traumas, Marquis's illness, matters of race and culture, and their relationship negative cycle make the work slower in stage one of EFT work. This couple gets stuck in negative interactive patterns because of the enormous stressors they have to manage, just as Marquis's illness limits his stress tolerance and his ability to be emotionally vulnerable. The following presents a very moving moment in therapy *(now working remotely)* which suggests both the progress of the couples work toward de-escalation and some of the challenges to assembling Marquis's emotions because of the cognitive confusion caused by his AD, when that is combined with his emotional vulnerability:

Anastasia: I think we are in a good place together, and it seems everything is gelling as a couple.

Guillory: Marquis, what is it like for you to hear that from Anastasia that for her it is a good place for you all? *(Lean into the remote screen and we're all smiling. Evocative question).*

Marquis: It is nice to hear. It was a particularly challenging week with Angelo's behavior, and there was a potential for things to go badly. I did start to escalate for us, and we did some things differently. *(Looking toward Anastasia).*

Anastasia: It was a classic start to our conflict . . . I had a knee-jerk reaction to something Marquis was doing with Angelo, and I said something sharp to Marquis. Marquis responded back sharply, saying "Don't correct me in front of my son." In that first moment, we were both reactive, but there was something else there, too, because of the work we have been doing in this therapy. We knew we were getting into the cycle. Marquis said we need to be gentler with each other, and that reminded me of the work we're doing here.

Guillory: Marquis, what happens to you inside as you hear Anastasia say that you reminded her that you have to be more gentle and softer to each other? *(Evocative question).*

Marquis: I don't have it in me to be anything but soft *(Smiling and turning to look at Anastasia).* It feels like my energy level is winding downward. At first I had to get away from the conflict, but I came back and our conversation after that went well *(He is starting to tear up as Anastasia is stroking his back).*

Guillory: This is an important moment. Somehow Anastasia heard you about Angelo and also about how you all interact; you stopped the cycle. She seems to be working on hearing you and getting it right with you. What's it like for you inside when you know she is taking in what you are saying? *(Anastasia is looking at him, stroking his back, and crying; therapist is heightening with use of observation and evocative question; EFT move two and setting up move three).*

Marquis: *(Nods and quietly says)* I appreciate it. It was such a difficult week, and it was nice to get some appreciation.

Guillory: Can you turn to her and say it again how much you appreciate it as you see her crying now? *(Facilitating an encounter; move three).*

(In a beautiful moment they pause and just softly look at each other. She is stroking his back and he is resting his hand on her leg)

Guillory: Marquis, I see you softly smiling at Anastasia; can you say how you're feeling inside? *(Using observation to softly encourage the encounter).*

Marquis: *(Long pause).* I'm struggling with the words... *(as he looks at Anastasia somewhat shyly and self-consciously).* Can I think about this and come back to it?

Anastasia: *(Nods that it's okay and reaches for him, saying softly)* Can I just say going to the heart is not easy. Particularly when we haven't been going there for some time, but I do feel that Marquis is letting me in again.

Given his illness, it seemed the right course here to merely reflect on their progress with changing their negative cycle of interactions. Perhaps if Marquis's AD was not a contributing factor to his cognitive confusion and this moment of vulnerability, I might have stayed with him longer, allowing him to find his words and continue to assemble his positive and loving feeling toward Anastasia. Nevertheless, this was a very tender moment. Soft moments like this have become a standard encounter in their therapy and have increased in length and frequency. Shortly after this moment, Marquis revealed that he had let Anastasia in earlier to attend a Zoom medical appointment with him and had found her presence helpful, and together they were able to successful advocate for Marquis to start a new medication. We all recognized this as a major shift in Marquis letting Anastasia stand with him in his fears. They remain in stage one of EFT couples therapy, and it is encouraging that they are accessing vulnerable feelings and reflecting on their negative pattern.

Reflections on Matters of Race and Culture

The stories about African Americans historically have described pain, hardship, and survival; Marquis's life story reflects this. It also seems that Anastasia's life has involved the historic hardship of poor Whites and religious minorities who emigrated from Eastern Europe. As part of a refugee family, Anastasia has been a social "outsider" most of her life. She survived by working hard to please her parents and doing well in school. Family nurturance was in short supply for her. She found comfort in academic achievement. Marquis grew up having a dual relationship with the African American community. Initially, his family lived in the midst of a Black community and then moved to the edge of a White area. While his brother and sister maintained their ties to friends and the old community, Marquis was too young when his family moved to have "insider" experiences within the Black community. His brother was more "street," and could be harsh toward him. In addition, the streets eventually led his brother and sister to have difficult lives.

Marquis had to straddle two worlds growing up and faced rejections from both; he wasn't Black enough in the African American community, and he was the only Black kid in the White schools. He has always felt socially isolated and different. He, like Anastasia, has been an "outsider." I wonder if this has created his alertness for reading social cues for danger and a deep loneliness and longing for connection. While he fought in schools with White kids with reactive anger, he maintained emotional control with Black kids on playgrounds because of his fear of violent fights. Controlling his emotions was critical to his survival as a Black man. It is as if his cultural experiences have made him allergic to strong emotional reactions. Wanting his children to control their emotions seems important and central to his belief about what Black children need to learn. His father embodied the values of inclusiveness and collective well-being seen in Black communities. Marquis shares those values, and it shows up in his work. Marquis reports having typical African American experiences of Black men in the United States: Whites avoiding him, racist comments made by random Whites, his pain medication being under-prescribed for him, and at times harsh comments and treatment by medical staff.

Anastasia's early cultural experience is one of rejection, too, as a member of a suppressed religious minority. Her family moved several times in response to "ethnic cleansings" violence when she was a child. There were also traumatic experiences within her family, as her father's personality "needs" left little room for anyone else's needs. Eventually, as a teenager, her family fled the country and stayed in refugee camps for over a year before relocating to a safer part of Europe. Of course, this caused a great deal of distress in her family, and she felt a sense of "survival" and anxiety day by day. As the family's interpreter in the new country, she had to learn quickly, and always felt on the spot to get it right for her parents. She experienced a great deal of social isolation in school because of her foreignness: her clothes, language, and accent. She has also felt "different" recently, as she works in a man's profession. As an adult, she has worked on herself in therapy regarding her relationship with her parents and her refugee experience. Therapy has enabled her to understand her anxiety, and she sees herself as less explosive with Marquis.

They both appear to be very loving, responsible parents. In their parenting, however, they trigger each other regarding the other's approach. Cultural differences play a large role in their conflicts here, and this is consistent with a major area of conflict between interracial couples as noted in *Couples on the Fault Line* by Peggy Papp (2000). Marquis feels that his five-year-old son is too aggressive, that both children are too close to their mother, and that Anastasia disrupts his Black parenting. That is, he worries that the world is dangerous for Black children who don't learn to control their emotions at home. Anastasia wants their children to have the accepting parenting she didn't have, with an engaged mother, and she fears imposing parental needs on the children. In particular, she wants her son to have freedom of expression.

Anastasia's past expressions of frustration, irritability, and annoyance, which have led to extreme yelling and throwing things at Marquis, have left a lasting dread/fear impression on Marquis. This impression is also influenced by his recoiling from aggressive behavior that he witnessed growing up. Both of them see their reactivity from a cultural and familial lens. She views herself as coming from an expressive culture where feelings, thoughts, and arguments were active discussions of points of views. Marquis's experience of disagreements is different. For him, too much feeling expression and arguments are dangerous; they cause him distress about their past, physical pain, and they lead to physical fights. He also experiences her intensity as racially demeaning. Neither saw their parents as models for communication.

Accessibility, Responsiveness, and Emotional Engagement

Accessibility

The external stressors and their negative cycle are overwhelming for this couple. The tension between them has been so high for so long. Their need to be heard by each other is desperate and pressing, causing their emotional reactivity to be strong, immediate, and loud. When vulnerable feelings do emerge, it is often Marquis expressing sadness about his horrible life. Anastasia reaches for him in those moments. Marquis seems to let her in briefly, but these experiences are so brief that they might otherwise go unnoticed. While access to vulnerable feelings is low, so is any ability to reflect on the other's brief expression of vulnerability.

Responsiveness

They respond to each other from their reactive negative cycle. Each partner's responsiveness is constrained by the other's reaction, which is largely reactive emotions of frustration, irritability, and anger. There are moments of lightness, however, when Marquis is play-acting Anastasia's stern, critical eyes and face, looking over glasses like a critical school teacher, or Anastasia describes the wonderful personality characteristics of Marquis. There are also moments when Anastasia seems to hear Marquis's sadness about his illness and life stress, and she reaches out to him with comforting words. From his withdrawn position, Marquis has a hard time reaching for Anastasia.

Emotional Engagement

The negative cycle limits the depths of their emotional engagement. There have been brief moments, however, when there seems to be enough emotional safety between them and then another positive cycle emerges. In these moments, they are likely holding hands and softly looking at each other. Typically, they both have been softly crying. Significantly, Anastasia tends to reach for Marquis in sessions, and he accepts her gesture for a brief moment. He is always a bit uncomfortable in these vulnerable moments. Over time, Marquis is beginning to reach too, and the duration of these soft moments is growing. As the therapy has continued, we have slowed the process down to linger on these moments. We have expanded these moments of touch to assemble their internal experience. They each have described a pleasant and warm feeling and a reminder of their love for each other; a return of softer feelings associated with their romantic past. Specifically, these softer communications start with noticing that one has reached to touch the other, and the therapist reflects, "I notice you reached for Anastasia. What happens for you inside just now as you reached for her? And for you, Anastasia, what happens inside for you as you feel his touch?" As the therapy proceeds, they seems to touch each other more, and this becomes a new pattern of emotional engagement. We have called this, "The Softness" where they can both give what the other needs.

Where the Future Work Is Going Stage Two of EFT Couples Therapy

The EFT interventions and moves have been working. This couple has a great deal of challenges that makes their cycle more intense and therapy slower. As they increase their moments of emotional engagement, Marquis and Anastasia are moving closer to de-escalation. Their stage two work will create encounters to increase the duration and frequency of positive cycles between them. This has to include a "felt sense" of more safety to allow for more significant discussions of fears and vulnerability. Specifically, this is likely to include discussions of Marquis's growing disability and potential for his premature death. This is the dragon that they will have to face together. They each will have to take risks that will challenge their working models of self. First, both need to risk vulnerability and having their attachment needs met with empathy and comfort. Neither of the family or cultural histories have prepared them for this. In this regard, both could have benefited from more maternal nurturance. Nevertheless, as they are able to stop their negative cycle and give clearer signals of attachment longing for comfort and affection, they are increasing their gentleness with each other. Second, as safety increases, Marquis can risk that he can "fall into Anastasia's arms" to help him face the dragon, and Anastasia can both embrace him and face her dragon of the AD realities for her. I remain hopeful that by promoting positive encounters, their love bond will grow and that in some vital way that will have a positive impact on their relationship and Marquis's health.

Case Discussion With Sue Johnson

Guillory: *It seems that this couple has been coping with a great deal of stress in their lives. To some degree I'm not sure I've done a good enough job of drawing attention to their cycle. What might you suggest?*

Sue Johnson: First, you have such lovely empathy and reflections with this couple. I think we create safety first in our EFT work with empathy, and all the interventions flow from that empathic stance. We find too often when we teach and supervise people who want to learn EFT that they want to know exactly when and why you set up this kind of encounter or that kind of encounter. It is more essential to develop emotional safety in our work, and lean in with empathy, and all the EFT interventions and moves rest on maintaining that empathic stance.

I was wondering with this couple—can they pull back from their conflicts and blame the cycle instead of each other? Can they say "We're stuck in this dance, and this is the dance we get caught in?" When this dance takes over the relationship, it goes bad. Nobody's a bad partner here. We say some version of "When you, Marquis, get worried, scared, you shut down, and when you, Anastasia, get worried, scared, you ramp up." You might even start the session off with "I've really been thinking about you guys, and how much you care about each other, and how you sort of miss each other. I've been really thinking about it, and it hit me that maybe we haven't talked enough about how couples get stuck in a negative dance. Every couple has a negative dance."

They both have fears, but their fears are different. His body sends alerts about fatigue and pain and primes him to hear her voice tone in a certain way, or his illness primes him to be reactive to his son's behavior. She seems overwhelmed with responsibility, and that primes her emotional reactivity. We have to track their disconnection flash points—the moments when something goes wrong between them. One block to their connection is their take on Blackness and parenting. She is saying, "I am scared of having my son lose his wild, lovely self, and I am pissed that to protect him, we have to corral him. And so I get angry at you, Marquis, when you come on strong with discipline." He is saying, "I'm scared that his aggressive behavior will only bring him trouble, and I have to teach my kid how to be safe." We have to stay here, linger, and assemble each of their fears. Anastasia, you watch him discipline your son and you say to yourself, 'I want my son to be free.' You get upset, and you step in to tell him to stop. And what happens to you, Marquis, is you hear that she's disappointed in you, and you're doing it wrong. I'm adding the attachment frame in this and the withdrawer sense of failure. The angrier you get, the more overwhelmed you feel. You feel you are failing at being a Black father, and failing at promoting free expression. This is where you guys get stuck, disconnected, and alone.

Guillory: *To a large extent, his illness is the predominant stressor impacting this couple. Sometimes I wonder if I've been too careful, not exploring their* *emotional flash point because he becomes ill/nauseous. Any suggestions for working with his emotions?*

Sue Johnson: It seems with him and his condition, you have to invite him to stay with an emotional flash point. "Can we stay here, because this is important." "Could you help me? I don't want to make you upset. We need to be here, but let's do it in a way that's safe for you." You have to normalize emotions with men, and perhaps Black men, in particular, have to learn to deal with their emotions by controlling them, as there are too many dangers associated with self-expression. Men have been taught to shut down, and he has a particular sensitivity because of his illness. His body gives him very big signals all the time, and that's upsetting in itself. We have to validate that, and then we ask his permission. "Can we talk about this for a little bit? You tell me if it's too much." His emotional responses are important to understanding him and his reactivity in the cycle. I think you are also saying, Paul, that greater emotional depth will tell us about his sense of Blackness, his awareness of dangers, his vigilance about his son's behavior, and his withdrawal in the relationship. When he says "The illness makes my brain get confused," we have to normalize this: "Many people who don't have AD get confused here with all these feelings. It's very confusing. You're in a relationship where you care, and you want to be close, but somehow, it keeps slipping away from you, so there are lots of feelings. And you get caught in this negative cycle, and end up feeling alone. That's confusing for everyone." The more his emotional experiences come out, that they are also somewhat blocked by his body sensitivities, the more we can understand his loving, protective feelings toward his son and his attachment to his wife.

So the continuation of this might look like *(using RISSSC . . . softly and always ready to pause when it is too much for him).* "Do you think she knows how scared and how it 'sucked' for you to be so alone and vulnerable as a Black kid trying to fit into a White school?" "Do you think she gets this?" "Can you help her, Marquis, . . . can you find a moment when it was really hard when you were a little guy and tell her what it felt like. . .? Tell her right now *(Get him to look at her).* "She knows there were no other Black kids, but how hard it was being so alone in all that Whiteness. Having different rules than the other kids, and how unsafe is was." "So you were alone and found a way to shut down your feelings." "This is kind of like what Anastasia was talking about, wasn't it? Losing yourself in that White setting . . . and you don't want your kid to go through that?" We have to validate his experiences and his fears and his hopes for his children to have a different experience.

It seems her flash point is different in their parenting. If I've got it right, her point of view is that she wants her son to have more of a range of expressions and behavior, but this is triggered by Marquis's restrictions and discipline. So we have to assemble her emotions: "What happens to you when Marquis says you intruded on his parenting?" And if she can't take it in because her flash point is about being criticized, we have to be prepared to catch the bullet (see Chapter 4), and I would run it by her again. For example, I'd say, "Let's just stop here for

Case Study

a minute. Could you help me? Your husband turns to you and says *(We repeat his words and very slowly say)* "I want to help my son learn how to manage his emotions. I don't want the outside White world to treat him harshly." And you have to be ready to repeat this, because you're trying to get her brain hear this message. This can be difficult that her Brain might be immediately triggered to hear something else. Sometimes, I think you have to say it again and again because she has been scared. She seems to have heard his protest differently than his intention, "Oh, this means something dreadful about me, and it's not fair." You might reply, "Yes, I know, but then you see he's wanting something more for your son, too. Both of you are."

You're trying to get her to hear above or below her level of reactivity. "He gets scared with your tone because you're the most important person in the world to him. And he longs for your approval." And that's true for all of us, but this man is, of course, scared. We're all scared that our partner might judge us or not feel good about us. That's human. We have to find ways to repeat this. . . "This man, if he loves you, he's going to be scared if he feels like he's disappointing you. That is just the way we wired as people." And he is watching you work with his wife, and he sees that if she gets triggered and you catch those bullets for him, that you have his back. He'll take more risks.

7   Case Study
EFT With One Spouse With Serious Depression

Ayanna Abrams with Paul T. Guillory and Case Discussion with Sue Johnson

This case study describes EFT couples therapy involving a pursuing/withdrawing couple dynamic, specifically focusing on engaging the withdrawer. The couple's negative cycle is driven by their reactive emotions. EFT interventions are used to explore these emotions and their roles in the reactive cycle. They are also used to increase insight into the attachment meaning behind each partner's response pattern. Although both partners identify as Black, it is important to note that they come from vastly different ethnic backgrounds and experiences. Their backgrounds are highlighted to show how dynamic Black culture is and that historically viewing it as monolithic has missed the deeper impact of differences in ethnicity, values, needs, and norms in Black romantic relationships. While not rare, this couple is unique in that they share various aspects and beliefs of Black culture but are vastly different in cultural values and norms of the American and Nigerian cultures. Additionally, Samuel initially presents with a serious and persistent mental illness (SPMI).

Description of Partners/Partnership

This couple exemplifies a classic pursuer/withdrawer interaction when they enter therapy. As therapy progresses, however, Cassandra becomes a "burnt out pursuer," exhibiting depressive symptoms in response to the lack of emotional or physical intimacy with Samuel. Cassandra initiated the therapy, and Samuel was hesitant but open to couples therapy in order to enable Cassandra to receive additional emotional support for her distress in the marriage.

Cassandra is African American, born and raised on the West Coast of the United States. Samuel was born in Nigeria and moved to the United States with his family at the age of 12. The couple met in a vocational program in their early twenties and began their relationship as friends, building this into a deep romantic partnership over the next four years. They have been married for eight years and have two young daughters, ages two and four. Samuel and Cassandra both work full time, which limits their opportunity to spend time together while raising their children. This situation also introduces an extended family dynamic that affects their marriage, sometimes pervasively. Neither partner has significant peer relationships outside of family connections, and they currently

DOI: 10.4324/9780429355127-7

reside with Samuel's family, including his parents, permanently, and his siblings intermittently.

Reason for Coming to Therapy

Cassandra initiated couples therapy, stating that there was little to no physical or emotional connection in the marriage for at least three years. She also described the ongoing adjustment to raising their children and the all-encompassing impact of Samuel's depressive episodes (diagnosis of bipolar disorder 15 years prior, with very minimal treatment at time of diagnosis). Samuel reported openness to treatment, given Cassandra's ongoing expression of marital dissatisfaction, his own lack of control of depressive and possible manic episodes, and largely desiring Cassandra to feel better in the marriage. He reported that he felt "fine" with limited to no physical affection or attention but understood why and how this impacted Cassandra negatively.

Cassandra's Attachment History

Cassandra was born and raised in California and described an emotionally detached relationship with her mother, her initial primary caregiver. Due to inconsistences in housing, income, and social supports, Cassandra was raised by extended family members. Older Black women in her family, including aunts and her grandmother, played major roles in her upbringing. She also described close relationships with some uncles who served as Black male role models. Cassandra noted intermittent contact with her mother mostly but remembers often feeling worried about her, desiring to be closer to her. When Cassandra became an adult, she wanted to help her mother. Her relationship with her biological father is estranged and she reports losing any desire to know or contact him when she was a teenager. She felt fully supported by older Black women in her family, and they taught her most of how she understands gender, sexuality, romantic love, spirituality and religion, family role expectations, marriage, and parenting. She had several role models of marriage in her extended family; however, she did not feel prepared for gifts and dilemmas that come with marriage, and did not learn much about sex, sexuality, or sexual expression due to strict religious norms in her family.

Cassandra's upbringing is largely comprised of mixed emotional attachments and detachments, the honor and love in parenting she received from extended family increased her sense of longing to be connected to, loved, and seen by her own mother, who has never been able to offer this to her. Cassandra's understanding of connection with her mother was through anxious searching, waiting, feeling disappointed and unloved, yet still engaging in the cycle, hopeful that she could do something to change this pattern. Her estrangement from her father was consistent with messages from the media and the larger community about Black men's presence in the family. Given that she was somewhat primed for disconnection from him, Cassandra reports that she did not grieve much about their relationship, though she does wonder about the overall impact of this absence of love and support.

Cassandra reports that when she became a parent she felt an increased desire to connect with her mother so her daughters could have a positive grandparent relationship like she did. She feels an empathic disappointment for her children about the grandparent relationship they are unlikely to experience. Feelings and behaviors initially acknowledged included abandonment, confusion, low self-esteem, and a persistent desire to fix and change others. She wanted to "get them to love me" by showing them how much she can anticipate and take care of their needs and forgive them if she felt hurt. Her estranged and pursuant relationship with her mother and previous romantic partners set the tone for how she relates to and desires to be seen and valued by Samuel. When this does not happen, it can begin their negative interaction cycle.

Samuel's Attachment History

Samuel was born in Nigeria to married parents. After moving to the United States, he was raised primarily by his mother while his father remained in Nigeria for several more years. Given that he is the oldest of six children, he took on what he identifies as a parentified role, with responsibility to care for his younger siblings while his mother worked. Samuel reports not remembering much about migrating to another country, except he did not feel prepared for the abrupt change and there was no conversation with his family preparing him or discussing the potential impact. When asked about whether he grieved or felt angry at his parents for this, he exhibited limited insight and redirected conversations to the role that he needed to play to re-stabilize his family, regardless of how he may have felt about it. He also did not report a sense of missing or longing for the cultural norms he learned in Nigeria. Samuel shared that he learned at a young age that emotions are not to be discussed, don't have much meaning when "things need to be done," and in fact, are a hindrance to moving forward and succeeding personally and professionally. Though wrought with intense emotion the majority of his life, Samuel did not have access to experiences where he could develop language or gain any understanding about emotions. Therefore, he learned to avoid feelings and use cognitive strategies to move through life circumstances.

Though Samuel indicated ways in which he has individuated from his family through going to college, creating his own family with Cassandra, and forging toward his career goals, he still presents as enmeshed with his family and within his family dynamics. He reported that the offering of emotional and financial assistance that he gives to his family of origin has sometimes blurred his ability to care not only for himself, but also his family of creation. His sense of responsibility and internalized narrative of being a "burden" to his family of origin anytime that he has needed or "taken" anything from them is evidenced by a significant increase in mental and emotional distress when he may ask them for support. Historically, if this distress is too overwhelming for him, he suppresses the "need" and goes without. The first instance that he remembered of this causing significant psychological distress was upon entry to college when he needed financial support to remain in school.

Describing himself as a burden who was already too much for his parents to bear, he developed a deep depression rooted in low self-esteem, anxiety about the impact of his financial need, dissociation from self, and suicidal ideations centered around 'how easy it would be for others (family) if he no longer existed. This chronic suicidality, though currently passive, was heightened during that time when he felt like a burden to his family of origin and is exhibited currently when he feels the impact of role strain between his family of origin, family of creation, and work demands. While his family of origin is unaware of his chronic mental health distress, they notice his bouts of isolation and tension but don't comment until he "reappears in better spirits." They seem to adjust during these episodes and take on tasks in order to help, with no mention or overt curiosity about what is happening.

Samuel's stress response and withdrawing attachment style prompt severe depressive episodes, emotional avoidance, and detachment from relationship demands and his marriage. Additionally, his sense of obligation within various roles that appears unmanageable at times prompts increased anxiety, burnout, and resentment toward responsibilities and those associated with them. He has described what seem like episodes of hypomania in the past, when he focuses on work, experiences insomnia, and has dysregulated appetite.

Negative Cycle Construction

When Samuel's emotional attachment to Cassandra feels strained and he feels overwhelmed by demands, he retreats from any emotional engagement. When Cassandra feels emotionally disconnected, often unseen or overlooked by Samuel, or when she notices that he is not taking care of himself physically or emotionally, she begins to pursue emotional connection with him through demanding conversation or intimacy or she begins caretaking. This takes the form of offering various self-care opportunities like food, water, time to rest, or peppering him with questions about how he feels in general or about her, their marriage, and parenting. When she receives "no response," and is put off by a text message, limited response, or limited affective response, Cassandra feels more anxious, probes more, demands connection, and then, when not comforted, begins to withdraw along with their daughters. She initially exhibited great difficulty in withdrawing from Samuel, noting that she felt sad, lonely, and scared about his mental health and emotional connection with their children. She also exhibited increased worry about her own marital dissatisfaction and lack of sensual and sexual exploration, and she felt less desirable in the marriage.

Transcript Tracking the Cycle of Pursuit and Withdrawal

Samuel: Cassandra mentioned our main issue happened just a couple of days ago. She felt like I might be going through a dip into depression, or at least in the way I was interacting with her.

Abrams: Okay. Can you say more?

Samuel: I understood why she mentioned something, and I saw the signs, too. I didn't necessarily go into it with her, and I wouldn't call it "panic mode." But I wasn't as worried because I know we're just going through some stuff right now and that it wouldn't last long necessarily.

Abrams: Samuel, can you tell me what it was like to hear that from her? Did that feel surprising? Did it feel like that helpful information we've talked about when this pattern has shown up before?

Samuel: Yeah, it was helpful for her to acknowledge it.

Abrams: Sometimes it's just helpful for you to see it from her perspective? Now I can take in what she is saying to me? (*Engaging with Samuel **by proxy**; using his internal dialogue to deepen his understanding of the experience*).

Samuel: Yeah, it was more helpful than anything else. The way we talked about it. One of the things I said to her was, "Yeah, I mean, I was feeling kind of funky." But usually it's on a cycle that's sometimes weather-related. I think it's a little too early for it to be depression. But she pointed out, it's maybe not necessarily linked to cycles. It's probably more stress-related than anything else. So I was like, "Yeah." I mean, there's definitely some truth to that, more than anything else.

Abrams: This is really important. It sounds like she linked it to stress, where you thought something else with it, but you didn't put up a defense against it, or any kind of pushback. Instead, you kind of pushed away, you said, "Hey, let me just see, let me just kind of reorganize this. (*Validating his reflective consideration of wife's perspective*).

Samuel: Yeah, I didn't feel it as an attack. I didn't get that impression, because in the middle of the conversation, she was asking, "Do you not want me talking about this? Are you uncomfortable?"

Abrams: What's your understanding of what you were experiencing? What did that feel like for you? (*Evocative questioning*).

Samuel: I mean, the way it sort of feels like for me is like, I still have stuff to do . . . but for the most part what I'd like to do is just shut down. I would just like no one or nothing to talk to me just for a period of time. And when I'm poked or prodded . . . I'm like, okay, how necessary is this? It's something I have to do? Then I'll do it. But what I'd really like to do . . . is to go back to being undisturbed.

Abrams: Sounds like there can be so many demands on you coming from different directions, some of it in your control, some not in your control. That must get so overwhelming. Is that when you say to yourself, "I just want to be back there—just be alone? So nobody can get to me. I just want uninterrupted time." I can take care of whatever it is, but I absolutely want to retreat after that. I want to go back into that space. Because that space give you something important, doesn't it? Can you tell me about that space, Samuel? *(Summary on internal experience with curiosity about withdrawal experience).*

Samuel: It's a retreat in many ways. I mean, for me, it's a strange perspective I have. Everything just starts to seem dumb. Pointless, is really just the best way to put it. It's like, I don't understand what the point of modern life is right now. Like, if I get one more email about how I need to update a credit card or, you know, or fix this. It's overwhelming that so many things need to be done.

Abrams: Yeah, many things seem more trivial, but demand your attention, and that weighs on you? *(Evocative question).*

Samuel: Exactly. That's probably the best way to put it. All of a sudden, everything just seems so trivial. And I'm like, but why, though? Why are all these menial things suddenly feeling so urgent? That's the thing. But they are. Because the thing is, if I don't update that credit card, that bill's not going to get paid, and then it becomes this whole other thing, you know what I mean? That example came up because I was literally trying to pay a bill today, and then the thing said the bank had rejected this thing I did, and I wasn't sure why. I was like, "Now I got to call the bank just to get this bill paid?" Seriously, what is the point of automating everything if I have to keep calling?" Why is there more to do when I try to make it so much less?

Abrams: If you have to be involved and it demands your attention, it does something to you inside? *(Reflecting stress and evocative question by proxy).*

Samuel: Right. It's thoughts like that where something else comes up, and like I said, everything feels really trivial. One thing that became an eye-opener for my associate at work was that I tend to pay attention to what the next problem is. Even if I'm in the middle of something, if you put something in front of me, I automatically go, "Let me solve this problem." She noticed that and gave me that feedback.

Abrams: We've talked about how that shows up in the pattern between you two in your marriage. That you go into kind of a "fix-it mode" and you miss Cassandra's point? *(Linking his coping to negative pattern in relationship).*

Samuel: Exactly. So I have a very hard time prioritizing. But because she's (associate) noticed that about me now, she's being more careful than she was in the past and she's not as surprised when she notices when it does happen. It helps me when she does say out loud that I'm doing it again, though.

Samuel: I really did not realize how bad it is. I literally get distracted by problems. I'm more conscious of it now. I was aware of it, but especially being able to sort of name it, it makes me more aware of it, and I didn't realize how habitual it was until I started noticing. "This is another thing that I need to do."

Abrams: That sounds awfully overwhelming. Like you always have to be the problem-solver. And even when that's not the scenario; it's not what Cassandra is asking from you. But the way you hear her say something, it can be terribly overwhelming for you because you hear her words as problems to solve. House, family, this brother, that brother, that family member. All of those demands, Samuel. It makes so much sense to me, now that you've shared that when all these things are problems in your mind, that's when you assign personal responsibility to yourself. And of course, sometimes, Samuel, you just want to get away from it. *(Empathically reflecting on his stress and coping, the negative pattern, and his action tendency toward withdrawal).*

Samuel: Yes. That's it.

This begins an important shift for Samuel in therapy and the marriage, as he is allowing me to reflect on his internal processing without shutting down, being confused by his own process, judging himself negatively, or deflecting away by sticking to his stories about work. Though he has a strong tendency toward "exiting," by offering examples, retracing his thoughts, and steering clear of emotional language, he *is* willing to stay with his perspective on stress and his view of himself. It was important that I stayed there with him for a bit and validated his experiences.

While there could be an opportunity to process his emotional experience with Cassandra, I chose to stay with his processes because he has historically struggled to be in touch with his feelings, locate them in his body, or talk about them like this. Typically, he might just say he doesn't know how he feels or he doesn't feel anything at all. This has been a challenging part of the work, but the therapeutic alliance helps Samuel to navigate in and out of his thought processes and emotions with my assistance. While my focus in stage one is assembling their emotional experiences, they often drift to focus on detailed examples of their experiences without deepening their internal emotional experiences. I aim to focus on their attachment communication and not specifically his health or extended family relationships. I also want to engage Cassandra in what seems like Samuel's increasing capacity to listen to her.

Cassandra: Absolutely. I notice the little things. Like, he'll snack incessantly, which in and of itself isn't a problem. Hey, I get those days too when I'm just eating junk food, so . . . whatever. But when he cooks, he spends hours cooking these meals for us (the entire family), doing meal prep, then you *(turns to Samuel)* won't eat any of it. You'll eat chips and salsa and popcorn, and just snack on that all day. I get so confused! It makes me wonder, and then I'll ask him directly, "Did you eat any of the beautiful vegan meals that you spent hours cooking? No? Why? It's sitting here. I can't eat it all by myself." It's so distressing to see when that happens.

Abrams: *(Acting as Cassandra's proxy)* I hear you. You're sitting there thinking, *"Wow!* You made this for us, and you're not even participating with us." This is what you see as Samuel neglecting himself for the family. And you want him to take care of himself. *(Validating how much she cares for him and validating her experiences, her caring).*

Cassandra: I'm just saying to him, "You need to take care of yourself. Because there's only one Samuel. I don't want him to get to a point where he's having a heart attack because he hasn't taken account of what's actually going on with him to such an extent that he's running his body and mind down. I just really want him to hear my heart, and not that I'm fussing at him.

Abrams: You're saying, "Man, I try to make it easy. I'm trying to take care of you. I make it easy in this way. But you react badly to me." So your panic goes up, Cassandra. You're so concerned about Samuel's health, and losing him, and your children losing their father to these patterns, aren't you? That's what gets really big for you, the second you notice that he's overwhelmed with tasks?

Cassandra: Yes, it's terrifying every time. I don't think I always realize in the moment how scared I am though. I just try to find what I can do to not even have to consider what this could turn into. It's not like we don't know the issues with Black men and their health. Like, why wouldn't you do more to not be the statistic they say you are? We can't do it all, but my God, can't we just do this? The day-to-day stuff to stick around? *(Cassandra becomes tearful)*.

Abrams: Can I slow you down right there, Cassandra? This sounds so important, and I get the idea that this isn't the conversation that you two have in these moments. The look on your face; you look so sad. It's like you're begging Samuel to stay with you, to stay alive for the family. And you're talking about the odds stacked against you. We've talked about these odds before, you know? These odds that impacted you two even making it to therapy with me. But these awful odds that Black people are stacked up against regarding our health. It's saddening. Maddening. And I'm seeing you ask Samuel to really align with you against these odds, right?

Cassandra: *(Still tearful)*. That's all I ask for, that kind of alignment. It's like we talk about the alignment but don't practice it, and then I'm holding all of this fear about whether this man will fall down from exhaustion in front of me and our kids. And if I can just get in there and help him get it together, this wouldn't be something ELSE that we're fighting in this world. Like, come on.

Abrams: I hear you, Cassandra. I'm really getting that. I appreciate your tapping into how deep this goes for you. And I know that in the moment, this is what you don't say to Samuel. Could you imagine turning to him today and continuing to tap into this? What do you think?

Cassandra: I can. *(Turns to Samuel, still tearful)*. I know what you see is me nagging you about what you're not eating, when you're going to go to bed, your eyes being glazed over. But what's happening for me is that I'm really scared that you're going to hurt yourself. That you're going to work yourself to death and not even live to see the work that you're putting out there. And since we don't talk much about what's happening inside your head, I just don't think it's on your mind. And I think I'm supposed to be the one to help you with that. But it's because I'm scared, not because I'm trying to control you. You mean so much to me and our family, and sometimes I don't know what else to do but to lay everything out for you and hope that you'll see it—that you'll see my trying to be there for you because I love you, not because I want attention or anything.

I just really worry that you're going to run yourself into the ground, literally. And that's awful to constantly have to think about.

Abrams: Samuel. Wow. I'm looking at your face and you look sad, too, while Cassandra is talking. What is this like to hear what's happening for her on the inside when she worries like this? She's not pushing food or self-care onto you right now, but instead she's really identifying how scary these moments are.

Samuel: You know, that's hard to hear, but really good for me to hear and to try to remember. Because I know that I can treat her sometimes like it's nagging, but it's really because I'm so wound up that I can't even think about when to incorporate some of her thoughts.

Abrams: Can you share with Cassandra what it means for you to hear her talk about her own feelings in these moments?

Samuel: Cass, I know I don't make it easy. And I love you for the ways that you try to take care of me when I don't do it myself. I didn't really realize that it's so scary for you, though. I know you're into a lot more healthy stuff than I am, and I'm thankful for that. But it's hard hearing that you're actually scared for me when I get like that. To know that you think about me dying and you raising the kids yourself is just . . . wow. I hadn't even considered that that's where this takes you when I don't sleep one night. That's what you've been holding all this time? That's not fair. That's really not fair and I'm glad I now know what's going on inside of your head—heart, too.

This is an example of an attempt to shift the conversation from the content of health-related suggestions to the emotional channel of anxiety and fear—Cassandra's worry about Samuel's depressive episodes, or worse. In prior discussions, we have talked about the health risk of Black men to strokes, high blood pressure, and heart attacks, as well as the limited models of how to better manage these very real health inequities. Samuel carries a high baseline stress in his body due to his felt sense of responsibility to his extended family, his own family, and work demands. While they both acknowledge that these are real health concerns for Black people, their reactive negative pattern has gotten in the way of talking about these acknowledged health concerns. It is important for me to slow their communication process down, and process each of their experiences. Both partners have to process their individual stress and engage each other's experiences. I validated their experiences and helped them develop emotional and attachment language that resonates with both. This constant validation and empathic reflection create the foundation for leaning deeper into their internal experiences and sharing those meaningful experiences with each other. This continues to emerge in the work over the next six months of treatment.

Samuel: Honestly, this takes mental effort, Dr. Abrams, to remind myself that someone is trying to help me. My initial reaction is, "What do you want?" Even though I don't do it verbally, that's automatically where I go. But then I have to learn to pause for a moment, play that back, and say to myself, "I think they're trying to help you." And try to feel thankful so that I can respond differently to them.

Abrams: I imagine that it takes a lot of work for you to reconcile that. That can be hard and stressful to do in the moment. *(Using first person, validating reflecting cycle, and evocative validation).*

Samuel: Exactly. It is hard. And I don't get it right a lot of the time, but that doesn't mean that I'm not thinking about it. Especially now that I understand it a little better, but the thinking about it to the doing it just doesn't land or doesn't land in time. So then it becomes *another* thing to think about. Trying to change my belief to seeing people as helpful or trying to help me; it's so hard to do. I guess it sounds easy, but it's so hard to do.

Abrams: Samuel, can you talk to Cassandra right now about what those moments are like for you? Just as you've shared with me? *(Evocative question and staging an encounter).*

Samuel: *(Turned toward Cassandra now).* There was a ton of work that I was still getting poked at, that I just was not able to get to because I had to spend most of the time with Alexandra, and thank goodness Mom was there to help alleviate a little bit of that. But it had more to do with that than what was going on with how I felt about you. And yeah, this is inconvenient. *(Cassandra recently hurt her foot and is less mobile)*, but I felt really bad that you would think that I would blame you for twisting your ankle. *(Pause as he gathers himself).*

Samuel: It hurt a little bit because for me, I just need someone not to need me for just a couple seconds. It would be nice just not to be needed for just a couple seconds. *(Samuel begins tearing up and emoting distress; tone of voice becomes high pitched).* Then to hear that I'm doing something that's making you feel even worse like that. That actually set me off in a harsh way. That's even worse because that's not what I intended. *(Heavy breathing, tearful).*

Abrams: *(Processes the encounter and emotional height).* Those moments are really hard. There is a lot of emotion here right now. *(Leaning in toward Samuel and using RISSSC with observing the emotional moment and using evocative reflection).*

Samuel: Then I'm saying, well, I now need to fix that because it's not what I meant to do. *(Speaking through tears).* And so—*(Long pause).*

Abrams: *(Soft tone of voice).* What's coming up for you right now, Samuel? Those moments are really hard for you. *(Staying with his emotional experience, evocative question).*

Samuel: It's weird because there's a part of me that's telling myself that this is "not that much," but after a while, it feels like a thousand things poking at me. It really gets to me, and I just try to get through it. I just try to make it through. *(Cassandra reaches out and holds him).* It sucks to hear that my efforts to just get through it hurt Cassandra or that I can't do my thing in my head and still make her feel less anxious about when this happens. I just don't know how to do both quite right yet. So it's like I have to choose one. I'll usually choose to go back into my head and just hope that she can roll with it. But the more we talk, the more I recognize not only can she not roll with it, but I can't really roll with it.

Discussion of Transcript

Samuel has been taking steps to become more emotionally engaged with himself and Cassandra. In this session, he is making himself more emotionally accessible regarding his overwhelming sense of stress. His internalized sense of hyper-responsibility and consequent withdrawal behavioral tendencies have resulted in depression and disconnection from his wife and children. In this session, I am disrupting their negative cycle of critical pursuit and withdrawal by slowing the interaction and underscoring it heavily with distressing emotions and self-talking in an effort to assist them in seeing how their assigned meanings to their partner's behavior can be adjusted. This gives them more opportunity to lean toward one another instead of withdrawing. By focusing on their emotional experiences—Samuel's stress in feeling demanded upon and not seeing Cassandra as a figure to lean on, and Cassandra's fear of loss of connection (at various levels)—an emotionally engaged moment happens between them. Safety is created by interrupting their cycle, preventing their interaction from taking place at a content level about healthy habits. Also, we focus in a more useful way about how they can be there for one another in the management of internal distress and as well as in their own interpersonal emotional experiences. Enough safety had been developed in the therapeutic alliance for Samuel to process his felt experiences of stress and for Cassandra to stay with her fear a bit longer before rushing to offer suggestions for health.

History of Couples Therapy Across Two Years of Treatment

Mainly, the couples therapy was biweekly, except during a brief period when we met weekly. Over the two-year period, both partners have shown growth in emotional engagement within and between themselves. The couples work treatment focused on understanding their negative cycle and assembling their emotions, thoughts, and behaviors. This process took some time, and I moved slowly with this couple for several reasons. First, neither had significant experience with therapy and emotional vulnerability. Building the therapeutic alliance through pacing and validation is especially important in our work with Black clients. This increases emotional safety and familiarity with therapy. Secondly, they had to experience a nonjudgmental stance with the therapist to validate emotional safety. Thirdly, Samuel and Cassandra presented with emotional traumas from their childhood/adolescence with significant people in their lives, so providing education about this is imperative to help them release feelings of shame and self-judgment, in their narratives about how they understood their experiences.

As each partner felt more willing to take risks to "stop walking on eggshells," as Samuel mentioned to Cassandra in one session, they received indications that the other could receive them without judgment and with empathy, openness, and longing to connect. Both continued to struggle at times with fear of how the other would hear their words and their own self-worthiness. Nevertheless, they also began to understand that some of their emotional reactivity was motivated to protect themselves or the other. Adaptive reactions were blocking their romantic connection.

Below is a session two years into our therapy:

Samuel: The truth is that I've always had this feeling of existential dread, and some of it is still there with me. The difference now is that when I talk about it, I can say, 'Hey, I know where that feeling is in my body.' I know where it's located, and I can picture it . . . I can imagine it. So it isn't like it has gone away.

Abrams: So you're saying "It is here, that feeling, and it has shifted. . . . The difference is that I'm able to name what I feel. . . . It's occurring in my body, and I'll take that as a win from our work here." . . . This has been a gradual shift, a change that you have become aware of? *(Speaking as if in first person with reflection and evocative question).*

Samuel: That's interesting because the way you put it, that sounded much more impressive *(We all laugh)* than how I would have worded it, but yes.

Abrams: Yeah. I think about this with you all, and how to offer back what you say. What has that experience been like for you? To engage in that kind of emotional location and naming of where and how you feel? And then making choices to share that with Cassandra? *(Evocative question with reflection and attachment framing).*

Samuel: It has been very good to have a trusted person to practice with. I hope I can do this in different situations, as well as with Cassandra. I can risk that sense of vulnerability with her, and I'm not as worried about being accepted.

Abrams: I have a hunch that this increase in sharing and vulnerability will continue to build quite a bit of trust between you guys. I'm wondering if maybe desire, too . . . at least space for or willingness to engage physically? Would you say that you have been building momentum between the two of you over the past few weeks? *(Reflecting on discussion of increased desire discussed in earlier part of session. Linking emotional closeness to sexual desire).*

Samuel: I think so; it has a lot to do with being a male in this society. You don't get a lot of practice or discussion about the emotional impact of sex. I think you get tricked into thinking that you just will react physically. That the male anatomy has a mind of its own. Which can be true. But what I've found particularly true for me as a result of the relationship we have . . . is that the feeling that you need, that connection for it to be really something that you want to enjoy and something you want to engage in is just as important or more than the physical aspect. . . . That closeness and connection we're building is feeding into the physical aspect.

Cassandra: So we have been talking about our past sexual history, and the lack thereof, and how much of that was associated with my church upbringing and religion. It was layered on top of a lack of sexual experience. I really had no knowing, no way to access how to enjoy sex or even explore it, and I carried that into my marriage. He took that to mean that I didn't enjoy sex, and he decided that sex wouldn't be a part of our marriage. Until we finally talked about it, I didn't realize that he had given up on sex and made a contract within himself to do without.

Abrams: What was it like for you to hear that he made this internal contract with himself without talking to you about that? *(Evocative question with negative pattern)*.

Cassandra: I didn't understand it before. So in hearing this now, I got a little worried and tried to bring him back to us. I was like "Oh, please no don't do that! Let's try. Let's explore." I understand how jarring it must have felt for him to hear me talk that way. He had no point of reference for this coming from me, so I got worried that because he decided that for himself, then this was also a decision for me and I would lose that access to him sexually and to myself.

Abrams: I'm wondering, Samuel, what was your experience like to hear Cassandra talk this way about sex? Was it actually jarring for you? What were those moments like for you? *(Evocative question and conjecture with evocative question)*.

Samuel: Jarring is a good way to describe it. And honestly, the other part was that I just had no context to make sense of it.

Abrams: So it landed on you in such a way that you couldn't even recognize. You had no model for what to do or language for what to say to Cassandra. *(Reflection of internal experience)*.

Samuel: No modeling, and I had no way to talk to her about this, so I started with the same language that I used in the beginning of therapy with you: "I hear what you're saying, but I don't know if I can trust it." I wanted to have fun at sex, too, but honestly I didn't believe that it was possible given our previous attempts." It always ended in a sense of rejection.

Abrams: So it seemed to you, so why are you thinking of making attempts again, only to open up the experience of feeling rejected? *(Empathic reflection with attachment fear)*.

Samuel: When we were first married and we were just getting started with sex, there was lots of foreplay which was something great, and I was into it, saying, "Let's have more!" I'll always remember when she said, "I'm not comfortable with that." It was like she was saying "We won't be able to engage in physical intimacy!" At that moment I knew two things: sex will only happen on her terms, and it won't be any fun for me." *(They both laugh)*. She's not comfortable, so that's it. It was written.

Abrams: So if I'm hearing you right, that moment had a serious effect on you going forward in the marriage. If I understand it right, you made an internal agreement, accepted it, and continued on, believing there was no way to change what was written. There must have been something else that was more important in this relationship for you than sexual fun. *(Reflection, assembling internal voice of emotion with attachment reflection).*

Samuel: Yeah. The idea obviously came from a place of love which is in my marriage contract. You know, the sickness and in health, until death do you part, part. So I just told myself, "We'll just have to see how this goes," and I just eventually added that additional clause of bad sex!

Abrams: Wow, you're saying a great deal more than we've been able to explore before. I appreciate that, Samuel. I know you two have been talking more and been willing to address the things about your marriage that you thought would or could never change. I know we've also talked quite a bit about your sense of worthiness; you being deserving of having self-satisfaction. You've been asking yourself "Do I actually deserve these things? Like fun in sex? Really?" So I know this goes pretty deep for you. *(Reflections on view of self and assembling internal emotional experience).*

Samuel: That's a whole other point and you touched on it. Yes, you're absolutely right. It's not as if I felt like I even deserved a good marriage.

Abrams: "I'm not even built for this in the first place." *(Engaging by proxy using his internal voice).* Of course, you're bad at this anyway, so when she says "This physical interaction is not comfortable," you're not going to push on that in any way. You know, Samuel, as you've said before, that as a Black man, you are particularly respectful of Black women. You don't want to make it uncomfortable for her because you're aware of the deep implications of that kind of experience. So you found a way to shut down physically and move away emotionally, too, right?

For you, Cassandra, this was different. You wanted to bring back the conversation about sex and offer some new attempts to be close to him. The challenge for you, Samuel, has been this internal contract you made to protect yourself. Self-preservation against rejection. No need to become tied to having or seeking self-worth and value. And pair all of that with no modeling. How risky it must have felt for you to even consider pursuing closeness when you have such a fear of rejection that is parallel to Samuel's, unbeknownst to you. Wow, you two. *(Reflective summary revisiting a defining moment of failure to communicate about and during sex, validating response, and reflecting on how the negative cycle was blocking possibility to adjust/correct now).*

Cassandra: But the difference is that we are closer now *(Cassandra is looking directly at Samuel)*, and the sex podcast helped me with the language I didn't have before. Because of my upbringing, sex was new to me, and I didn't understand enough to say to you that it was literally too overwhelming, stimulating for my body. I didn't know what to do with those feelings. No one had ever touched me in this way before or gone that far. I had to shut it down. All I had ever learned was that having sex was against God. All I could say at the time was "It's uncomfortable for me." I didn't have the ability to say "But I want to get past it, I want to find a way to get more comfortable. Let's just practice feeling pleasure and enjoying each other's bodies."

Abrams: This could be something different between the two of you now. This is creating something new and you're saying, "Let's create this together in a collaborative way that feels right for the both of us and has relationship depth to it also." It may feel risky at times, and it may have new feelings, but we can add layers, and safety, and pacing to the physical intimacy, just as you all have done with your emotional intimacy. What's it like to hear what I just said? *(Reflecting on the attachment closeness and new positive cycle, empathic reflection with linking emotional engagement with sexual intimacy).*

Samuel: Honestly, it makes me realize that I had lacked some compassion. That I made a contract with myself to avoid rejection and decide what our sex life was going to be, and I didn't see that she was afraid or lacked knowledge. *(Talking directly to Cassandra).* Now it is so obvious as she talks about it. I went off protecting myself and making an internal contract, and it could have been a different conversation. I'm learning about compassion for her, and how to show more of that to myself.

Cassandra: For me, it has been learning that pleasure is good. Pleasure is okay and allowing myself to have it and be responsible for my own pleasure. And being a partner with him for his pleasure. We can do that in a uniquely Black way, too. (*Looking at* Samuel) We are in a relationship and your pleasure is important to me, too. This is totally different.

Abrams: It is a new pattern you all are working on for yourselves. Allowing yourselves to have pleasure. And even just connecting to your bodies. And on some levels, it requires a grieving process from past difficulties, the lack of models, the right terms, and what society and the media have taught us about our bodies. How revolutionary that the two of you are searching to learn from each other. To offer yourselves the beautiful curiosity that says, 'What's the language for us?' *(Empathic reflections and promoting emotional and sexual engagement, using culture as connection).*

Therapist's Reflection

As you can see from the transcripts, their evolving communication has improved. This EFT therapy has been successful in reconnecting them in ways that they could not have imagined before treatment. Both partners are committed to and motivated for continuing couples therapy. They both experience less internal anxiety and are far more satisfied with their marriage. Samuel reports a significant decrease in depressive symptoms, increased awareness of triggers, and a decrease in duration and intensity when he does begin to experience a depressive episode. Cassandra also reports decreased depressive symptoms, more awareness of herself and her needs in general and related to the marriage and parentally, and she has deepened her spirituality in response to understanding more about her needs, both ancestral and in her family of creation.

This couple has made major strides toward emotional engagement. When they started therapy, Samuel would become emotionally overstimulated with some felt sense of stress or emotional dysregulation and shut down. This was a long-standing pattern of coping that pre-dated his marriage. This avoidance style of coping was to withdraw emotionally and physically go away to protect his family—parents, siblings, and other family members—from himself. That became harder for him when he was married and had a child. His beliefs about his emotions were that they got in the way of doing. Feelings to him were not useful or important because "they don't get things done." As he grew up, he came to understand that feelings would eventually go away, and after a few days of sadness or depression, those feelings would go away. This coping pattern wasn't working in the marriage, however.

The therapeutic tasks of this couple's treatment have been to offer consistent and repetitive messages of self-worth, validation of their individual experiences, the importance of hearing them, and using their internal voice to express emotions and thoughts. Their family histories included patterns of being silenced, and both of them lacked role models to teach healthy curiosity and exploration in marriage. Each of their histories involved limited understanding of mental and emotional health. As a result, this meant at times a bit more focus on brief psycho-education about feelings, thoughts, emotional impact, and interpersonal behavior. It also meant leaving room for practice, and staging encounters through me, instead of their talking directly to each other.

Work with them involved a lot of "kayaking tango," which describes a rhythm of attempts to focus on his feelings, and then he would exit that focus to talk about details of stressful experiences at work. Then I would bring him back to his feelings. This was an ongoing rhythm to develop his emotional experience. For example, given his multiple demands at work, I would say "That must have felt really stressful for you," or "Man, I could only imagine that you must have felt really sad to be in this place alone. Everyone's out there doing their thing, and you're isolating alone in the bedroom." He stayed with that a moment and shifted to talk about all the demands on him with lots of details unrelated to feelings. Slowly, it became easier to bring him back to his feelings. With a great deal of evocative conjecture and questions, he eventually started adding feelings to his own stories.

Softening Cassandra's pursuit helped to increase her distress tolerance and to depersonalize Samuel's own journey with parenting and his expressed love for her. As he became more engaged, she could stay increasingly present. It was important for Samuel to know that when he showed up, Cassandra could hold space with him. She has alternately found strength in her own resilience, takes more time to herself while Samuel works on himself, and hears him for what he is saying about himself without interpreting that he must believe less about her. Cassandra's internal work also included receiving and seeking out her own assistance with having a close loved one with severe and persistent mental illness. She has found social and educational support, which has been beneficial.

Reflections on Race and Culture

First, this Black couple, like most in my practice, chose me as their psychologist for couples therapy because they hoped to experience a safe place to work on their marriage with a Black therapist. Building the therapeutic alliance through pacing and validation is especially important in our work with Black clients, to increase emotional safety and familiarity in the relationship through practice and education about the process. I spend time talking about the process of therapy and what the couple might expect during the process such as exploring their emotions, their attachment bonds, and their cycle of interactions. Second, they chose this modality of therapy as well as me specifically, as a Black clinician, for a culturally responsive space to examine their gaps. Some of those cultural factors include their specific cultural backgrounds, their unique family experiences, the religious differences, and particular experiences in the world as Black people. Additionally, both are interested in social justice matters related to race and ethnicity. During treatment, we have also addressed the emotional and possible physical impact of community violence, police brutality against African Americans, sending their child to school, and feeling safe and seen as they move in and out of various social/community circles.

The working alliance is a process of continuing to show this couple, and other Black clients, that I show up as therapist not to penalize, judge, or admonish them for their experiences. Instead, I am there to actively explore their unique emotions and perspectives and help them to lean into the therapy and their relationship with each another. It seems a safe working alliance was enhanced by a number of factors: (1) a nonjudgmental attitude of the therapist that was demonstrated with validation and empathic reflections; (2) continual curiously about their unique experiences as Black people and not assuming any stereotypic Black notions of their Blackness; (3) a gentle but relentless focus on their emotional experiences in order to help them to develop increased awareness of the emotional experiences and emotional engagement between them. This EFT therapeutic stance was particular useful because both Samuel and Cassandra presented with emotional traumas from their childhood/adolescence. They were responsive to naming the emotional traumas and to receiving some education about the impact of traumas. Validating their feelings and gently reflecting on cultural practices and discrimination were helpful in countering shame and self-judgment.

There are cultural differences and some profound similarities between Samuel and Cassandra. Samuel's parents and sometimes one or more of his brothers lived with them in a separate house behind their home. While Samuel's early years were spent in Nigeria in a village, Cassandra grew up in Southern California.

Samuel had immediate access to several family households within a short distance from each other, and likewise, Cassandra had access to her grandmother, aunts, and uncles who lived nearby. This access to many caregivers in their early development mirrors the idea of collective attachment bonds suggested by Otto and Keller (2014). Samuel's family migration to the United States, mirrored to some degree African American family migration out of the South to Southern California. Samuel's father stayed in Nigeria working, while his mother and sibling moved to the United States. Typically, African American families had to travel out of the South separately so as to not experience White violence during the migration. Often fathers came months or years earlier to find work, and the family followed. Samuel's family living close by is a familiar Nigerian experience for Samuel and also a familiar African American experience for Cassandra.

Both welcomed the opportunity for multigenerational family living, and to both it was reexperiencing a cultural norm. While there has been significant tension at times between Cassandra and her mother-in-law regarding child-rearing practices and healthy food versus African dishes, this has significantly improved with couples therapy. Specifically, as Samuel became more emotionally assessible and engaged with Cassandra, she has come to understand that he is on her side and standing with her. Previously, when cultural differences would show up between Grandmother and Cassandra, Samuel would be silent because he felt protective of both, but Cassandra felt abandoned and alone. He would only want to stop their conversation. There was a felt sense of mutual dislike of Grandmother and Samuel. As Samuel shared the stuck place he experienced with not wanting to make the situation worse between his mother and wife, and his lifelong felt responsibility for taking care of his mother, and his loyalty to Cassandra, she both felt included and together. Moreover, as Samuel became more expressive and engaged with Cassandra, he was also able to become more engaged with his family. Samuel's accessibility, responsiveness, and emotional engagement seemed to increase the spirit of cooperation in the whole household. They have more open discussions about childcare practices, and healthy family diets that also include African foods.

There was a very important moment that happened in their developing emotional engagement. In this important moment, Cassandra took a risk, talked to Samuel about the matter, and was delighted to get his emotional support. This event was a threat to Cassandra's racial identity, sense of belonging, and likeability. She goes to a Black yoga studio that is for her self-healing. One day she became tearful during the yoga positioning and was off-putting to the yoga instructor. The trainer pulled her aside and reprimanded her for emoting, and it was a problem for others in the class. The Black women in the yoga class were conservative, but she was beginning to feel a part of the community. So the reprimand deeply hurt her feelings, and she wasn't sure she could go back. Samuel was able to stand tall for her and said, "Man that sucks, I'm sorry that happened to you." This was such a shift for her—to take a risk with being vulnerable and for him to just be there for her in her moment of distress. This was a deeply emotional experience for Cassandra and so moving to her that Samuel was there for her. We processed this over a number of sessions, and Cassandra seemed to heal from this deep wound.

Case Discussion With Sue Johnson

Guillory: *Ayanna rarely used encounters as an intervention in her work. She does an exceptional job, creating a great deal of safety with relentless empathy, validations, and empathic reflections. Each partner also seems to own their roles in their negative cycle of communications, and as a couple, made efforts to develop a different positive cycle. I wonder if more encounters might be helpful in setting a more solid platform for stage two work.*

Sue Johnson: Well, I think the point is that in couples therapy, your client is the relationship. You're trying to change the nature of this relationship. Yes, Ayanna demonstrates beautiful empathy. She works with one person, then the other, and talks to them about each other. This couple, like all couples, can gain insight. This man has gained insight about his depression, and has worked on that. He has also worked on his withdrawing behavior. The wife in this relationship has also gained insight on her anxiety. These insights and work on their negative cycle have impacted, positively, their relationship. I would still want Ayanna to change how this couple dances together. Our task here as EFT therapists, is to translate new emotions and new ways of understanding the self and other into new connections and inner connections within a new interpersonal dance. And the only way you do that is to create an encounter, a new kind of encounter. And what we know is that new drama that the encounter creates is often on a different level than the couple usually interacts on. That's what changes the way they see themselves with their partner, and the way they see their partner. That's what changes how they dance together. It changes the dance from a dance of disconnection to a dance of connection.

The other issue is that we are attachment theorists, and we believe in the power of attachment. Before attachment theory impacted psychotherapy, therapy was based on the idea that it is the messages from the therapist or the way the therapist directs the client that is going to be healing. What attachment theorists and EFT started as a couples therapy is different. So from our point of view, which is what attachment says, the most healing element in the room is the response of the other partner, not the therapist. Therapists have a role; we change the music. We create safety. We do all the EFT interventions, but the partner—the messages from the partner have huge healing potential. We can validate someone as a therapist, and hopefully you do it well. But when the partner shifts from not understanding or being withdrawn, or even being rejecting and dismissing into accepting a message from their spouse, and being touched by a message from them, and responding to their message, that is huge. And that spouse's brain takes that in on a survival-oriented level in a way that is different from the way that spouse takes in your messages, because you're not a significant attachment figure. And so your messages don't have the same level of significance. I mean, hopefully if you're a very attuned therapist, you can have quite a big significance to your messages. But still, it is the partner. And you see that with traumatized couples.

The therapist's acceptance is important, but the partner's acceptance not only changes the relationship but also changes each person in the relationship. When the relationship dance changes at the attachment level, it changes the dancers, too. We have seen in attachment research that when my husband comforts me, that is a different channel of emotional and physical comfort than if a nurse pats my hand and says something comforting to me. It can change my world. I can change how I see myself and how I see him. When you have responsive, engaged encounters where both partners are accessible, responsive, and emotionally engaged, it adds so much to survival significance. You learn that "Oh my God, someone has my back. I'm not alone." And you feel that in your body, and learn that "I'm worthy of care. I'm important to this person." And we learn that "There is someone in this world I can trust." This is a huge message as attachment therapists. It is very simple and very profound. The message is you are not alone. These encounters transmit very powerful cues. The loving images of our partners looking into our eyes softly, hearing the tenderness in their voices, and feeling their vulnerability. These are powerful cues that are bred into our nervous system, and that's what we are activating. I recall falling in love with my husband's voice when we had a long-distance relationship. I could hear the tenderness in his voice, the humor and inquisitiveness, and presence and intellect. Even today, after years of marriage, his voice has a calming impact on me. If I'm in a bad place, I think about his hands on my face. When we create these powerful encounters, we're activating that knowledge of primeval drama associated with basic survival needs and cues. These encounters are our most powerful moments of change, these new encounters, it's a process; so yes, we have to create them.

Guillory: *It seems to me that EFT trainings have shifted over time. When I initially learned EFT, there was more of an emphasis on the nine steps and three stages. This is how Ayanna and I were taught. Now, the training is more focused on the five moves of the therapist, the tango moves. It seems the role of encounters and changing the relationship conversation has become more central.*

Sue Johnson: You're absolutely right. Earlier in EFT training, we focused on the process of the client. What we used to do was focus on the client's process, not the interventions of the therapist. And the tango really came out of my frustration with how caught up therapists would become in the nine steps. Well, we focused on the process of the client, and so we did nine steps. The client would shift to steps toward emotional engagement. My teaching experience over many years was that therapists would get obsessed with these nine steps and think about them all the time. And somehow, one evening when I was preparing a class, I thought, "These nine steps, I use to teach a process, but it's not the most efficient way to do it. What's wrong with it?" And then it somehow clicked that "it is the client's process. What is it that EFT therapists do in therapy?" And then it was obvious. I'm a tango dancer, so it was obvious to me to call it the tango. So then when I outline the tango, I thought, "Oh, this is much simpler for people to learn. It's focused on the therapist's interventions, not the client's process. This works." So then I started teaching the tango, and people respond to it much more easily. I think it's because I'm focusing on what the therapist does, not what the client goes through, which is a bit sort of vague and more difficult to identify. So yes, you're right. The tango I think is easier. And the steps are still useful. You hear people say, "Should I talk about the steps?" I say, "Well, you can talk about the steps, as this is the client's process that we used to focus on, but I want you to learn the tango."

And then people get all focused on the structure of the tango: "Okay. Do I always have to do the complete tango and in this sequence?" No, of course not. Doing therapy is an improvised dance, not a set choreography. You sort of play around. I spent a whole session on move one in my last session. My client is a very severely traumatized woman and she'd had a very heavy session the session before, and I was concerned about her. I went in and did move one. Just stayed with her experience, but really, I just touched on a few emotions and I spent most of the session in move one, normalizing, validating, integrating, validating, validating, integrating. Ayanna had to do that with this depressed man. We stay close to where the client is, and we only assemble as much emotion as the client can tolerate.

I use the metaphor of the dance to conceptualize couple interactions. Music moves dancers to engage a particular way, and emotions are the music of couple interactions. The steps in partner dancing are how dancers rhythmically move together. Tango dancing, for example. If I'm going to teach you tango, I've got to teach you the steps, but learning the steps is not dancing. At first, people say, "Oh my God, this dance is so hard," because you have all these intricate steps and moves. But as you learn to dance, any dance, there's a certain moment when you realize that the steps are not the dance, that the steps are a basic structure of the dance. Dancing starts when you realize that the steps move you, and that you can flow. Within the dance you can play with sequences, and you use the music to stay connected in movement.

In tango dancing, the music is the structure. In EFT, the emotion is the structure. The emotional music is the structure. And you move more fluidly within and between the partners. The process has choreography, and you still have the structure and steps in the background. So the structure goes to background, rather than foreground. The foreground is the emotions and couples dance. We track their conversational patterns and their attachment moves. First of all, you need, "Oh, okay. What does an 'ouch,' the first flash point of distress, look like? Again using the dance as metaphor, "I turn my body, I step with my step, I bring my other leg, I put my foot down." (Or in Ayanna's case, I feel the stress from work, and her telling me I have to take care of myself . . . as pressure and stress, and get alarmed and I shut down, and go into the bedroom and close the door.)

And then after three years of marriage, your body just does it this way. We call this withdrawal. The point is to stay with your client and follow them. We can change this dance by focusing on the music, the emotions, and their moves, and suddenly they find they are doing something quite different.

Basically, if you think about the tango, as soon as someone puts something together in a new way or gets in touch with a new emotion or clarifies an emotion, that's relevant. I always then tend to think about turning it into an interpersonal signal. So it could be very short and small in the beginning. It could be a man who says he doesn't feel anything. And then he talks—suddenly, I'm talking to him and I do a little bit of affect assembly, and he admits that he's intimidated by his wife, right, and that's part of why he shuts down. And so this is new. So then if it's a first couple of sessions, I might say, "Oh, could you help me?" Because it's the first few sessions, I won't go into that in huge depth because he's not ready, but I might just say, "Oh, right. I hear that." And I'll normalize and say, "Oh, well, we all get a little intimidated if we think our partner is angry at us." And then I might say, "Have you ever told her that?" And he's bound to say, "No, I don't think I have," or "She knows."

And I say, "Well, maybe she doesn't. I think that's important. Could you maybe just look at her and tell her right now that what happens in these moments is that you actually get intimidated by her anger, and you don't know what to do with it, so you withdraw? Could you tell her that, please?" So I'm always looking for opportunities to start encounters, but knowing the most significant change moments will occur in stage two. Stage one encounters are important too. Encounters in stage one help with de-escalation. In stage two encounters, I'll load the affect. I'll do a big affect assembly, get a moment of vulnerability that will evoke a new response in the partner. I'm looking for a message that may evoke a new response in the partner. I'm trying to expand the drama, expand the dance, and send a new signal—get the person to send a new signal that they've just put together that may move, shift the partner. Right? So that's what I'm doing all the time. So in that case, I'll load the affect and once I've got a new way of dealing with vulnerability, then I'll get them to say it to their partner. So you're always looking for opportunities for the partners to share vulnerability in a way that creates connection.

8 Case Study
EFT Withdrawer Re-Engagement

Yamonte Cooper with Paul T. Guillory and Case Discussion with Sue Johnson

This case study is an example of a stage-two, withdrawer-re-engagement (WRE) in EFT couples therapy. WRE is a part of the stage-two process of restructuring the bond and creating deeper levels of accessibility and responsiveness. This entails a set of enactments in which a withdrawn partner fully experiences and coherently expresses their core fears and needs to the other (Johnson, 2019, 2020). This is an African American couple struggling with issues of infertility and a pattern of disconnection. Their negative pattern of interaction leaves them feeling abandoned/rejected and helpless/lost, with both partners feeling painfully alone. The attachment traumas in their early lives impede their ability to turn toward each other during times of distress. Their feelings of rejection and helplessness get triggered regarding the importance and meaning of having a baby together, ultimately leading to disconnection in the relationship. Their disconnection gets stuck in a rigid negative pattern that continues in a downward spiral of demand and withdraw. The core struggle is related to the meaning around having a child, their negative pattern of engagement, and emotional availability and responsiveness. The couple dynamics include race, trauma, and fertility that inform the couples therapy.

Description of Partners

Eric and Kam have been together for nine years and married for three years. Kam is a 38-year-old African American social worker. Eric is a 36-year-old African American who works in an oil refinery. Both of them were born in Los Angeles (L.A.) and met at a mutual friend's party. Eric and Kam do not have children and they live together in L.A. Both of them are bright, reflective, caring, able to access primary emotions, and very motivated in therapy. They came to see me for EFT couples therapy because they were experiencing a lot of conflict around attempts to conceive a child. They described themselves as feeling disconnected and drifting apart. During many fights, Eric would leave the home for hours, impacting Kam and raising doubts about whether they should conceive. Historically, in moments of disconnection, Kam pursues and Eric withdraws from engagement. They came into therapy stuck in their reactive modes related to having a child.

DOI: 10.4324/9780429355127-8

Reason for Coming to Therapy

Kam called to arrange couples therapy, as they were experiencing a lot of conflict regarding attempts to conceive a child; she described them as feeling disconnected and drifting apart. In moments of disconnection, tension, and conflict, Eric and Kam tend to get into an EFT pursue-withdraw cycle. Kam is the pursuer; when she feels disconnected from Eric, she becomes anxious, panicked, and fearful that Eric will abandon her. Further, she questions whether Eric can be there for her during times of need. Kam often feels alone, unwanted, and vulnerable. Kam then protests by telling Eric what to do and how to change, criticizing him, and asking him a lot of questions while threatening to discontinue pursuing pregnancy. This was a coping style she developed growing up as a result of anxious attachment and experiencing the adults in her life avoiding ownership of their emotions. This situation ultimately created a sense in her of empowerment, though feeling powerless. The pursue-withdraw cycle started with Eric drinking alcohol, gambling, staying out late with friends, or not being emotionally present. Eric felt criticized by Kam, and would get quiet, shut down, and withdraw. He developed this coping style when he grew up in the foster care system. He received the message that displaying emotions was a sign of weakness, and in order to remain safe, one could not be weak; this contributed to his anxious attachment style. When Kam became angry and more critical, Eric did not know what to do. He felt like he could never get it right with Kam, and that he was bad and inadequate—the same way he felt in his family of origin and the foster care system. As a result, his only recourse was to shut down and withdraw. At times, he would leave the house and stay away for hours. Being away from Kam was painful for Eric, and often left him with a deep sense of despair and hopelessness. When Kam attempted to contact him, he ignored her communications. When they first came to see me, they were unaware of their cycle, but they knew they did not feel emotionally safe with each other.

Eric and Kam's Cycle

Eric's attachment distress cues are criticisms from Kam about his leaving, drinking, and gambling. Kam's disapproval is a trigger, along with suggestions that they should consider adoption. In moments of couples distress, Eric withdraws. He also has a racial distress cue that gets triggered regarding the adoption system.

When he withdraws, Eric becomes quiet, pulls away from the conversation, leaves the house, isolates himself in the house, and at times, withdraws by drinking. His internal self-appraisals when they are disconnected are harsh. Examples: Something is wrong with me. I am the problem, and I will never get it right with Kam. My feelings are bad. I am bad. I need to be by myself to have my feelings. If people know me, I will be rejected. Avoid making it worse.

His reactive emotions during disconnections and conflicts with Kam are frustrations that he has gotten it wrong again, annoyance that he is being criticized, and anger that he is being rejected.

His attachment emotions are fear of being inadequate as a husband, and rejected by Kam as a person. He fears losing Kam. His attachment needs to feel safe in order to have his feelings. He needs acceptance, empathy, comfort, and a felt sense of belonging.

Kam's attachment distress cues are criticism and Eric's withdrawal behaviors. When she feels distress, she pursues connection.

Her behavior when they are disconnected is to complain and criticize Eric for his behaviors, ask many questions about his intentions and thinking, and demand attention. Kam will sometimes use food to numb her anger and sadness. Her internal appraisals are associated with self-worth: I am unlovable and alone. I will be abandoned by Eric.

Her reactive emotions are disappointment in herself and with Eric, and anger toward his behaviors. Kam's attachment emotions are fears of being abandoned by Eric and of being alone. Her attachment needs are to be engaged, responded to by Eric, and attended to by him. She wants Eric to comfort her during times of distress. Kam also wants to feel safe to feel her vulnerable feelings and have Eric be there for her.

Their cycle: The more Kam reaches for connection by commenting on Eric's withdrawal behaviors, the more Eric withdraws. The more she experiences his withdrawals, the more she comments. And the more they struggle as a couple with conceiving a child, the more they struggle with feelings of being failures, Kam as mother and Eric as father. Their dilemma as a couple is that each one has difficulty articulating attachment feelings. Each has learned coping strategies to protect against the expression of vulnerability from their traumatic past; this impedes their connection and ability to repair disconnections.

Eric's Attachment History

Eric reports that he grew up in the foster care system. At the age of seven he was removed from the care of his mother due to her drug abuse and neglect. His father was never present in his life and after being removed from his mother's care, she discontinued being present in his life as well. Eric recalled living in multiple foster homes without ever feeling like he was loved and cared for by the various foster families. Eric felt like he was bad, unworthy, and inadequate as a result of his parent's absence in his life. This impacted his attachment style in that he tended to be anxiously attached and sometimes questioned his self-worth. Eric felt ashamed of his feelings and sensitive nature. He felt that he had to hide this part of himself—otherwise, people would abandon him like his parents. He also hid his vulnerability in order to maintain safety in the foster care system. While growing up in foster care, he received messages that having feelings and expressing them or any other vulnerabilities were signs of weakness and could leave you open to being harmed and taken advantage of by others. This belief system was solidified from witnessing people being taken advantage of when they displayed emotions. He disclosed during a session that his mother once told him that the police take pleasure in seeing Black people hurting and crying;

she warned him to never allow them to see him cry, as it is a source of humor for them. Eric had a twin brother who was placed in the same foster home with him. They forged a deeper sibling relationship as a protective factor due to the trauma of being removed from their mother's care and placed in the foster care system. This strengthened their bond, and Eric's brother often relied on him for protection. They had each other in the midst of feeling constantly monitored and exploited. As Eric grew up, he often would socially abuse alcohol. During times of vulnerability, he would withdraw, shut down, and isolate himself. He often found it difficult to feel safe with his feelings and reach out for Kam. Sometimes he overindulged in alcohol for comfort and numbing.

Kam's Attachment History

Kam reports that she comes from a critical and verbally abusive background. She describes her mother as warm and loving but as someone who struggled with drug abuse throughout her life. Kam stated that due to her mother's drug abuse, she took on the role of being a parent to her mother. Unfortunately, her parents divorced when she was young. Her dad remarried, and as a result of her mother's drug abuse, she lived with her father and stepmother full-time. She grew up receiving a lot of criticism about her weight and parental surveillance regarding what she ate. This resulted in conflict with her father and stepmother and left her feeling ambivalent about being loved, as it appeared that love was conditional and revolved around her weight. As a result, Kam suffered from anxiety and depression and struggled with self-acceptance. Kam has invested a lot of time in self-acceptance through Black feminism (womanist), and has come to a place of self-acceptance around issues of weight and body image. Black feminism helped her to gain a deeper understanding of how Black woman are often sexually objectified and their bodies evaluated as a function of sexism. She grew up in a predominately Black community in Los Angeles. The community was tightly knit, with adults actively present in the community and in the lives of the children. Further, her grandmother was an active and influential presence in her life; she felt unconditionally loved by her. Kam has had a couple of significant relationships with two boyfriends; she is still friends with one of them. Overall, Kam displays an optimistic disposition. Often, she feels unsafe about being with her feelings or reaching for Eric and will seek food for comfort and numbing instead.

Stage-One EFT

During stage one work, I established an alliance with them and used a lot of validation, reflection, and RISSSC to help them focus on identifying and understanding their cycle. We explored their secondary behaviors, underlying the primary emotions, and attachment reframes. When we began meeting, Eric expressed apprehension and frustration and found it difficult to be present with Kam. Sometimes he left their home for hours and refused contact with her.

Therefore, Kam would get angry and question moving forward with having a child. I reflected these behaviors and action tendencies and helped them to see their negative cycle. I also validated and reflected their internal, softer primary feelings of sadness, fear, and aloneness. I helped them to see and discern their external behaviors and action tendencies, and to see and feel their internal, primary feelings. They were open to attachment reframes and were willing (with my support) to do enactments. After some time, they were able to interrupt their negative cycle within and outside of sessions.

Cooper: Yeah. I get it. That makes sense. So with this process and throughout attempting to get pregnant, often, Kam, you have felt like you've been doing this on your own and there's a part of you that feels rejected, as well as sad and afraid that you mentioned you would be alone in this process... *(Kam nods).*

Cooper: ... and wanting Eric closer to you, while you're going through this process to ensure that you're safe, and you're supported in this process. And during those moments when you're not feeling safe and supported and you feel rejected, then you get scared and you start arguments or start picking at Eric or criticizing. *(Walking them through the cycle).*

Kam: *(deep sigh).* I guess so because really it's deep down, I wasn't sure if the relationship is going to be able to withstand this. Is he going to fall out of love with me? You know, go find somebody else to have a baby. So then I just end up trying to I guess act like it's not bothering me *(pause)*, and then that's when I get irritable.

Cooper: And, you get afraid? *(Validating secondary and offering primary).* *(Kam nods).*

Cooper: The part of you that gets afraid that he might fall out of love and there might be someone else at that point. And you want him to see you, and value you. So you say, "Hey, I'm over here. I need you to be a part of this process with me. I need to know that."

Kam: Yeah. And maybe, and maybe that's why I do bug him a little bit with the adoption stuff. I guess that's like an attention thing, too.

Cooper: And then you, Eric, when this happens, how you get caught up in the cycle is you don't want to lose her. You don't want to lose Kam, and so you shut down. You might physically leave (Kam scratches and then rubs her leg) for fear of escalating the situation and not being able to resolve it. Does that, does that fit for you? Does that make sense? *(Helping them to understand their cycle).*

Eric: It does, you know. I mean, I'm not an argumentative person. I mean, I can be, but I choose not to. You know, I guess (slaps knee with hand) to me the best thing to do is to retreat into my own little comfort zone. I don't want her to think she's alone (gestures with hands) because she's not. I mean, we've been doing this for quite some time. I think if I was going to step out, I probably would have stepped out by now.

Cooper: But can you tell her that, "I'm not going anywhere. That you mean everything to me, and I don't want to lose you"? *(Seeding the enactment).*

Eric: I just want you to know I'm not going anywhere. I mean, we've been doing this for quite some time. I mean, we've been riding through this storm for quite some time, I want to ride through the storm together.

Discussion of Transcript

This brief transcript reflects their cycle reactions and their positive engagement with couples therapy. Eric is starting to understand that his withdrawing behavior is have a disturbing impact on Kam. Kam is able to articulate the distress she is experiencing with the process of conceiving a child, and she needs to feel connected to Eric. When he withdraws, she is alone and scared, and she fears she could lose him. What adoption means to Eric has not been completely articulated by him at this point, but it is a point of disconnection. Kam and Eric are engaged in their couples work, and the working alliance feels strong. While both have some difficulties talking about their feelings, they will explore them and engage in enactments. They are actively engaged with reflecting on and changing their negative cycle.

Stage Two of EFT Couples Therapy

As we moved into stage-two work, Kam became more aware of her need to fight and become angry, the only method of communication she saw growing up. She learned that fighting and protesting were how she was able to survive. As Eric learned about his fear of being blamed and rejected and his subsequent withdrawal, he was able to stay more present with his deeper, more primary feelings of sadness and fear. I continued our work in stage two with heightening primary emotions and reflecting attachment related fears. I worked on slowing way down, using their words, and guiding them into softer, sweeter interactions (enactments) to help lead to more bonding and secure attachment. We created new patterns of interactions, with Eric able to stay more engaged and connected to his primary feelings and needs. Kam has begun softening as Eric is more engaged. We are currently working on Kam's softening, accepting disowned aspects of herself, and creating new bonding experiences. The following is an example of our stage-two withdrawer re-engagement.

Withdrawer Re-Engagement

Stage two of EFT involves the deepening of emotional experience and expression. Attachment emotions become more aware to each partner, and their emotional vulnerability becomes more specific. At this stage of the work, the couple has become increasingly safe with their partner and the process of therapy. While all of the same EFT interventions from stage one, such as empathic reflections.

validations, evocative questions, heightening, conjectures, and tango moves are used, there is greater depth to the processing. In withdrawer re-engagement, the EFT therapist focuses on increasing the withdrawer's presence in the room and their ability to reach for their partner and ask for the response they need from them. The withdrawer's felt sense of safety increases to reach and express needs assertively. As withdrawers feel safer, they are less shut down, indifferent, numb, or present as not caring. As depth in tango moves increase, withdrawers talk about their fears and needs.

Example of Stage-Two Transcript

Cooper: So we have been focusing on you lately, Eric, and how you get caught up in the cycle and what you are experiencing emotionally in those moments. Is that okay, Kam, if we continue with Eric? *(Inviting permission to return to discussion about the cycle and his emotional experiences). (Kam nods).*

Cooper: Okay. So we've been talking about how you become afraid, and you move into a place of sadness. You feel alone when Kam is having those moments of feeling alone herself. This process of attempting to have a child together is hard. And you have acknowledged feeling sometimes like you're not able to help her when she's feeling alone. You're not able to help her when she feels rejected or inadequate. She gets sad in those moments when the relationship with you seems doomed and you both move into a place of sadness about not having a baby together. Can you talk about that? Can you talk about the sadness and the fear of potentially losing the relationship and not being able to fix the problem of having a child together, and connecting during those moments when Kam feels like she's doing it by herself? *(Summarizing some prior work while identifying the cycle and primary emotion, and evocative questioning, EFT move one).*

Eric: Most of the time, I do get sad. I get very sad because sometimes I think you're by yourself, you know. I can only do so much as a person, you know. And I'm trying to do the best I can to be a support system for you. But even then, I don't think that's enough, you know, I'm not doing much, because at the end of the day, I don't know what it's like to be a woman, to go through the fertility process. And so sometimes I remind myself to kind of really slow down and make sure I'm more empathetic, *(Kam scratches face and nods yes)* be empathetic about your situation.

Cooper: Can you talk to her about the sadness and emptiness that you've mentioned, of being by yourself on this island at times? *(Tracking Eric's part of the cycle—RISSSC—Using his words seeding enactment).*

Eric: I know sometimes when I get sad, whether it's here or out there or even with myself, sometimes it's like sitting on this little island in the middle of nowhere and I just feel like it's, sometimes can be difficult to kind of escape. *(Kam nods head slightly).*

Cooper: So in this middle of nowhere there are times that you feel by yourself, alone, not able to escape and then you're just out there by yourself. *(Empathetic conjecture, heightening, tracking the cycle—slowing down to stay in the present emotional moment, move one).*

Eric: But I know sometimes when I hear your voice, you know, you really bring me back to reality which makes you a very strong woman that helps balance me out. And I appreciate that.

At this moment, Eric shifts away from going deeper into his sense of being alone and to his secure base with Kam. It is important to stay with him, and to be empathic to his need for safety. While Eric is expressing his feelings more, he still has long-standing protective instincts against vulnerability.

Cooper: So in those moments you feel supported . . . and it kind of brings you out of being on that island by yourself. *(Validating, reflecting, empathetic conjecture) (Eric nods and looks toward Kam).*

Kam: Well, I'm glad I can be that for you. That makes me feel nice, that makes me feel good. So I am glad I can be of support and help you feel loved and supported and like you're not alone, because you're not alone, I am here for you.

Eric: Yeah. And I appreciate that, you know. *(reaches out and holds Kam's hands).* I appreciate that very much.

Cooper: And what does that feel like to know that you don't have to be out on the island by yourself, that you have this strong woman that has your back and so you don't have to do it alone and that she's here to help you where you both can figure it out together. *(Attachment-related frame and sensing Kam's responsiveness to his reach, evocative question, move one).*

Eric: It makes me feel good knowing that I have a beautiful Black woman like this. That will go out of her way to help me out when I'm kind of lost. And so, I mean, it's not like the whole family is lost. I mean, once we got each other like you're saying, like you were saying earlier, this is bigger than the baby. It's about us. So I appreciate that. It makes me feel really good to know that.

Cooper: Can you tell her about the feeling of being lost, what that's like being lonely out there? *(Returning to attachment emotion, with the idea of setting up the enactment).*
With some sense of having Kam along with him on his journey into his internal sense of loneliness, I'm wondering if it is safe for him to talk to Kam about his fears—tentatively returning to his sense of isolation, exploring gently.

Eric: It can be lonesome sometimes, you know, because it's like confusion, you know, there's a lot of confusion and there's a lot of anger. But sometimes it brings me back.

Cooper: Okay. And what's that like for you to share with her the, the sadness and the feeling of being lost at times? *(Evocative responding and reflecting to particular moments of lost, move two).*

Eric: I don't do well expressing myself, so it's a little different, you know, out of my little comfort zone. *(voice just a bit shaky).* Because I just do well if I just shut down and move on.

Cooper: Yeah. *(Validating and leaning in).* But you took the risk just now. What was that like for you to have Kam there for you? *(Validating, evocative responding).*

Eric: It felt wholesome, you know, beautiful.

Cooper: Yeah. I can imagine that it feels good, right, to know that you're not out there by yourself? That you have her. . . *(Validating, reflecting attachment bond)* . . . and to be able to rely on. *(Reflecting the attachment base).*

Cooper: Yeah. Can you tell her that? *(Setting up an enactment).*

Eric: It feels good to be able to have somebody to rely on. To have you to rely on, someone like you when I'm in my darkest moments. *(Kam nods head in the affirmative).* I appreciate you for that.

Cooper: Yeah. Can you, can you talk to him, Kam? Well, how was that for you to hear, by the way? *(Evocative responding while staying with processing the enactment).*

Kam: It was nice, and I appreciate hearing that, I welcome that. Hearing you say that makes me feel very appreciated and loved and supported, as well as assured in the relationship. Knowing that I'm not in it alone in terms of doing the work. This transcript started with his reaching out to Kam with his vulnerability, fears, and sadness. At least a couple of times, Kam has reached back with acceptance and they have emotionally engaged. Again, tentatively, I return to his deeper attachment emotions.

Cooper: Can you talk to her about the sadness of potentially not having a child together? Can you talk to her about what that sadness does to you? *(Validating, reflecting, heightening, setting up the enactment, move three).*

Eric: I mean the sadness, it kind of slows things down, you know, puts me out of the loop out of people who are having a family, who are having kids. So, it kind of freezes me up as if a full stop. Displaced and feeling lost. I'm unable to do that, so that's what the sadness does. I'm trying to make a bright day, but the reality is that the sadness kind of really makes it gloomy.

Cooper: It kind of freezes you up where you feel like you're stuck. Feeling displaced and lost. Because it means a lot if you could have a child together? Can you speak to Kam about that? How important it is for you to have a child with her? *(Empathically reflecting the meaning of attachment bond; setting up the enactment with attachment frame, move three).*

Eric: This is important for me, as I hope it's important for you, that we can be able to kind of grow our family, you know. Create something that we can kind of really mold together. And also, be able to kind of share with our loved ones and our friends and our family, just like they're sharing amongst themselves and their joy, their bundles of joy. So, this would mean a lot for us if we could have a kid. I know reality is that *(moves hands back and forth nervously)* due to situation that may not be, but this is where I'm coming from.

There is a great deal of his history here. His desire for a family with Kam, his healing attachment wounds of his past, the struggle they are experiencing in conceiving a baby, and his love for Kam. *(See discussion later in this chapter).*

Cooper: Yeah, but stay with why it's important to you to have a child with Kam. *(Maintaining focus on the attachment meaning, move two).*

Eric: Because I love you and would like to expand on our family. So that's why this is important.

Cooper: What would that mean for you? What would that feel like for you? Because obviously there's something important about having a child with Kam. *(Heightening attachment focus, move two).*

Eric: Well, it's important because it's a part of life. It's part of our family. Having a child is very important because it's part of life. It's a family. You know we're trying to establish a family. To teach cultural values and social values. So that's why I think it's important.

Cooper: So there's this, this idea of continuing your legacy together with each other? *(Reintroducing concept of legacy, that has racial and cultural meaning discussed in prior sessions and reflecting on attachment frame, move two).*

Eric: Our legacy, yeah. To continue our legacy. So yeah, that's why it's, it's important.

Cooper: And, Kam, can you speak to him about what you heard and how you would like to be there for him when he is sad? That if you both will not be able to potentially have a child together which leads him to, at times, feel like he's alone in the relationship and not able to connect when you are having your own struggles as well? *(Summary of Eric's attachment vulnerability and reach, and seeding the promotion of acceptance, move three).*

Kam: I do hear you. *(Cooper: "Can you talk directly to Eric?")* And I am definitely here for you. It makes me sad as well to know that there's only so much *(gestures with hand)* really either of us can do to make sure that we have a child of our own. But it makes me feel good knowing that he's fully committed to the process, and that he does just really want to have a child with me. So, it makes me feel good to know that you are committed to the process and that you really want to have a child with me. Like you said, a piece of us to carry on.

Cooper: The legacy you all have been talking about building?

Kam: *(Laughs).* Yes, our legacy *(looking toward Eric and Eric nods in the affirmative).*

It is especially important for Eric to be able to develop his legacy. Legacy means creating a natural Black family of his own. A family that is stable, secure, and outside the reaches of the foster care system. The foster care system was a source of racial trauma for him, and he wants to avoid that system's involvement in his life—with White social workers and their negative evaluations. His coping strategies to protect his vulnerable feelings seem to link to his racial traumas as a child with White social workers. His lifelong allergy to "weak" emotions has been a central problem regarding intimacy with his wife and has hampered his emotional expressiveness in couples therapy.

Having an intact family is not only a priority but a strong attachment longing and symbolic of the family he never had—one he belongs in that is safe, secure, and loving. Eric wants to protect his family; that is essential to his sense of self as a husband and father and his identity as a Black man. As Eric reveals more from his internal world, Kam is reaching back with acceptance and responsiveness. Kam desires to have a family, although having a biological child is not as important to her as it is to Eric. Unconditional acceptance and love are important to Kam, as she often felt judged, manipulated, and controlled by her father and stepmother, particularly around her weight and food. This often left her feeling unloved, with complicated feelings toward men, and an inability to express her emotions. She often talked about developing the "Strong Black Women Schema" where she avoided emotions and placed her attention and efforts on serving others. Instead of feeling, she would focus on being strong and powering through tough situations. This essentially meant that Kam had to control her distress feelings, and endure. Kam expressed that this would leave her traumatized, angry, bitter, and lonely. The following occurred a few minutes later in the same session:

Kam: So that makes me feel really good and helps me to understand where you're coming from at times. *(Eric nods in the affirmative).*

Cooper: Can you talk to him about how you want to be there for him when he's in that place of feeling sad and feeling alone, as well as empty? *(Returning to emotionally difficult moment for Eric and his attachment need for her acceptance and engagement).*

Kam: I do hope that after this you are able to share more with me when you are feeling sad and alone or afraid so that I can be there for you.

Cooper: During those moments of sadness and fear and helplessness *(pause)* Kam, you're saying that you will be there for him. *(Heightening, reflecting his underlying emotions, and her attachment bond, move one).*

Kam: Yeah, it's not really a place of helplessness because, you know, at the end of the day, I do need *(Eric places his chin on his fist)* to make this work, regardless of what we decide *(play with her hair).* So you are very much a part of the process.

Cooper: Can you, can you talk to Kam about what you're most afraid of? *(Returning to primary fear of Eric, and helping him explore deeper fears, move two).*

Eric: I'm afraid probably that you won't be able to conceive a child, you know. That I'm going to have to kind of really rethink my reality. That's not to say adoption is bad, it's just there's so much that comes with adoption, you know, not just a child, but the system. And I don't think a lot of people who go through the process tell you *(moves hand back and forth nervously)* the ins and outs, the pros and cons, but the reality is, and the fear is that you won't be able to conceive, which means we won't be a so-called *(makes air quotes with fingers)* a complete family. And then if we do the adoption, then we'll be some kind of add-on family, you know.

Cooper: So the fear is that "We won't be able to conceive," right? That "We won't be able to conceive and that then we won't be able to carry the legacy forward through having a child together." And so there's a fear of potentially a loss, a loss of not being able to have a child together through the connection, through the bond, and the meaning of not being able to bring that into fruition and what that means, that loss of not having that child . . . and continuing the legacy, the family legacy? Yeah. Can you talk about that with Kam? That fear?

(Heightening primary emotion connected to multiple level of attachment and empathetic conjecture, the legacy as his freedom to create belonging, move three).

Eric: Well, like I was saying, the fear of not being a complete family.

Cooper: And how you feel about that, if that was a reality. So it sounds like, ah, there's a part of you that wouldn't feel complete as a family without having a child together and that, that can be very scary. *(Heightening by focusing on his fear and using evocative questioning, move two).*

Eric: Right. So I guess my fear is the fact that if you don't have a child, we would not be a complete family. The other fear is adopting a child and adopting the system that comes along with the child. *(Kam nods head in the affirmative).*

Eric experienced the foster system as a system dominated by White people who did not care about him. He felt that the social workers he dealt with did not see him as human and treated him as such. Their involvement in his life was a source of racial trauma. Eric described White therapists with racial biases that were apparent in their handling of him during therapy sessions. He often referenced these experiences as traumatic and coming from White people who were entrusted to care for him. Eric felt that these White professionals cared more about confirming their beliefs about Black pathology than his humanity. He was just another thing for them to exploit in their professional roles, and at the time, he was just a scared little boy. This is a deep fear, perhaps dread, too, of racial White appraisals of his life.

Cooper: So talk about what that leaves you with, that fear of potentially not having a child together. *(Heightening the attachment significance and primary emotion, move two).*

Eric: It would just be a *(slaps knee)*, I don't know, a very *(pause)* it would feel, uh, I don't know how to describe, maybe a hopeless, a helpless type of hurt.

Cooper: So there's this hurt? I imagine potentially it would be a helpless hurt. This hopelessness of not being able to have a child together. *(Heightening, empathetic conjecture, move two) (Eric nods).*

Cooper: This helpless feeling, and what do you imagine you need, what do you need from Kam? What would it be like to tell her? *(Kam sits upright and looks toward Eric; setting up the enactment, move three).*

Eric: I guess just for you to continue to remain strong, you know. Continue for you to think very positive, trust in me, to know that I am your foundation and your shield, your rock, you know. Despite the fact of our ups and downs. I need to know that you have my back. That you're here for me just as much as I'm here for you. That makes me feel safe, and makes me feel comfortable.

Kam: I definitely have your back. Regardless of what comes out of the process, I'm not going anywhere. So from my perspective *(points to herself)*, you know, we're good either way. It would be disappointing inside, but that wouldn't change how I feel about you.

Cooper: Can you let him know how you want to be there for him when he's feeling helpless or hopeless, and sad and afraid? *(Leading with attachment frame and heightening the engagement, move three).*

Kam: And, yes, I definitely want to be there for you when you're feeling hopeless, sad, and afraid. So I just want you to know that you can talk to me about that.

Cooper: *(Looking toward Eric).* What does that feel like to hear her say that? *(Processing enactment, move four).*

Eric: It felt good to know that she's there to support me. That we have each other. At the end of the day, that's all we have is each other. And so we need to confide in each other, trust in each other, and support each other.

Kam: Even when we do have a child, we still have to rely on that strong foundation.

Cooper: And you both are building that right now in your relationship. How you both are connecting and reaching out to each other in ways that you haven't before. And wanting to be there for each other. (*Eric and Kam nod heads in the affirmative. Empathetic conjecture, framing in context of attachment needs, and acknowledging their work together, move five).*

Kam is consistently reaching back with acceptance to Eric's expressions of fear and sadness, and his dreams of family. She clearly gets his needs for a secure Black family and his attachment bond to her as a secure base.

Eric: It's a good start. It is a process, and I think we'll make it through.

Kam: *(Laughs and nods, looking approvingly toward Eric).*

Cooper: So with the connection that you two have and knowing that you have someone that has your back, that leads you to feeling safer where you can consider other options as well. *(Empathetic conjecture, reframing in context of attachment needs, move four).*

Eric: So I'm going to still love her, you know. So you'll still be my baby, you know. We'll still be a family. It won't change how I think about you, definitely not that. But like I said, it is what it is. Life goes on. We just have to make this work.

Cooper: But I, I think it's so powerful how Kam has been able to connect with you and let you know that she's there for you and that you don't have to feel like you're out there alone. That she wants to be there for you. *(Empathetic conjecture, framing in context of attachment bond and needs, move five).*

Eric: It felt good. It felt good that I have you, good to know that I have a strong woman. You are a very strong woman. I respect her strength. I mean between your work every day, you come home, you handle stuff at home. You know you do stuff in the community. I respect you. You're a very strong woman. You're not easily knocked down. And then when you do get knocked down, you get back up. Find your way to get back up. I respect that.

Cooper: So you don't have to be on that island, feeling helpless or hopeless. You really admire her strength. That she doesn't want you to feel that way and she wants to rise to the occasion to meet you there when you're feeling that, then you can reach out to her and she'll reach out to you. And what does that feel like, knowing that you don't have to do it alone? That you have your partner here to be there every step of the way? *(Heightening, empathetic conjecture, reframing in context of attachment needs, move five).*

Cooper: What does that feel like for him to tell you this? That he has a lot of admiration for you. As I look at your smiling face, it seems it makes you feel good inside. *(Evocative responding, processing enactment).*

Kam: It feels nice. Like I said, it's good to be appreciated.

Cooper: Can you tell Eric that?

Kam: Yeah. *(turns toward Eric)* It definitely *(motions with hand)* brings a different feeling from before where I was afraid and worried, and, yes, angry all the time. Hearing you say that definitely makes me feel good, and I guess calm where I don't have to feel so worried about the relationship and whether or not I'm being appreciated or whether or not you see me. So it just feels good to hear you say that.

Cooper: Yeah. So it makes you feel safe? And that you, you know that he has your back as well. And you're not in this alone. That you both have each other. *(Reflecting, empathetic conjecture, attachment related reframe, move five).*

Kam: And we have love.

Eric: *(Turning toward her)* I love her, you know. I love her. I feel good about it and it makes me feel good that I now can really acknowledge you and tell you how I feel.

Cooper: I would like to commend you both for the work that you did today. You really have gone to some places that in the past were difficult for you. And to witness that and be in the midst of that, I feel honored in the work that you've done, and how you've traveled to some areas that were difficult for you to previously travel. So I really commend you on the work that you both are continuing to do and how you're working to go to those places to be able to restructure your cycle. *(Tying the bow, move five).*

Discussion of Transcript

During this segment, we see Eric feeling sad and alone because he can't comfort Kam during her moments of feeling sad and alone. Both of their fears are salient as they feel alone, disconnected, and inadequate. Kam, who is the pursuer, needs support in the form of Eric being A.R.E. (Accessible, Responsive, and Engaged) while she undergoes the medical fertility process. Eric, the withdrawer, needs to feel that he has the ability to provide comfort and support, coupled with the significance of having a biological child of his own while feeling seen and accepted. Kam feels rejected, fearful, and sad when Eric is not able to provide comfort and support. Eric discussed feeling lost at times without a child of his own due to his own feelings of loneliness while growing up in the foster care system.

During the session, I identified the cycle and Eric's primary emotion. I employed RISSSC (Repeat, Image, Simple, Slow, Soft, and Client's words) while tracking the cycle. The EFT micro skills of empathetic conjecture, heightening, validating, reflecting, evocative responding, and attachment reframe were utilized in exploring Eric's sadness and loneliness. Enactments are set up for Eric to reach out to Kam and tell her how important it is to know that he can reach out to her during times of loneliness, and that she can provide comfort and support. Other enactments explore the loneliness Eric feels as a result of not having a child and the meaning of having his own biological child. Moreover, Eric discloses the fears of adopting a child and being connected to the foster care system that bring up past trauma. The enactments set the stage for more loving interactions, a deeper bond, and a safe haven.

Therapist's Reflections

Throughout the sessions, I attempt to deepen emotions and facilitate emotional engagement with Eric, while accessing fears and needs. This proves difficult at times, as it was challenging for him to stay with emotions. He later disclosed that "it brought up all of the past trauma with White therapists while growing up in the foster care system." Eric is able to experience emotional engagement for brief moments and touch on his pain, fear, and needs. But he often resorts to creating emotional distance through language and narrative. I consistently deploy EFT micro skills such as empathy, validation, and reflection, while attempting the tango move two of assembling emotions while maintaining presence and attunement. Kam has softened and is emotionally accessible, responsive, and engaged; therefore, the focus during this session is on WRE.

Reflections on Matters of Race and Culture

Race shows up not just because this is an African American couple but due to systemic anti-Black racism. Systemic anti-Black racism includes redlining, residential segregation, their parents being locked out of the labor market, and the backlash against the civil rights movement of the 1960s. This backlash included mass incarceration, the war on drugs, and the resulting despair that set the scene for the crack epidemic. This impacted Black families and removed large numbers of Black men and boys from their communities, creating relationship and generational ruptures.

Eric's and Kam's mothers were addicted to crack cocaine. As a result, Kam lived with her father, and Eric was placed in foster care. Eric grew up in foster care and had many experiences with White therapists during that time. The foster care system in the United States has a history of being connected to enslavement and the removal/separation of Black children from their parents' care. Moreover, Eric grew up with Black foster parents who helped to instill cultural pride and identity in him.

But he experienced issues of colorism because he was dark-complected. Thus, he experienced unfair, harsher treatment than other lighter-skinned foster kids. Further, he developed a healthy mistrust of White people as a result of the negative, exploitive experiences with social workers and therapists. Eric ultimately experienced these therapists as exploitive because he felt that they were not invested in him as a human being but objectifying him as an inferior thing. These racial traumas as a boy contributed to his reactivity to Kam's suggestions about adoption. Kam reported growing up in a predominantly Black community. This shaped her sense of self in relation to her Blackness. She reported that she did not focus on her Blackness until she went to a predominantly White college and became more conscious of being Black. Kam indicated that this was imperative in order to protect herself from discrimination and advocate for other Black students. Being darker complected was highly valued in her family and the Black community where she lived during her formative years. This helped build her self-esteem around her skin color. As a couple, they enjoy each other's dark skin.

Eric landed in the foster care system because his mother became addicted to crack cocaine. Crack cocaine began to proliferate in the Black community as a result of economic blight and the resulting despair. The response from the government was one of punishment and mass incarceration, even though there has been some speculation that political expediency were part of crack cocaine being trafficked into Black communities during each of their parents' early adult lives (Alexander, 2010, Jones-Rogers, 2019; Pettit, 2012).

It is remarkable that Eric has not rejected all therapists, and his willingness to engage in reflecting on himself with his wife is impressive. I suggest that it also had a great deal to do with our conversation about the impact of racial discrimination in the geographic area and nationally. Throughout their couples therapy, I have reflected on my own empathic reflections on the broader social inequities and discrimination and the direct impact on this couple. I validated the depth of his distrust and his rage toward his former White social workers. Beyond validation, I encouraged both to talk about his angry feelings toward White people in general. From this relentlessly empathic stance, it was easy for me to reflect that some of the behaviors or appraisals were not the fault of the couple and made complete sense to me. I validated the assaults on African American communities. At times, I respected their pushback to my exploration of their vulnerable feelings out of respect for their resistance/blocks that helped each to survive past traumas.

Currently, Eric and Kam are continuing to do well. They are able to recognize the negative interactional cycle that used to take over their relationship. They can recognize the cycle more often than not and short-circuit it before it becomes all-absorbing. Through stage three (consolidation) work, they are more confident in their ability to weather the emotional storms that life may throw their way. Eric and Kam turn toward each other more often, creating a secure bond with A.R.E. Although they are still attempting to conceive a child, they know that they have each other through this process, regardless of the outcome.

Case Discussion With Sue Johnson

Guillory: *As I read the attachment history of this withdrawer, it is surprising that he is even willing to come to couples therapy, or any therapy. It makes so much sense that he is a withdrawer. He has a traumatic history, and the fact that he is engaging his fears in this therapy is a testimony to Yamonte's attunement and his love for his wife. He is bringing his fears to the conversation. What should we expect regarding assembling his emotions and the struggle he has with vulnerability and feelings?*

Sue Johnson: Well, that's interesting what you're saying, because I think one of the things about this withdrawer is timing. So what hit me looking at Yamonte's case with a guy like this, especially a guy who's been traumatized and who needed to shut down and numb out to survive, is we do not start in EFT with questioning where this person needs to go. We start with where this person is. How can I join with them? We go into where people are, and we validate where people are. So we validate this guy's need to shut his feelings down. However he names it: to push them aside, to numb them out, to go away. People have their own phrases for what they do with their feelings in order to turn away from them. We validate that as a way of managing their feelings. We validated that it takes time for this person to tune into themselves. We validate that managing his feelings was a survival strategy, and we start by putting that in the cycle. We start by having them talk about how he manages his feelings with his partner. It seems Yamonte has done a wonderful job with RISSSC, validating and empathically reflecting to create emotional safety with this man. And then we say, "Have you ever told your partner, 'I'm slow to get in touch with my feelings, I need more time. I know sometimes that's difficult for you. I need more time because it was so important for me in my life to be able to shut these feelings down to survive.'" And I've made it clear and specific when I say this. I say, "Have you ever told her that?" And he says, "No." Then I say, "Good. Could you tell her now?"

And that's a move three, and let's be clear, you've gone from move one to move three. You haven't really gone into lots of emotions. You've gone into, "This is the way it is for you for very good reasons. And could you just talk to her about that a little bit?" On the one hand, it's a very low-key encounter, but it's still saying, "Yes, I accept." You're telling her you're different from her. You're telling her that you had to learn to shut down your feelings. You're telling her you need some time. And you're talking about the process of the dance; you're not evading it and just doing it and thus sending a distorted message to her. So the message is, "I needed to learn to shut down. I want to be with you. It takes me time to turn back." And the therapist accepts that, and validates. And that is still very reassuring for the partner; she is listening to us say that in the room, and it's a shift. It's not a great big shift like moments of vulnerability, but it's important because it starts by looking at the position in the cycle and saying to people, "Yes, of course. This is your dance. This is the position you take in the dance. There are very good reasons for it." Which is kind of a move one. But then you say, "Could you tell her, 'I do shut down. I shut down.' *(which is a stage one move)*. 'I do shut down. I learned to do that when I was very young to protect myself. And it does take me time to know what I'm feeling.' Could you tell her that?" And it's very simple. And he tells her.

And usually, these kinds of guys have never just told that to their partner. Their partner says, "You don't care about me. You turn away." No, he's struggling to get in touch with his feelings. His immediate response is to numb out if there's something negative going on between them, and he's struggling to get in touch with his feelings. And I think, in general, we've trained men, and I'm sure this is even more true with Black men because they live in a hostile universe, a more hostile universe. We've trained men to push their feelings aside. So in a way, it's eminently reasonable that when they're trying to tune into the emotional music in a dance with their partner, their timing is probably going to be different. It's not true with every man, of course, and there are some women for whom this is true, too. The trouble is, if you can't talk about the dance and say, "Oh, I don't know what to do when you put your foot there," the fact that you don't put your foot next to the other person's leaves a huge gap of ambiguity for the other person to interpret. So then how does the other person interpret it? Well, unfortunately so much is at stake in love relationships that the other person interprets it with, "You don't care about what I just said. You don't see me. You don't want to reply." "No, no, no, I'm trying to—I'm trying to be in my own skin so I can turn toward you. It's just taking me some time." "Oh, all right. This is your process, it's not that I'm not important to you." I mean, that's huge. That's a real different signal we bring forth and have him talk about.

So yes, as Yamonte does, we validate, and normalize. You say, "Of course you had to shut down," and say to him he deserved better. That life has been unfair. And that "I'm impressed by how you're fighting for your relationship with your wife." And, I love when Yamonte says that you use the African American experience to counter shame and promote a positive view of African American history. I love that. You go into a bigger context. And I do that all the time. Especially with traumatized people. To a military vet, I'll say, "You're a warrior. And you went overseas to help people and to represent Canada, and you're a warrior. And you tried so hard, and you did your duty, and you were a good warrior. And then in this moment, everything fell apart, and somehow you say to yourself, 'I failed,' but actually what you're telling me is you are a good warrior, a reliable soldier. You are a loving responsible man. You helped lots of people when you were over there." So yes. And that's for me, part of normalizing and validating. And you make the picture bigger. The person focuses down on, "I shouldn't have acted this way in this situation, and the fact that I didn't protect my buddy well enough means that I failed. It means I'm a bad person. It means I'm a bad soldier." As Yamonte does say in this case, you say this happens to Black families during mass incarceration and the war on drugs era; it created huge problems with drug addictions and Black children going to foster care. In effect, you said to him, "This was unfair to you. It made your life hard, and you had to confront racism alone. So it makes sense that you shut down. You have done well in your life. And you were always a good person, and you have an opportunity to build a legacy with this woman. It makes total sense that you would not want White social workers in your life, but you would do so for this woman, for a family with her."

Trauma backgrounds can take longer in each stage of EFT, and that's why we have three stages, too. The tango patterns can be different, and you have to be flexible with the tango. Pacing can be different, and timing can be different. And some withdrawers, once they kind of start to feel safe, they can kind of come out. And I mean, I've had occasionally a withdrawer come forward so fast and start leading in with their internal voice, and "Oh my God," and they race toward their partner, and then suddenly the pursuer is running away. So it's sort of like, "Oh, no, wait a minute. Wait a minute. Wait a minute. I don't know what—are you doing?" I mean, but that's unusual. It does take time and it takes time for the pursuer to be less perhaps strident in their protests, and start to shift their signals and their emotional reality. And that's why it takes time for emotional engagement. But we have a map and we know where we're going. We know what home looks like: accessibility, responsiveness, and emotional engagement. So because of what I just said, even though it is a process, basically, we still do this really powerful multilevel change type therapy. If you're working with a trauma couple, it might take longer, but it's still pretty efficient from my point of view; it's a pretty efficient intervention. In our crazy society, everyone's in love with quick fixes. Unless you actually believe that, it seems like somehow our culture wants immediate fixes for huge, complex problems. Well, that's nonsense. There's no such thing.

Guillory: *I was wondering how deep to go with withdrawers who have traumatic histories. While some of his withdrawing behaviors have been harmful to the marriage, his avoidant defenses have been the foundation of his survival and protected him from perhaps crushing self-appraisals.*

Sue Johnson: This depends on the couple, and I can't give a hard and fast rule. My response is that you go as deep as you have to go to mend the relationship, because in couples therapy, what you're about is creating connection. So does he need to tell her more about what happened to him as a child or his struggles in life? Yes, he does, because it's this sort of block that prevents engagement. Does he need to tell her every single thing that happened as if he was in individual therapy? No, he doesn't. He needs to tell her about parts of his life, and how it impacted him, and how it translates into how he dances with her and his sense of self. He needs to be able to say to her, "I say to myself every moment of every day I should have done something different, or I wish I had a different life. And it means something terrible about me, and so I hide. I hide from you. I hide from the world." He needs to be able to tell her that. And then he needs to be able to look up into her eyes and see that his pain matters to her. That he matters to her. And that she accepts him, whether he did the heroic thing in that moment, or not. So that's what heals the relationship. In couples therapy, the client is the relationship. So you go into that trauma history when it's useful to heal the relationship, but it's not like individual therapy where you're going to go deeply, deeply into a core trauma scene in order to shift the emotional reality of that scene.

And the other piece, though, which is really important is when we use the attachment lens, we are using the most powerful healing element, the most powerful antidote to trauma that human beings have. You place that person in contact with the love and support of their partner for the traumatized self. And the love and support of the partner for the traumatized self is an incredible, incredible healing element. It's fascinating to me. You read the trauma literature, everyone's going on about the fact that maybe there's a new drug from a jungle somewhere that can give people a psychedelic experience. You can have them listen to music. You can do EMDR with them. You can do all this. Yeah, all right, you can. But you know what? If I'm going to put my money on something as the most powerful antidote to trauma, it's real simple. We all know what it is. And it wasn't available often in the original traumatic event, which is why people develop PTSD. When it is available, people don't develop PTSD. What wasn't available as an antidote was the acceptance and presence and love and care of another human being.

And when you make that available in couples therapy, I mean that, I've seen it so many times. People come in, they've done every therapy and drug under the sun. And of course, they're still trying to deal with their trauma all alone because they can't connect with their partner, and their relationship distress increases the impact of the trauma every day. They face everything alone. Then you switch that, and they're able to open up, and their partner understands them, understands their traumatic vulnerability, and their partner responds. Well, they're no longer facing that dragon alone. That changes everything. I've seen such shifts and transformations in people, because suddenly the partner is able to be there with them. And it gives them what they needed, which is comfort, support, and validation. The fact that their frailty renders them lovable and more precious, not somehow unworthy of love, that's a powerful thing. So when you create relationships, when you heal relationships, you create relationships that heal the partners.

9 Case Study
EFT Pursuer Softening

Denise Jones-Kazan with Paul T. Guillory and Case Discussion with Sue Johnson

This case is about an African American couple who enter couples therapy with significant relationship distress. Their conflict is punctuated with intense disruptions and deep emotional withdrawal. Each partner has an attachment trauma history: their parents struggled financially and coped at times with heavy drinking. While each of their backgrounds is different regarding race matters, both suffered from significant challenges to their racial identity development. Combined, these race-based contextual matters pose significant threats to their relationship. As a result, their couples therapy is intense, and their stage one, de-escalation EFT work takes a great deal of time in order to develop emotional safety. This is a case that demonstrates the EFT model of couples therapy with an African American couple who advance to stage two work, pursuer softening. There are two major changes in the couple's work in stage two: withdrawer re-engagement and pursuer softening. While the withdrawer did become re-engaged in this couple's work, the emphasis in this case will be to highlight the pursuer's softening.

Stage one of EFT focuses on de-escalation of the couple's negative cycle and seeding the development of attachment needs and longings. Stage two builds on the safety created in the earlier work to lean more on the felt experiences of attachment needs and longings; their expressions and emotional engagement are central in this stage of couples work. With pursuer softening, the pursuer is encouraged to feel their attachment needs and longing and to express them from an internal felt sense of vulnerability. The increased emotional safety that comes with de-escalation in the relationship allows for greater accessibility of attachment emotions. When the withdrawer signals greater availability for response engagement, it also helps to create more safety in the couple's therapy for leaning into vulnerable feelings.

The use of a culturally competent, skillfully attuned EFT therapist enhanced the successful work with this African American couple. Relentless validation, acceptance with a nonjudgmental stance, and consistent patience help to create a safe working alliance. Racial attunement helps to facilitate their exploration of deeper levels of emotional expression and counter the impact of historical racism and implicit bias. Racism impacts this couple's perspective in the negative cycle, as Yvette says to herself, "I am all alone" *(no one stands for Black women)*, and John says to himself, "I can never get it right with her" *(just keep quiet, it is*

DOI: 10.4324/9780429355127-9

never safe for a Black man to be vulnerable). Their negative cycle exacerbates a lack of attunement and connection between them. As their relationship bond was enhanced, so, too, was their racial identity development. Later in therapy, Yvette would say, "I think anti-Blackness is pervasive in all other cultures. It is always there in the interacting with people. We . . . John and I had to also unlearn internalized anti-Blackness as well."

Reasons for Seeking Counseling

Yvette and John initially came to couples therapy to pursue pre-marital counseling. They are a millennial African American couple who met after college. They identify as Black Americans and attribute their strong racial identity to their families and the neighborhoods in which they grew up. As undergraduates, they attended integrated schools in the South and both of them excelled academically. They came to the Bay Area to work and currently hold professional jobs. During our initial session, it became apparent that there was a significant attachment injury between them, and they lacked the ability to work through it successfully. They also stated that they had difficulty communicating with each other. In the early phase of this couple's therapy, Yvette often started the session with protests about John's withdrawal. She complained about her unmet attachment needs: "I'm not important to him," and "I don't matter," or "I can't reach him!" She presents with intense anger and frustration, often with uncontrollable tears. Her primary emotions are hurt, loneliness, fear, and anxiety. Her view of self was wounded as a child, and re-injured as she experiences not being important to John—particularly as she witnesses the importance to him of his mother and friends.

John presents as very quiet, withdrawn, and sometimes confused. He often feels that no matter what he does, it's never enough for Yvette, and she doesn't believe him even when he does express his feelings. He is very thoughtful and careful, and his responses often have long pauses. His reactive, or secondary emotions, are frustration, anger, and bewilderment. His primary or attachment emotions are feelings of hopelessness, despair, and depression. He also feels betrayed by Yvette's attacks on his character and for not believing him. His view of self is that he is not trusted or believed.

Yvette's additional unmet attachment needs are that, "[T]here is no one there to protect me," and that she will be abandoned. In therapy, she frequently says, "John is not my cheerleader." John's unmet attachment needs are that he is never going to be loved and cared about for who he is, and he perceives Yvette's complaints and protest as a lack of commitment to him. He was nearly always alone as the nerdy Black boy who was different because he was bright, introverted, and not popular.

Stage-One EFT Work

My initial goals for treatment were to create a safe space for them to talk about their relationship and to assess their attachment style, while observing the manifestations of their commitment to each other. My first task is to form a working alliance with them while assessing the ongoing struggles in their relationship. Second, I want to understand their negative cycle and their positions in the cycle. Yvette presented as a critical pursuer and John as a confused withdrawer. Third, I sought to reflect and validate their reactive emotions in the negative cycle and seed access to their primary emotions that underlie their patterned negative interactions. Fourth and last, I reframed their conflict in terms of their underlying emotions and unmet attachment needs. In sessions, I encouraged them to identify their attachment needs and accept each other's experience while creating a new, more functional cycle.

The following transcript of our early sessions illustrates the attachment injury themes that were often present with this highly escalated couple. Yvette often felt that John was gaslighting her, and she had intense reactions to the idea that he was intentionally causing her pain and distress. These early sessions were intense, and Yvette often became triggered, yelling and storming out of the room. Yvette's reaction to John would leave him startled, confused, and not sure what to do. John is a naturally quiet, introverted person, and he would withdraw into himself and focus on his work. Yvette in this session, as shown in the following transcript, is attempting to explain her appraisal of John and the meaning of her gaslighting experience:

Yvette: That is, you lead someone to believe that they are the cause of the problem when you're the problem.

Jones-Kazan: Okay. Thank you. Can you say more about that. Help me understand that between you and John. *(Validating with curiosity).*

Yvette: Yeah. It can, it shows up in a number of ways.

Jones-Kazan: Mm-hmm (affirmative).

Yvette: And John's not the person that introduced me to the concept, just the term, to be clear. And it happens a lot with like victim-blaming and shaming and things like that.

John: Sure.

Jones-Kazan: So just to kind of summarize a bit. John, you started off having a conversation about Yvette wanting to obtain yoga training certification, to help increase participants in her yoga class. You were offering her some suggestions about business strategies. All of a sudden, the discussion started to take a left turn; she got triggered in some way. And then it started going in a different direction that left you kind of feeling confused and then frustrated. *(Summary attempting to understand their cycle of disconnection and the distress cue that signals John to withdraw).*

John: *(Nods affirmatively).*

Jones-Kazan: So for you, sometimes, you can say supportive things and they're felt as supportive by Yvette. And other times, you can say something that you intend to be supportive, but she does not hear it that way. I know this can be confusing. *(Empathic reflective of his experience and validation).*

John: Yup.

Jones-Kazan: And who brought up the term gaslighting? Yvette said that you were gaslighting her. *(Returning to distress appraisal to understand their cycle)*.

John: *(Both nod affirmatively)*.

Jones-Kazan: Okay, John, you were confused and frustrated by this experience. You were trying to be supportive; it went quickly downhill in an ugly direction. I'm wondering if there are any other underlying feelings you had that caused your frustration and confusion, because, John, you start out wanting to offer her some support and some business strategies, and then it takes an ugly turn and goes downhill really quickly. And, John, you're left feeling really confused and frustrated. And I'm wondering what else might you have been feeling. *(Summary again of distress moment of disconnection. Staying with John to encourage his participation in therapy, and validate positive intentions. Also empathically reflecting on his experiences, and ending with evocative question.)*.

John: Um *(John looking uncomfortable, and confused . . . long pause)*.

Jones-Kazan: You said that when you started out you weren't happy about the way this conversation went. Right? *(Using RISSSC directed toward John, who is looking down)*.

Yvette: Yeah. I mean I, I guess like, as was with these types of interactions, especially recently like I just feel like disappointed.

Jones-Kazan: Can you help me understand your disappointment? *(Deciding to give John some relief from his discomfort and shift to Yvette with evocation question)*.

Yvette: Just disappointed that we like keep, that we like end up in that place.

Jones-Kazan: You both end up disappointed it seems. *(Looking back and forth at both of them)*. Can you say more? *(Empathic reflections with evocative question)*.

John: Usually it's like a long kind of arc of like, building up to like this good place. And then it like goes on for a while and then it goes downhill. This one was like a really quick turnaround; it was like in one conversation like it literally started off like great. And then it just like turned around really quickly.

Jones-Kazan: It turned so quickly, and what happens for you when it turns? *(Looking toward John, nodding and validating his experience and exploring cycle with evocative question)*.

John: Um *(pause)* so yeah just, it's just disappointing.

Jones-Kazan: Yeah, it's disappointing. John, can you help me understand the disappointment? *(Validating and evocative question)*.

John: We end up in this negative place, but it otherwise could have been a good interchange, a good note between us.

Jones-Kazan: Right, not a good place, and Yvette, you're left feeling unsupported and John you're left feeling confused as to what happened. Am I getting that right? *(Empathic reflecting their cycle and their emotional distress experiences).*

John Good day, really. *(Softly under his breath sarcasm).*

This reflects the typical pattern of communication between them, in which Yvette was left feeling invalidated, mistreated, and unsupported by John. Her appraisal was that John was intentionally doing something to her, gaslighting. As I tried to track their pattern of interactions, it was unclear how the interaction turned ugly for Yvette. John seemed very uncomfortable revisiting the situation and on the spot to talk when he would very much like to hide. At this point, therapy does not feel safe to John, and I'm encouraging him to engage by validating and reflecting his experience. John seems confused by this experience with Yvette, and typically finds himself misunderstood by her. His safe strategy has always been to withdraw, and he seems to want to remain as withdrawn as possible. He is engaged enough with the therapy and seems to look toward the therapist for support. He is confused by Yvette's big reactions to him and critical of them. In the beginning of therapy, John was emotionally illiterate, he had not developed a felt sense of his emotions and could not name feelings. Evocative questions would fall flat with him, and it became clear that we had to work toward exploring his internal emotional world. It took many sessions to develop his emotional experiences. Both John and Yvette appear to have ended this disconnecting moment feeling miserable, alone, and wondering about the viability of the relationship.

The following excerpt from the same couple's session only several more minutes into the session exemplifies the continuation of the ongoing conflict and disconnecting cycle. From prior work, John shared that he belonged to a think-tank group that also included two of his friends, Debra and Melody. The goal of this group is to motivate each other in their entrepreneurial projects. Melody left the group and John had an opportunity to advocate for Yvette to join, but he did not.

Jones-Kazan: So I want to just kind of summarize again, I think the continuing question for you, Yvette, seems to be "Is John there for me?" You don't feel like he shows up for you and fights for you in the way that you need him to. Do I have that right? *(Using attachment frame to capture Yvette's appraisal of her longing and disappointment).*

Yvette John is there for me, he's just, I'm just not at the top of the list. And that's what I think he, he struggles with when he says, you know some days it's good some days it's bad.

Jones-Kazan: Right, so you're saying you're on his list, but not at the top? *(Reflecting her appraisal).*

Yvette Like, nobody's denying you're there for me, I'm just not number one. I can be a fan of somebody. Let me put it this way. I'm a fan of Beyoncé, I'm not her biggest fan.

Jones-Kazan: Mm, this is important—can you say more? *(Curiosity about her appraisal).*

Yvette: Put it another way. Her biggest fans are the ones who show up, with dollars and more dollars, they're in the VIP seats. They're doing behind the scenes, and they pay for that. Others just show up and they still support Beyoncé.

Jones-Kazan: Right that sense of importance that you were uppermost on his mind? *(Reflecting attachment need).*

Yvette: What I'm saying is John is not, he's not in the beehive, he's not number one buying VIP, shelling out dollars. He is not that. He's a fan in section 100 maybe.

Jones-Kazan: Right. And this recent situation of the think-tank group reinforced that feeling to you. That you are not a queen bee? *(Returning to emotional moment with the attachment significance).*

Yvette: Absolutely.

Jones-Kazan: That you don't feel like he fought for you and advocated for you to join that group, when you had stated that was your desire. And the reason for that is that the conflict with Debra has never, ever been resolved? *(Reflecting attachment significance and exploring distress cue).*

Yvette: And he admitted that it would make, it made him uncomfortable.

Jones-Kazan: Right, that it made him uncomfortable. *(Validating).*

Yvette: And then on top of that is, even if, let's say you guys don't think I'm a good fit. At least have that conversation with me.

Jones-Kazan: At least think of me in the conversation. *(Reflecting and validating attachment significance).*

Yvette: . . . and that comes back to this connection that we're supposedly establishing. Like we're, how are we in sync and how are we close as a couple when you can't even tell me of all people; I expected you to be the one to deliver bad news to me.

Jones-Kazan: So, Yvette, you found out on Facebook that you were not invited to join the group. That was awful. And for you it made you think you're not at the top of John's list. This hurt you deeply. John continues to blame you for the rupture that happened at your wedding with Debra. You had expected that John would have talked to Debra about her behavior and that she would apologize to you both by now. You were hurt so deeply by what happened and still feel terrible. *(Summarizing her appraisal of John's disappointments. Validating her emotional experiences, her distress cue, and the depth of her emotional pain).*

Yvette: In two weeks it'll be six months, by the way, since the wedding.

Jones-Kazan: Wow, it's been that long. Okay, so did I summarize that correctly? Did I get that right? *(Validating and summarizing emotional experiences).*

Yvette: *(Nods her head affirmatively looking toward John).*

Jones-Kazan: Okay, John... *(John interrupts).*

John: Wait *(pause)*. Debra has pretty much been at arm's length for me. I don't really interact with her at all outside of the think-tank group. I don't really know how to resolve this thing with Debra and me and Yvette. I just don't know... *(voice trailing off).*

Yvette: *(Responds very quickly with anger).* So don't do it!! I'm not worth the unknown. I don't know how to be married, but you're worth it.

Jones-Kazan: So for you, Yvette, it involves just having you in mind, thinking of you first. That is the painful part for you, that you were not in his mind. *(Using RISSSC to slow the process down, and returning to attachment significance).*

Yvette: Why wasn't I the first person that came to mind when you guys reached a group decision, yup we're going to add people. It's because you're not fighting for me, you don't ever fight for me, you never fight for me. I'm tired of not being fought for. You don't fight for me with your family, and it's constantly in my face. So yes, Thursday I—I did a big fuck you, don't ask me shit about my business. Because it's mine, it's one thing I have for me where I don't have to worry about anybody advocating for me but me. It's back to the Yvette that doesn't fucking trust you. That's what it meant.

Jones-Kazan: Okay, so that came first that he is not fighting for you and that gets you in touch right now with your anger and maybe your hurt. You have to take care of yourself. *(Reflecting on his appraisal and action tendency to cope with feelings).*

Yvette: *(She nods).* But I don't see the forest for the trees. Contrary to what you might believe, I see all of it, and see how it's all linked because it's still fucking unresolved. Like, if you fix something then it will go away. But if you don't fix it, it's just going to linger. *(Her voice gets louder, and she becomes more agitated).* And you started the issue, even on your birthday, you made up an excuse about me being the reason why you couldn't talk to your think-tank group. That's what you did. *(Voice getting louder with hand gestures toward John).* That is in fact the essence of gaslighting. And how you don't see that is beyond me. You didn't try to say, "Oh, well, you have access to me at home." But that's not the point of the think-tank group, I don't just want you, I want other resources. I see them doing great things, I want to be a part of that.

Jones-Kazan: So Yvette, can we slow it down so I can understand all of what you are communicating? There are a lot of feelings here. Let me try a recap *(Leaning forward, using RISSSC, and using hand gestures to have her focus come to me).*

Jones-Kazan: What feels like gaslighting in this situation is that John continues to blame you? (pause) for the conflict that happened with his friend? And as a result, he didn't feel comfortable fighting for you to be a new member in their think-tank group. Yvette for you this is like him not fighting for you with his family? *(Validating, empathically reflecting on attachment significance and needs)*.

Yvette: Yes, and I would say John makes me the problem. I'm the reason why resolution is not possible.

Jones-Kazan: This is the distressing part for you. He doesn't fight for you, and then you become the problem when you say something. This is so painful for you, and you can't get him to understand that. *(Empathic reflections, attachment frame, evocative reflection with distress cue)*.

Yvette: Yes, he continues to blame me for the situation.

Discussion of Transcripts

It is clear in this segment that Yvette's protest is mulilayered with a number of incidences in her story about her relationship disappointments. As she attempts to relate her stories, she is hurt that John has neither thought about her at critical moments nor failed to place her first in his thinking. Yvette has appraised that she is not important to John. As Yvette relates her story, it has a perspective of building a case to support her view; the many ways he has failed to support her. As I validate her perspective and emotional experiences along with reflecting the attachment significance of her experience in the therapeutic relationship, I am also trying to create a safe place to be heard. On several occasions in subsequient sessions, Yvette would become so intense that she would abruptly leave in protest, vowing never to return. John would often sit in bewilderment and not have a sense of what led to Yvette's intense reaction.

John did not understand the impact of his withdrawal on Yvette. While they could have good conversations about topics unrelated to their relationship, when the conversation became about them, John would retreat emotionally. What became clear early in their couples work was that John was at best, emotionally numb and unaware of his attachment anxiety. In this matter, he had no way to talk to Yvette about his feelings—that he could not feel himself and had no words to describe his experience. I needed to create a safe space to validate and reflect on John's lack of awareness of his feelings and his lack of emotional language.

Initially, their distress centered on John's relationship with his mother and close friends. Yvette perceived that they did not like her, and John would take their side or fail to protect her. Another major issue was that John would not always pay bills on time, and that would send Yvette into a rage. These two predominant themes colored many of our sessions during the first two years, resulting in a negative cycle that was often escalated. Over time, Yvette revealed that there was a pattern of a lack of physical intimacy, and she wondered if John was addicted to porn. I encouraged both to enter their own individual therapy to address family of origin themes, and encouraged John to explore his porn-related behavior while remaining in couples therapy with me.

I continued to work on de-escalating their negative cycle, with relentless validation, emotional exploration with John, and slowing down Yvette's emotional reactivity. I also encouraged them to engage in enactments to express their attachment-related emotions. Slowing down the acting out of anger and frustration in-session was also a major focus. Over a couple of years together we were able to create a safe space where their enactments were growing in depth, John was growing in his emotional expressiveness, and their reactivity was decreasing. John, the withdrawer, was coming forward with his attachment needs and emotions, and Yvette accepted his experiences and new responses as valid and true without disavowing them.

My focus as an EFT couples therapist is to heighten their awareness of their negative patterns and promote their more attuned, softer engagements. In those softer moments they create enactments and thus, enhance their emotional engagements. These repeated enactments of attuned moments allows them to become more connected in a safe and loving way. After many enactments, John became much more communicative about his internal work; this eventually led to Yvette's pursuer softening (see stage-two work later in this chapter).

Attachment History: Yvette

Yvette has a history of developmental trauma. She is the younger of one biological brother and three siblings from her father's prior marriage. Her mother was seriously injured at her job, and has been disabled since Yvette was in high school. During the next few years, her mother struggled with heavy drinking but went into recovery a few years later. She has remained sober since that time. Her biological brother has a serious substance abuse problem and was always the "problem child" who demanded a great deal of attention from the family. The family's constant focus on his behavior left Yvette feeling neglected by her parents. Yvette's mother also had to become a caretaker for her niece and nephew, adding financial pressure on the family.

According to Yvette, her family experienced periods of poverty and a lack of financial security. They lived in a poor African American community. Her father worked off and on as an automobile mechanic. He could only find work, however, in Black-owned automobile repair shops, businesses with cyclical financial stability. At times, he sold marijuana to earn money for the family. Her father drank heavily at times, and she thinks he has been a problem drinker throughout most of her life. Her parents would get into loud arguments, typically about money, and sometimes it would end with her father becoming violent. These were some of the worst moments of her childhood, and with her other siblings, she would hide in her bedroom. Her parents have been divorced for ten years.

In grade school, Yvette, but not her siblings, was bused to a largely all-White, affluent school. She has always done well in school and her test scores gave her the opportunity to attend integrated schooling. She recalls the impact of these mixed racial experiences. In many ways, she felt special for being selected, and for learning and adapting to "White culture" (the way White kids acted). That also led her to become more critical and demeaning toward her sister and brother who she began to see as too "ghetto" for her. At the same time, at the White school, she was being treated more negatively than she had ever experienced. While she continued to excel in school, this was despite what she perceived as her teachers' bias against her. She recalls a racially defining moment in first grade when a White boy bit her cheek in class; he wanted to know if she "tasted like chocolate!" She was startled and yelled out. The teacher sent her to the principal's office, and her parents were called. Despite Yvette protesting, "Why was I pulled out of class?"and that of her parents, the boy remained in the classroom, and Yvette does not believe there were any consequences to him for his behavior. She also had a sense of being unprotected throughout grade school and high school.

Yvette grew up in the Black church where she heard strong messages about how Black people should act. She refers to it as "respectability" politics. That is, she had to be a positive representative of her race at school regarding her behavior as "a good girl" and be at the top of her class academically. The messages were clear, that she should not attract negative attention to herself. That was true even if the attention or accusations were unfair. In addition, for Black girls, that also meant that there were strict policies about not being promiscuous. According to Yvette, she became very conscious of race and how not to be a negative Black girl at the age of 11.

Yvette has an insecure anxious attachment with her mother for not protecting her from her father's rage. To Yvette, the house was calmer when he was gone, and as a child, she did not understand why her mother would let him back. She also had a sense that her mother was not available for knowing what was going on in Yvette's childhood world in school or regarding her developing self-esteem. In many matters, Yvette's wants or needs (like hair products, friendship problems, or clothing) were ignored by her mother. Sometimes even the basics like food were also ignored. Yvette has an insecure avoidance attachment with her father.

Attachment History: John

John comes from a single female parent household and was estranged from his biological father until late adolescence. He was very close to his paternal grandparents, aunts, and uncles who lived nearby and spent most of his time with them. He lived with his mother and younger sister. According to John, his mother has worked as a paralegal at a sizeable firm in the South for nearly 20 years, and she works for a series of bosses who have been very hard on her. The oldest child and only son, he has an enmeshed relationship with his mother.

He suggests that her boss is racist and has limited her opportunities to advance professionally. She is good at what she does, and that has been very helpful to the firm. John thinks the discrimination she experiences at work largely contributes to her drinking problems. He functioned as a co-parent to his sister, as his mother often depended on him for emotional support when he was young and for financial help after he started working. While he came to accept that his father was not in his life, at times, he longed for his father's presence. Even as a boy, he thought his life growing up could have been easier. After reuniting with his father, they both made efforts to build their relationship.

John suggests that his family has always recognized his intelligence and actively supported him. His family understood that he was introverted, nerdy, and very smart. He has always excelled in school. As a boy, he was drawn to math and computers. When he was young, his small group of friends were like him, except they were White. He was an outsider regarding Black kids because he was clueless regarding Black culture, sports, and social activities. Nevertheless, he felt positive about being Black, and being a smart Black person. While his family protected him from race matters living in the South, he did encounter issues. One recurring problem was when he became bored with his school work, and his teachers would suggest that he was lazy. John would say he was not being challenged, and his family advocated for him. Only White people assumed he was lazy or not smart. He would also get harassed by his aunts to engage with more Black kids, and they criticized him about not acting Black enough. Not being Black enough was also a message he received in high school, and it hindered his relationship with other Black students. John found a way in his college years to attend two schools: one for his math and computer interests, and a historically Black college to engage with Black students.

Significant Attachment Injuries in the Relationship

As stated previously, John had to take care of his mother and sister financially and emotionally. This, combined with a strained relationship between Yvette and his mother, resulted in numerous attachment injuries. Yvette felt pitted against John's mother, especially around financial agreements that she made with John. We spent several sessions focused on a broken agreement she and John made to take his mother off of the family cell phone plan. Yvette wanted his mother off their cell phone plan and felt that she should pay her own bills. John was unable to face Yvette by telling her that he wanted to continue to support his mother on their cell phone bill. This dynamic resulted in a huge rupture between them due to John's desire to avoid conflict with Yvette and to continue to support his mother. Yvette perceived that John cared more about his mother's feelings than hers. John felt that he couldn't express his feelings to Yvette due to her constant attacks and that he should not have to choose between his mother and her. I worked with his negative cycle to help Yvette be heard by John and to enable John to come forward with his emotions.

Ultimately, they agreed to leave John's mother on their plan and work out a more agreeable transition for her to get her own plan.

Therapist Reflections on Race

Race-related matters have impacted multiple layers in this couple's experiences, as well as their parents' lives. Both of their experiences in grade school and high school led them to attend the historically Black college where they met. Race has also influenced their perceptions of each other when they are in a negative cycle. Significantly, in an extremely positive way, racial identity development has been enhanced with their increased emotional engagement. As an African American therapist working with an African American couple, it has been a wonderful experience to see their love develop.

It was important in the beginning of therapy to hear Yvette's protest about not feeling protected in the relationship. Historically, African American women are often stereotyped in their role as "strong Black women." That is, Black women are expected to handle everything, including being the financial providers and caretakers of the family relationships. To the extent that "the Strong Black Woman" exists in marriages, their emotions, like Yvette's, are dismissed, minimized, or invalidated. The literature suggests that African American men generally learn as boys not to allow their emotions (except anger) to show because that demonstrates "weakness." To some extent, those themes played out in this couple. It was important to allow Yvette's reach and calls for closeness to be heard by John, and for John to come forward. It was also important for John to have a safe place to be vulnerable and to have his needs met.

We had many discussions about race matters. I shared with them my views about the legacy of racial oppression and how it defines roles in African American society. I wanted to create a different experience for them using the EFT model of couple's therapy while recognizing the impact of racial stereotypes on the lives of African Americans. Yvette and John actively reflected on the racial issues and experiences in their past and current circumstances. As their relationship became more safe, they also delighted in sharing their dreams of protecting and parenting children who could be free of negative stereotypes and might experience new freedoms. Their enactments about their Black parenting were wonderful and deeply moving (see later in the chapter).

In working with African American couples, I am constantly aware of and curious about the impact of racism historically and currently in their lives. It seems that Yvette and John have taken some huge strides toward healing each other. They have come a long way since they began therapy. I had to be relentlessly patient while working with John as a deep withdrawer and with Yvette as a dramatic, desperate pursuer. As I never gave up on them, they never gave up on each other.

Description of Stage-Two EFT Work

My goal in stage-two EFT was to help Yvette and John continue to access their attachment needs and come forward with their attachment emotions while promoting their accessibility to each other. I had to balance Yvette's need to be heard and seen by John with his ability to come forward and be heard. As a culturally sensitive EFT therapist, I was aware that often, African American women's needs are placed on the "back burner." Of course, this happened to Yvette growing up, as the family had to focus on a sibling's negative behavior. This also happened to Yvette when she attended an integrated school where she felt the negative and neglectful glaze of White teachers. John's withdrawals from her tapped into that same deep well of feeling alone and abandoned. Like Yvette, John's responsiveness grew exponentially. With each enactment, she was able to reduce her defensiveness, allowing John to experience a softer side of her. For the first time, Yvette's vulnerability began to surface and she allowed herself to be taken care of by John, something she once thought impossible yet desperately craved.

Yvette and John's cycle has de-escalated significantly. We continue to work on the salient components of their relationship. They are now able to communicate with each other, and the negative cycle is something they stop and talk about.

John often felt that Yvette personalized every slight or misstep that he made in their relationship. He also felt that she perceived his intentions were to harm her. As John gradually came forward and began taking a stand against the criticism he perceived from Yvette, he also revealed more of his internal experiences of their relationship. As he became more emotionally available to Yvette, he also began to own the damaging impact his withdrawing had on their negative cycle. The following transcript highlights a session in which he reassured Yvette that he had no intention of harming her, and it is a good example of John's stage-two work:

John: I'm definitely glad that you're not taking what I do for my mother personally. . . . I mean that I think when you do, it just escalates things. It makes things worse, and of course it's not a personal thing toward you. I wouldn't do anything like intentionally to bring harm to you and our relationship. I do understand how you thought about this before. I really do understand that.

Jones-Kazan: John this is so important, can you turn to Yvette and say that directly to her? *(Initiating an enactment; EFT move three).*

John *(He turns to her and pauses and then with conviction says)* I would not intentionally do anything to bring harm to you or our relationship.

Jones-Kazan: What's it like to say that to Yvette that way? *(Processing the enactment; EFT move four).*

John: Awesome. It's good to be able to reassure her in this safe space where hopefully it's received in the same way it's offered.

Yvette: I think it's important to be reassured because my love language is words of affirmation.

Jones-Kazan: I'm hearing you say that John's reassurance is so important to you it's what keeps you going, right? His connection feeds your soul in a way?

(Attachment meaning with evocative question and continuing to process the enactment; EFT move four).

Yvette: It also helps me from filling in the blanks when he is silent or withdrawn, which is like a pretty dangerous place for me. Without his presence, I go to a place where I start to make meaning of the blanks that is ultimately dangerous to our relationship. I am trying hard not to do those things. Where I struggle is with John being more the withdrawer in our relationship. When he is more intentional and forthcoming with what his intentions are, it helps me.

Jones-Kazan: John when you hear that Yvette's enjoys being more connected, knowing more about your motivations and intentions, what's it like for you to hear that? *(Continuing to process enactment; EFT move four with evocative question).*

John: It makes me a little bit anxious. I'm not used to communicating outwardly. This has been new for me. I was always worried about how it was going to land with her, to make her angry and go badly. My not communicating made it worse.

Discussion of Transcript

A benefit of couples' therapy is to provide a safe space and container where vulnerable feelings can be shared between the individuals. As the therapist, I can facilitate the sharing of these vulnerable feelings in a safe way. John's vulnerability allowed Yvette to become more comfortable with him and understand that it causes him anxiety when he is accused of not caring about her. As Yvette came to understand the attachment meaning of John's behavior, and John's anxiety about sharing his feelings, she saw that John's intentions were not to harm her. His withdrawal was largely driven by her importance to him, and his fear of being wrong that would cause her to be angry with him. John has continued therapy about his porn addiction. He is committed to a 12-step online recovery program. He appears to be maintaining abstinence from that addiction. He is able to come forward and share his recovery progress with Yvette.

With small enactments after enactments, they appear to be moving closer and more attuned to each other in sessions. There is room for John to disagree and express his feelings, and for her to listen attentively. Yvette also stated that she "feels more heard by John" and he is more of a "cheerleader for her now." When their old cycle appears, they are better at de-escalating it and not attacking each other. They understand the roles they adhere to in their cycle that cause feelings of disconnection and misattunement.

In the following transcript, Yvette discusses how she can revert back to old behaviors she learned in her family of origin that cause her to mistrust John's intentions. Her reflections about her tendency to misappraise John represent significant softening, along with her ability to hear his perspective.

Yvette: I feel like John is being more gracious to me. I feel like John now knows why I respond to things the way I do. That it has a lot to do with the ways my parents related to each other. He knows that I am consciously trying to change those things. The way I react . . . he is already a very forgiving person. He is even more forgiving in those moments when I am not at my best self. I recognize that I am not a very forgiving person. Like he knows that my family is not a very forgiving family at all.

Jones-Kazan: Yvette, can you turn to John to tell him how it makes you feels about him? That he is so forgiving. Can you tell him how that makes you feel? *(Initiating an enactment move three with evocative question).*

Yvette: I think he already knows this, but I'm happy to tell you that you're probably the most patient and forgiving person that I know. I know there were times when I overlooked those attributes in you to the detriment of our relationship. *(She begins to tear up).*

Jones-Kazan: John what is it like to hear Yvette say that that you're the most patient and forgiving person, and that is what she loves the most about you? *(Processing the enactment; EFT move four with heightening and evocative question).*

John: *(Long pause with water in his eyes, he struggles to respond).*

Jones-Kazan: *(Softly and slowly; RISSSC).* John, you have said that you wondered if your unconditional love for Yvette was taken for granted. I am wondering if it is a bit overwhelming to hear how appreciated this is by Yvette. This is the new edge of love you all have been building? *(Evocative questioning with attachment frame).*

John: *(Turning toward Yvette).* I appreciate that you recognize my patience and forgiveness as something that is a good quality of mine and something that is of benefit to you, and something that is good for our relationship.

Yvette: I understand John's skepticism to step into this new space. It's your space. It's our new space. Like the challenge for me is to be patient with him. Like me getting comfortable with that space for John to step into. This is new territory for us. *(This is new territory for Yvette, allowing herself to be vulnerable with John).*

Jones-Kazan: This is terrific, you, John, and Yvette—this is beautiful what you have been doing with your relationship. Both of you took a risk and shared with each other in this loving way today, something that you could not do before because one of you would get triggered and the cycle would take over. Both of you are creating space for each other and the relationship. *(Summary, with new attachment meaning and positive cycle, "tying the bow;" EFT move five).*

Discussion of Transcript

The transcript demonstrates the calming of their negative cycle. John is able to come forward in ways he never did before. Yvette now appreciates John's patience and support, listens to how he feels, and trusts his perspective.

176 *Case Study*

They both have greater recognition about where they go emotionally when triggered by their cycle. Yvette perceives that she goes to panic, fear, and anxiety when threatened with attachment injury, and John knows that he goes to fear and despair when he feels misattunement with Yvette. It feels safer for them both to turn to each other for emotional support and regulation. At times, they continued to experience moments of disconnection, but they report more ease with being able to repair their cycle. Ruptures to their union signal an opportunity to deepen their connection with each other.

Yvette and John are in the process of starting a family, something that would never have seemed possible at the start of our work together. I am hopeful that their bond will continue to grow as they remain committed to EFT work to resolve issues that impact their connection. As I present this case to you, they are currently pregnant with twins. Both partners have an understanding of their roles in maintaining a positive cycle. There is a willingness to try new skills and behaviors in order to mitigate the pitfalls in their negative cycle. The following transcript demonstrates this willingness to allow each other to have a voice in the relationship.

John: I guess when we have these kinds of bad riffs or when I feel really bad about our relationship, I feel really bad in the moment, but I have this faith or expectation or whatever you want to call it that at like some point things will get better. Like at some point, Yvette will kind of see this the way I see it. Like she'll come around in her own time.

Jones-Kazan: This is such a tender moment between the two of you. You each have worked to make this happen between you. This is really beautiful, and both of you have worked hard to change the negative pattern. You have created a new pattern here. *(Empathic reflection with attachment love reflected and promoting new positive cycle, move five).*

Yvette: That's reassuring, because the way I interpret that is throughout the time of our relationship is that part of the hopefulness is also anchored in these manifestations that things actually are changing. . . . So it's kind of like this ongoing process, which I would consider growth. We cope with distress differently. When times get hard between us, John goes to a space of trying to find hope, and I go to panic. So in the past, when I felt panic I would push for my point of view, and I feel like it was easy to set the tone and tenor of our relationship, right? Because I'm in control, but part of relinquishing that control means that I am in a different posture. Now I'm trying to listen to John, where I can receive his reassurance and hopefulness in our relationship even if I am in panic, that I allow him to reassure me and reaffirm his hopefulness for both of us.

Jones-Kazan: Yvette, can you turn to John and ask him what you might need from him to feel less panicked in those moments? *(Initiating and enactment; EFT move three with an attachment frame focused on developing a new pattern of emotional engagement).*

Yvette: That when John could acknowledge my feelings, it de-escalated the protests and pursuits in a situation. The shift is that when I am starting to panic, I feel like I'm losing John. I'm needing reassurance from him that we're okay.

John: *(Talking directly to therapist)* I fear that she won't trust me when I say that I'm okay, or we're okay.

Jones-Kazan: John, can you turn to look at Yvette and ask her about that? Will she trust you when you say "It's okay"? *(Encouraging the enactment of his fears and his blocks to responding).*

John: So if I say that I'm okay or if I say that we're okay, will you trust that's actually the case? If I'm not okay, I think I can now reciprocate your bravery in that moment by sharing how I feel as well. I can do that for us.

Jones-Kazan: WOW! You all continue to be so impressive with taking steps toward each other. That is so beautiful, John. You reciprocate Yvette's bravery with your bravery. Taking risks and moving closer to each other. *(EFT move five, tying the bow highlighting new patterns).*

Discussion of Transcript

It seemed with each enactment that they were taking small steps toward each other. Clearly, John being more present for Yvette had a huge impact on calming Yvette's reaction in the negative cycle. It seemed also true that Yvette's less-charged reactions to John were allowing him to feel safer to come forward with his feelings and perspective. I had a growing sense of hopefulness about their marriage.

Another change in their cycle was when John could begin to acknowledge his feelings and affirm Yvette's feelings They are beginning to understand their cycle and how it gets triggered. John would have historically withdrawn from Yvette, not sharing how he actually felt. Yvette also had difficulty tolerating John's anger, causing her distress. The following transcript demonstrates a shift in this dynamic.

John: What was different about this argument was that there was space for me to be angry at her, and she could remain present and not escalate things or blow things up in a way that was often not reparable.

Jones-Kazan: What felt different this time? *(Curious about his experience).*

John: I could see that Yvette was coming from a different place. That she was trying to achieve something different, not trying to make herself right and me wrong.

Jones-Kazan: Ah, that is different from the old pattern—the feelings and the meaning are different? *(Empathic reflection with evocative question).*

John: We could talk things through, say what we were mad about, and what we liked about what the other person was saying and figure out a solution that worked for both of us. I don't think we would've gotten there if Yvette hadn't landed in a different place.

Jones-Kazan: Wow, that was a shift in how you both handle strong feelings between you, and you, John, have changed too, and Yvette is able to stay with you even when you are angry. You all continue to handle your strong feelings in different ways. It is so wonderful to experience these moments when you are engaging each other with love. *(Empathic reflection with summary that highlights the differences between the old negative cycle and the developing new pattern of emotional engagement, move five).*

As their cycle changes, they are able to see each other's true intentions and see that they are in fact there for each other. Often, when African American couples present for treatment, they don't feel comfortable expressing their vulnerable emotions, something the EFT model emphasizes for healthy attachment and repair of the negative cycle. As an African American EFT therapist, I am sensitive to the need to hide vulnerability as a survival strategy for African Americans. The men are taught not to show fear within the family structure as a survival strategy from the dominant society.

Therapist's Reflection

Yvette's family of origin had a great deal of unpredictability and many traumatic events. There was her father's substance abuse and rageful violence toward her mother, periods of extreme poverty that would require help from extended family, and mental and physical health issues of extended family members. John was parentified at a young age to emotionally support his financially and emotionally vulnerable mother. He coped with his private longing for his father with internal loneliness. In the early sessions, Yvette would become triggered in sessions and experience "fight or flight" responses to perceived threats to her safety. She would exit sessions abruptly, often vowing to never return. In the beginning, my work with John and Yvette was to de-escalate their negative cycle by providing a calm, stabilizing, and supportive environment. This took at least a couple of years.

I used relentless reflections to normalize and validate their feelings. Creating emotional safety in a nonjudgmental and accepting therapy was my primary focus. This involved relentless and repeated EFT interventions. I facilitated the use of enactments in sessions to provide opportunities to calm, correct, and stabilize their emotional experiences. I held hope for the relationship, even when they lacked hope that their marriage could survive. During so many stage-one sessions, there were times when Yvette would abruptly leave, threatening divorce, and John would be baffled about what had happened. He would be clueless as to what had happened to cause such extreme measures by Yvette. Yvette's trauma history and struggle with anxiety often activated her defenses to flee or fight. She became increasingly aware that it wasn't only John's behavior, but strong triggers from her past that contributed to responses in therapy and to John. She accepted a referral for individual therapy to a colleague who specializes in trauma. This allowed Yvette to develop coping skills to address her anxiety and resolve childhood traumas. John continued in his individual therapy to address his porn addiction. I continued to work with them concurrently in couples therapy.

John's instincts to avoid conflict and withdraw confounded the negative cycle in their relationship, influencing their reactivity. Early sessions were often fraught with feelings of hopelessness and defensiveness which made it challenging for them. John could not understand that his lifelong coping style of withdrawing had a negative impact on Yvette that felt punishing and left her feeling extremely alone. Yvette could not understand why her angry expressions of distress were not understood by John as a cry for help. I aided them in reflecting on their internal experiences, allowing them to see their mutual distress and sadness. I instilled optimism that they could repair their relationship and engendered hope that they could respond to each other's needs with empathy, support, and compassion. I never gave up on them and their resilience to persevere and navigate the murky waters in which they swam. I had faith in the EFT model of couples therapy that they could reimagine a relationship they never thought possible when we began our work together.

During stage two of EFT couples therapy, the couple's negative cycle has de-escalated and often, John, the withdrawer, is able to come forward with vulnerable feelings, enough so that Yvette, the pursuer, feels seen and heard. The couple has better insight into the origins of their attachment meanings ascribed to each other and are better at seeing their part in the maintenance of their cycle. A new cycle is emerging in which they both feel safe to explore their feelings and attachment longings with each other.

A Final Transcript Just for the Beauty of Their New Bond

Yvette: Since I've been pregnant, John has shown me why he is my perfect partner. Pregnancy has been a lot. I have been just tired. I don't have the energy.

Jones-Kazan: Can you turn and tell him how he's shown you that he is your perfect protector and partner? *(Initiating an enactment; EFT move three with attachment frame).*

Yvette: This is the hardest thing I've ever done, this pregnancy. And John, you're doing everything without a complaint, without a need for recognition. I know a lot of cisgender men look for recognition in things that they are doing in a relationship. You'll just ask 'What do you need? Or 'How are you feeling?' It inspires trust.

Jones-Kazan: What's it like for you, Yvette, knowing John is just here for you and ready to support you? *(Processing the enactment; EFT move four with evocative question).*

Yvette: I'm happy I could tell him that. I've been trying to tell him that a lot. I mean not that I don't think John was capable of this. . . . It's just like I never knew I would feel so scared, it was very stressful. And he would be so present and engaged.

Jones-Kazan: John, what's it like to hear Yvette say that you have inspired so much trust in her for you? That you've shown up for her and been there for her through some scary times? *(Continuing to process the enactment; EFT move four with heightening and evocation question).*

John: It means a lot. We've been in such a good place. I really thought a lot about our negative cycle. The really bad parts of our negative cycle. When we're in that, trust is an ongoing issue. It has been positive moving in a positive direction. Just glad that we're doing well and supporting each other through this process.

Yvette: Just thinking about the work John and I have been doing together and separately, learning and unlearning a lot things that are harmful attachments around our Black identity actually makes me feel more optimistic about what type of children we'll raise as parents. I really have come to terms with positive Blackness, and I want to shape and cultivate our babies' views of their own freedoms and joy as Black persons.

I have continued to see them once a month after the birth of their twin girls. It is so awesome to experience their growth as an emotionally engaged couple.

Case Discussion with Sue Johnson

Guillory: Denise has addressed some very difficult moments with this case. She experienced some dreadful moments when the wife had some flash points as a pursuer, became overwhelmed, and stormed out of therapy. I'm wondering what you say to yourself and the couple when this occurs?

Sue Johnson: That is a great word. They're overwhelmed, and that's a word I used again and again. None of us has a huge number of options as human beings when we're overwhelmed. There really aren't. I mean, we think we're such sophisticated, complex animals, but if you really look at us when we're overwhelmed, it comes down to fight or flight. Occasionally we freeze, which is kind of a flight, but that's what it comes down to—"do I scream louder and louder and louder," or do I find a way to distract myself, shut down, move away, or numb out? I mean, that's it. So when people get overwhelmed, they're going to do whatever they're going to do. And the therapist has to keep their balance and say, "Aha, you were overwhelmed. That's right. So in those moments, you say to yourself, 'I have to get out. I have to escape." Or some version of "This is never going to get better. It feels terrible. I can't bear it. I have to escape." And you get up and leave. I understand. And to the husband you say, "And you just stay and can be confused as to what just happened."

The message I give them when this happens is that it's understandable and it's workable. These moments of vulnerability are manageable and workable. There's no quick, easy solution, but the vulnerability is workable. And that's what a secure person knows, and a very insecure person doesn't. The secure person is still fragile at times, is still vulnerable. That's who we are as human beings. But the secure person has a sense that vulnerability can be handled and it's workable and it's manageable, whereas the insecure person who is facing that vulnerability alone just gets overwhelmed and says, "This isn't manageable. I've got to just fight like hell, fight for my life or numb out." So you kind of have more options. There's more flexibility involved with security, and all the research says that.

The therapist's job is to keep your balance and go get the person in the waiting room. Or keep your balance, calm down the other person who is left in the room getting upset. Call the partner and say, "Yes, I understand. It was so upsetting for you. There's nothing you could do, except stand up and leave. And next time when you come back, we're going to talk about what happened and we're going to understand what goes on." So the point is sometimes, especially with trauma couples—and I'm assuming that if you're dealing with African Americans, you're going to have some racially traumatized couples too, because they have lived in a much more hostile world—there will be moments when one or both are overwhelmed. Even with a great deal of progress in therapy, sometimes people are going to become overwhelmed and blocked emotionally, and they're going to have relapses.

So what I always talk about in trauma couples is that you're going to get breaks and relapses when you have to stop and reassure, go slow and consolidate, and you go over the cycle again, and then kind of wait for them to be ready to start moving forward. The point is that in EFT we know the way forward and we know where we're going. And that changes everything. Denise does show a great deal of patience and trusting the model.

Now that's the map we have, which is larger than EFT interventions. Thinking about security, insecurity, being overwhelmed with their vulnerability. But you're also talking about therapists keeping their balance. So what do you do in those moments to keep your balance? And I am not really talking about the self of the therapist, here. It is largely having the model, which is the map, and knowing this is an overwhelming moment, and there's some level of insecurity in that moment for the client.

Now to some extent, it is the self of the therapist, but I think it's also largely trusting the model. And I think that it takes time for people to learn EFT and grow in confidence. EFT is not something you teach in a day. It's not a sort of technique, a sort of slick technique that you teach in a day, and then you go out and practice it. EFT is a whole way of being with people, and it takes time. And the good thing about that is it's more complex and it's deeper, and it takes longer to learn, but the experience of most of the people who do EFT—I think this is fair to say—it gets deeper and deeper and deeper. And it's an amazingly satisfying way of intervening with people. And the research shows it's effective. So for beginning EFT therapists, you're learning something new, and you're not quite sure where it's going to go. EFT can feel complicated, and you have to learn to trust the model. And hopefully, you've read the literature, attended workshops, and obtained supervision. In those forums, someone like me says your job in this situation is to keep your balance and just recognize that the person became overwhelmed. It's part of the cycle, and you just bring them back.

Guillory: *This couple, despite their progress, is temperamentally very different. The wife is spontaneous, emotionally expressive, and quick to criticize. The husband, with help from Denise's focus on his emotions, is now emotionally engaged but still very contemplative—so much so that he seems a bit detached. How might we continue to work with this expressive woman and her classically introspective husband?*

Sue Johnson: I think the important point here is that their differences, in and of themselves, don't necessarily create disconnection. We're all different, and I know difference is relative. He's a computer nerd, and she's a passionate lady. But actually, that is very common in some ways, in that differences attract us as well. Because they are different, they fascinate us. Maybe if she was with another passionate person, it would all be too much. So differences in themselves don't create disconnection; it's how you deal with them. I mean, they can talk in therapy about the fact that he's got a different timing than hers in his processing. He has to consciously tune into emotion. And she can give him a clear signal that she needs him to do that. Can they make clear signals? This couple has made substantial progress with the frequent encounters they set up, and they are giving each other clearer signals about their attachment experiences. They are moving toward being a more secure couple. And when you watch secure couples, they have clear signals. Denise's couple reminds me of one of my own. The wife there, too, was a pretty passionate lady, and her partner was a pretty shut down, introverted guy. And they got to the place in stage two when she was able to say to him, "When I look at you and put my hand on your arm and say I need you here, what I want you to do is turn toward me, and hold me for a while, and then listen to me for five minutes," and he says, "I can do that."

So it's like they can send clearer and clearer signals. They can deal with their differences if they recognize the places where they get stuck, and if they recognize each other's vulnerabilities. And she needs to recognize, perhaps, that her passion sometimes overwhelms him. And he needs to recognize that his apparent detachment sometimes scares her. And that's part of their cycle. So differences, shmifferences. It's like everybody's basically incompatible.

As this couples therapy with Denise progresses nicely, Yvette continues to increase the depth in her understanding of her role in the cycle. She can be passionate, and she may remain critical of her husband in some ways. From an attachment point of view, the critical/blaming is a form of distorted pursuit.

I mean it is, "I'm poking you." As my client would say, "I poke him and poke him and poke him to get a response from him," and he ends up being aggressive and pushing her away. So we say pursuer because we see the attachment reality underneath the blaming or criticalness. But a successful blamer softening, I mean, it's written in the literature very clearly. First of all, you have to have a minimally responsive withdrawer. You don't want the blamer to come out and get in touch with their deep vulnerabilities and needs and put them out, which makes them even more vulnerable to a partner who can't respond at all. So you have to have an engaged withdrawer in this stage-two work. Denise has transcripts showing a bit of that work with this withdrawer. What I have shown in my writings about pursuer softenings in *Hold me Tight Conversations* and in my other books is that the pursuer goes into their fears, owns them, accepts them, and is able to present their vulnerability to their partner in an accessible, authentic way that then pulls loving attachment responses from the partner.

And the pursuer ends up in that safety zone being able to ask for what they need in a way that pulls the partner toward them. And when the partner responds, you have a classic bonding event. So you have a "hold me tight" conversation. And the point is that we're pretty specific about the moments of change in EFT. Pursuer softening is a big one. In fact, I can't think of another therapy across any modality that is more specific about what happens in these key moments of change and how these moments in nine studies predict success at the end of therapy in terms of a changed relationship. The research on pursuer softening encounters also predicts good follow-up three years later, security of the attachment three years later. This speaks to the fact that we really have put our finger on a powerful transformational moment.

10 Summary
Emotionally Focused Couples Therapy With Cultural Humility

I've known rivers:
I've known rivers ancient as the world and older than the flow of human blood in human veins.
My soul has grown deep like the rivers.
I bathed in the Euphrates when dawns were young.
I built my hut near the Congo and it lulled me to sleep.
I looked upon the Nile and raised the pyramids above it.
I heard the singing of the Mississippi when Abe Lincoln went down to New Orleans, and I've seen its muddy bosom turn all golden in the sunset.
I've known rivers:
Ancient, dusky rivers.
My soul has grown deep like the rivers.

("The Negro Speaks of Rivers," Langston Hughes)

African American Love

There is a hidden story about Black love rooted in the attachment nature of human beings. Attachment runs deep in our fiber and is hard to destroy, even if only preserved in the heart and soul, because it is the essence of being human. Attachment was there when Africans were stolen from their families and friends, there in the belly of the slave ships, there when they were sold away from their families into slave labor camps, there during the great migration fleeing the cruelty of Southern states, there in the harshest of anti-Black laws/codes of the Jim Crow era, and still there today. This is a story of Black attachment bonds, Black love, and threats to African American romantic relationships. Emotionally Focused Therapy (EFT) is grounded in the principles of attachment theory and science. It is an evidence-based model of couples therapy founded on the principles of attachment to promote, encourage, and enhance love. EFT therapy creates pivotal bonding moments in therapy. This book has viewed the African American experience and history through an attachment lens and makes the case for using the EFT model with Black couples.

DOI: 10.4324/9780429355127-10

THREATS TO BLACK LOVE RELATIONSHIPS

History is clear. There were and continue to be race-based traumatic wounds to African Americans from past and present cruelty, oppression, and discrimination. There are also major disparities in their current quality of life as a result of race-based practices in education, housing, income, employment, and wealth. Race-based, anti-Black psychological views explained all of these practices just mentioned as the fault of Black inferiority. These notions about Black people have been circulated and actively promoted for over 400 years. In day-to-day living, Black people have died and continue to die, carrying an additional burdensome stress in their bodies because of White conscious and unconscious adherence to these racist beliefs and practices. These structural disparities, active discrimination, and anti-Black stereotypes have a direct and indirect impact on the quality of Black marriages.

These structural disparities have to be appreciated and anti-Black ideas seen as two deep rivers that must be explored in therapy with cultural humility. But couples don't come to therapy with these issues in mind. They come with their presenting problems, and therapists have to build a working alliance honoring and addressing those concerns. Therapists make a damaging mistake, however, assuming that race is either unimportant or not an attachment issue or emotion. As Hardy and Awosan (2019) suggest, these assumptions may represent deep, unconscious, race-based trauma wounds. Hardy, Pinderhughes (1989), and Parham (2000) further suggest that it is incumbent on therapists to have enough working knowledge about African American experiences to effectively integrate a healthy knowledge about race into therapy. I would add that there is a deep unconscious love, resistance to unfairness connected to spirit, intelligence, and knowing of White American culture that also survived generations of the worst human cruelty. The therapist's curiosity about these deep rivers, racial wounds, and adaptive beauty, will significantly enhance couples therapy.

Stress and Its Impact on African American Life

Racial discrimination as a stressor among African Americans has been well documented (see Chapter 2). Its consequence is a higher stress burden on the "lived" experiences of being Black. The structural aspects of race also contribute to increased baseline stress, including segregated housing and schools; a racially influenced implicit bias toward hiring, firing, and promoting in employment; over-policing; and unresponsive policing. Of course, childhood traumas and traumas unrelated to race also contribute to narrowing the window of emotional tolerance. As a result, developmental histories are particularly important for understanding the lived experiences of African Americans. While diversity of backgrounds is very likely, there are some circumstances that flow for the structural racism described here. Socialization practices are also harsher and inner-city community life is harsher compared to that of the average White community.

These harsher approaches privilege stronger emotional expressions. The boy or girl who can fight makes their playground safer, compared to the Black kid who is afraid. Particularly, Black boys and girls learn to hide emotional weakness (Pinderhughes, 1982; Boyd-Franklin, 2003); this has implications for expressions of vulnerability in therapy (Boyd-Franklin, 2003).

Racial events in the lived experiences of African Americans also have been described as racial traumas. At one end of the spectrum, these events have led to death, rape, and serious injuries; at the other end, are microaggressive comments. I suggest that there is a race-based emotional alarm that operates in African Americans—a sociobiological phenomenon developed over generations. This emotional alarm signals the need for active vigilance in order to appraise danger—it is a historical, adaptive warning signal that indicates a Black person's survival is threatened. This unique evolutionary signal is a feature of 400 years of race-based assaults and violence.

Context of Couples Therapy

Black couples come to therapy for the same reasons couples from other ethnic groups seek it. It is most often due to communication problems, affairs, unresolved disconnections, and conflicts. While couples vary regarding their specific goals, they usually hope to improve their emotional intimacy. Typically, couples enter therapy after some defining moments of disconnection, disloyalty, or distressing conflicts. The task for the therapist is the same: to create a safe place for each partner to tell their story, help them de-escalate, and improve their intimacy. Of course, couples of any ethnicity are diverse, as are Black couples. The effectiveness of couples work can depend on a number of factors, including the couple's individual and mutual motivation for change and the therapist's couples therapy training, experience, and ability to establish and maintain a working alliance with both partners.

Couples Therapy With African Americans

Black couples are likely to bring additional challenges to couples work that other racial groups do not bring. Typically, other racial groups do not have the persistent history of racial assaults in their individual backgrounds or in the historical backgrounds of their families. Moreover, they are unlikely to have a history of health disparities, educational obstacles, and employment discrimination. This additional race-based stress increases tension in day-to-day life and in baseline stress, along with presenting greater need for emotional support. Other racial groups do not have a 400-year history of White self-serving, anti-Black social stereotypes that have justified the economic, educational, and health disparities (see the section "Racial Identity" later in this chapter). Those stereotypes have a direct and insidious impact, priming negative appraisals that are threats to intimacy and the worthiness of Black men and women. In moments of vulnerability, often fear-based, these stereotypes are likely to be activated within a couple and their therapist.

Individual histories of trauma compound the presenting problems and the couple's negative cycle and can make couples therapy much more difficult. It is not uncommon for Black adults to have experienced harsh discipline while growing up that is based on the legacy of slavery. And Black girls/women face the particular harshness of disrespect as the most devalued females in American society. These uniquely Black situations can increase the intensity in sessions, sometimes with a preoccupation to be heard and seen. This is a by-product of being socially invisible or hyper-visible when perceived as a threat (Boyd-Franklin, 2003). These "burdens of Blackness" will likely make couples therapy more intense, longer, and harder. While relationship healing is the primary goal of couples therapy, we should also consider enhancing the Black couple's ability to create a safe harbor from race-based events and microaggressions.

The Cost of Coping: Self-Care and Therapy

Many Black couples, likely more than White couples, use their health insurance for payments for psychotherapy, as they don't have the same amount of disposable income to privately pay for therapy. The practical result of this income disparity is that individual sessions are shorter, 45–50 minutes compared to 75 minutes for some who pay privately. And many couples therapy providers do not take health insurance, only private-pay sessions. In addition, real estate discriminatory redlining has forced Black families into largely segregated communities, which are not typically areas where therapists have treatment offices. Black couples also lack the same disposable income to manage stress by owning their own homes, living in safe neighborhoods, taking "getaway from stress" trips together, adequate health care, spas, gym memberships, and meditation training, along with other stress-reducing opportunities that are available to people with more money.

Literature on Therapy With African American Couples

The literature on Black couples in therapy is sparse. The research that does exist suggests that couples therapists need to know African American history, the context of racial disparities, the interpersonal dynamics of power, particular issues associated with Black women and men, their challenges to relationship trust, and microaggressions in interpersonal communications (Boyd-Franklin & Franklin, 1998, Boyd-Franklin, 2003). Typically, this literature describes these issues associated with Black couples; how they are to be explored or integrated into therapy, however, is not clear. A straightforward reading of EFT theory does not include references to power and gender roles. In practice, however, these couple dynamics are explored as the EFT therapist maps the negative cycle of interactions, distinguishes between intentions and impact, and validates and reflects on the individual experiences of each partner.

The unique dance of each couple within their cycle of pursuit and withdrawal (as the EFT therapist explores the intention of behaviors and impact on each other) sheds light on these contextual issues. Of course, these issues can be uniquely associated with race matters. At the macro-level, race has impacted their parents' lives, where they lived as a child, where they went to school, their medical treatments, and their employment experiences. All of these factors have influenced each partner's racial-identity development, baseline stress, and attachment relationships. At a micro-level, each partner's racial identity and attachment histories have impacted their interpersonal stress tolerance and the intensity of their negative cycles, and at times, it has triggered their race-related distress cue and attachment longings.

I suggest that these issues are embedded in the negative cycle, each partner's view of self and other, their attachment needs, and experiences of race-based events. The Black couple's interpersonal dance occurs in a social context of a higher baseline level of internal stress that comes from being Black, having parents who were Black, and the legacy of being Black in the United States. These macro- and micro-stressors can make couples therapy with Blacks more intense and a longer process. Therapists should assume that these factors are "baked in," even if the couple does not lead with these stressors. And sometimes, they are not "baked in." Nevertheless, this suggests that EFT therapists modify their case formulations and treatment approaches when necessary to be effective. At the very least, it is important to assess for race-related experiences, bring a curiosity about racial identity, and offer more validation and empathic reflections within a relentlessly nonjudgmental stance.

Racial Identity

As Helms (1990, 1995) suggests, racial identity development is strongly associated with sensitivity and meaning about one's view of self and others. She also suggests that racial identity plays a role in African Americans' selection of couples therapists. Helms's model is a stage model. At one end of the continuum, some Blacks avoid nearly all discussions of race matters as too threatening for them and maintain internalized negative stereotypes. At the other end of the spectrum, African Americans have a balanced perspective on race. In Chapter 2, I suggest that Helms's model in some ways seems more useful as a dynamic model of stress and attachment. In that way, it might inform therapists about the felt sense of threat (as in race-stress cue, see the section "Race-Based Cue," and meanings of a race-based event). As Black EFT therapists are more closely aligned with Helms's mature or balanced view of race, they are more likely to integrate race material appropriately into their clinical formulations (with learnings about the Black experience). Helms also suggests that White EFT therapists who have a mature racial identity (and knowledge of Black culture and their own culture) would more likely address race matters effectively compared to White colleagues who have a less-developed White racial identity.

Race-Based Cue

A trauma-based view of African American historical development suggests that there is an unconscious post-traumatic stress syndrome associated with slavery and racial assaults. This is often referenced as the residual or legacy of slavery—the enduring damage created by conditions of slavery. This concept offers an important contribution to African American psychology. As traumatized as Black people have been, with intense pain and cruelty that might have left only a sliver of faith and love, in the end, love and faith survived. Nevertheless, the traumas associated with and the perspectives shaped by the legacy of slavery might align with the more dynamic use of Helms's model. That is, we consider that there are race-based distress cues (triggers), and being Black in America generates higher baseline levels of stress (see the section "Cultural Sensitivity and Negative cycle Revisited" later in this chapter). This will impact couples by placing a greater need on the Black couple to be accessible, responsive, and emotionally engaged with each other when there is an external trigger. When there are race-distress cues that occur within the couple relationship, it intensifies the negative cycle. In this regard, African American couples may need to grow in acceptance of their racial identity differences and promote each other's healing from race-based events. To this end, EFT therapists need to process raced-based distress cues in depth, consistent with the tango moves that are applied to attachment-base distress cues. The goal here is to promote acceptance of racial identity differences, heal racial identity wounds, and enhance a healthy, balanced view of self with respect to racial identity.

Residual of Slavery: White Identity Development

There is another part to this story. And while this story is beyond the scope of this book, it seems reasonable to suggest that the "residual or legacy of slavery" is an American phenomenon. That is, the residual of slavery also exists in White communities. Some recent books offer perspectives on this; *White Fragility* (2018) and *White Privilege* (2015) offer guidance for therapists' understanding of White racial identity. Perhaps less popular, but also relevant "The 1619 Project" (NYT, 2019) and Acharya, Blackwell, and Sen (2018) suggest that White anti-Black attitudes toward African Americans are influenced and shaped by Whites' participation in slave labor camps. They suggest that these attitudes reflect a harshness toward Black behavior, a lack of empathy toward Black pain, and racially motivated aggression. The authors suggest that it is important to understand the "legacy of slavery" for all Americans, Black and White, that has been passed down from generation to generation. This might offer greater insights for promoting the quality of African American relationships and trainings for therapists who work with them (see Chapter 3 and section "Threats to Developing EFT and Race Interplay" later in this chapter).

The EFT Case Studies

While these case studies are in no way representative of the diversity and complexity of African Americans who present for couples therapy, they do represent Black EFT therapists' attempts to use the model of EFT in working with African American couples. These couples also represent a small sample of Black couples in the caseloads of the presenting therapists. Each couple's negative cycle, course of therapy, and life experiences are unique. Each of the Black therapists' life experiences and training in EFT are also different. These case studies, however, do offer a deep dive into the process of EFT couples therapy, with Black EFT therapists attempting to integrate cultural responsiveness and the EFT model.

While each case's presenting problems are centered around communication difficulties, their core distresses are different and include challenges such as physical illness and vulnerability, spousal depression, fragile trust, emotional unavailability, and issues related to conception. The couples vary regarding age, work, whether they have children, and age of children. They are all heterosexual. One couple is interracial, and one couple is intercultural. These cases vary regarding lengths of therapy, with one being four years, one at least two years, and the other three for at least one year. It seems clear that these are not short-term therapies, and the intensity of their negative cycles contributed to the length of therapy. Each therapist is using the standard EFT interventions of validation, empathic reflections, heightening, and empathic conjectures. All are attempting to slow down the process of communication in order to track the negative cycle, assemble emotions, and move through the EFT tango.

Across the cases, the Black men had a harder time initially talking about their feelings. Of course, each therapist slowed the process down and focused on developing the accessibility of these men's feelings. There were different blocks to accessing feelings for each man. Marquis's medical condition has his body in constant pain, and deep dives into feelings or prolonged immersion into them would cause him physical discomfort. John has a lifetime of introverted internal processing and no language or bodily sense for feelings. Samuel's depression has created a numbness for life and a dread of overwhelming responsibility. And Clifton's allergy to any felt sense of "weakness" only allows him to be "uncomfortable," "impatient," or "angry." Finally, Eric learned in foster care to block his vulnerable feelings and not to express any weakness, so a careful process of gently developing a felt sense of safety with his wife let him discuss his fears. There was a harshness in each man's childhood and not a great deal of tolerance for their emotional expression. All of the couples reported lacking good role models for marriage.

In each case, however, as the therapist spent time exploring, naming, and processing feelings, these Black men became more in touch with their feelings and able to express them to their partners. There was variation in their depth of expression, and the focused work regarding their feelings did increase the length of therapy. While all therapists are EFT therapists, the process or the flow of therapy in each case is different due to the intensity of stress in the couples' lives and their negative cycles. It seemed helpful to slow the process down with relentless validation, empathic reflections, linking their feelings to attachment and integrating the Black experience (see section "Threats to Developing EFT and Race Interplay" later in this chapter).

All of the Black women were described as strong Black women, yet their histories and experiences are so different. Anastasia could also be described as a strong White Eastern European woman. All of these women faced traumatic experiences at young ages that pushed them to be self-reliant. They have a deep love for these men that seems connected to the family they want to have or the family they do have that includes children. They presented with a longing to be seen as lovable women. Except Monique, they are all pursuers. Monique has a unique capacity to withdraw and also reflectively understand that this pattern has created interpersonal difficulties for her. Her difficulty with processing her emotions seems largely culturally influenced by the threats of showing weak emotions as an attractive female in an inner-city community. Except for Cassandra, they all become large and loud when triggered. Cassandra tends to become more of a gentle, quiet pursuer and is fraught with self-doubt. Taken as a small group with notable differences, their backgrounds have a great deal of family trauma and distress. This seems to create more intensity in their cycle and relationship distress. As a result, it makes the couples' work longer and more difficult and intense. Nevertheless, each woman responded to EFT interventions and responded positively to their partners' accessibility and emotional engagement. As encounters deepened, so did each woman's emotional engagement.

Traditional EFT Training and Integration of African Americans

The foundation of EFT therapy is that emotions and attachments are universally human. The universal image of John Bowlby's attachment is that of the mother's responsiveness to her baby. Babies' cries are calls or signals for their mothers to respond; mothers' repeated caring responses over time create safety and secure attachment. While race might be important contextually, it is viewed as content, such that if we singularly focus on the essence of EFT, the processes of emotions and attachment, all is good. Questions that people of color might have about the impact of race on couple interactions are typically validated as important contextual content but not central to the treatment process. I suggest that while attachment might be universal, different cultures have different models of attachment bonding, and those differences can also lead to secure attachment. One attachment style from West Africa, and perhaps effective under the conditions of the slave labor camps and anti-Black laws/codes, is that of the collective (see below for implications). In this attachment model, the collective is uniquely responsive to their babies' cries. Under some of the worst conditions, a mother might work in the slave labor fields, so an elderly Black woman and children would respond to the cries of Black babies. As Black husbands, wives, children, friends, and other family members were sold off to other slave labor camps, the collective responded to the pain and loss, and those who were sold off were comforted by the collective of Black people in slave labor camps. Pinderhughes (1982) suggests that the spirit of the collective, along with other value systems, continues to operate in African American communities.

How Cultural Diversity Training Is Traditionally Taught

Most clinical trainings about diversity, and most books on the subject of race in therapy, are not designed to teach Black therapists how to work with Black couples. They instead seem to focus on teaching White therapists what they should know about Black culture. In effect, they are designed to give agency to the Black experience in order to help White therapists understand the context of Black development and obstacles to Blacks' quality of life. Many Black therapists want to work with Black couples and are largely left on their own to integrate theories of therapy and culture. This sets the bar low regarding what might enhance the clinical work. Books about couples therapy, training videos, and training examples largely feature White therapists and couples. When people of color are teachers used in video presentations or are clients, there is little to no attempt to integrate race into the assessment, case formulation, or couples therapy. An interplay of race and clinical work would begin to set the clinical bar higher.

While contextual differences might be presented, therapy training proceeds as if any racial or cultural differences are inconsequential. When Black clients are used in presentations, race is described as demographic information without clinical implications. I suggest that there are clinical implications, including racial identity and clinically relevant historical information regarding race inequities. This information is helpful for understanding the interplay, together or independently, of the attachment distress-cue, and the racial distress-cue (see the earlier section "Racial Identity"). Of course, these different distress cues trigger emotional arousal at some moment of couple disconnection. I suggest that understanding the nature of distress-cues enhances the understanding of the negative cycle of couple interactions. Further, racial identity helps therapists understand race-based appraisals (what Black people say to themselves and the meanings they make of triggering events) that can be integral to the view of self and others. These factors help therapists understand the intensity of disconnections and the unique stress cues of African American couples.

Toward a More Culturally Humble EFT

The essential techniques and clinical stance of the EFT therapist help to create emotional safety and the foundation for exploring vulnerability, attachment meanings, and behaviors. It is essential in the early sessions to understand and explore the couple's presenting problems and respond to their concerns. While creating emotional safety, EFT therapists build a working alliance related to the couple's mutual goals for therapy. It is important to give couples an overview of the nature of EFT, and explain that therapy will include exploring their pattern of disconnections and conflicts. I point out that therapy will involve exploring their emotional experiences, particularly moments of distress, what they each say to themselves at those moments, and tracking their behavioral responses. During the first session, I mention that after two or three sessions, we will engage in a structured interview to explore their individual histories. I also state that there will be at least one session in which I see each one individually.

Typically, both partners are present for the structured interview. I use the Adult Attachment and Racial Identity Questionnaire (see "Attachment and Culture/Race-Related Interview Questions" in Appendix). It consists of 17 open-ended questions. Seven of the questions were taken directly from the Adult Attachment Interview by Mary Main and Nancy Kaplan (available online). The other 10 questions I developed to explore race-related matters. I follow the clinical exploratory method of the Adult Attachment Interview. Typically, that method is designed to provide structure and allow the clinician to ask follow-up questions to understand a respondent's memory, event, or point of view. Race-related experiences are explored to assemble their emotional experiences as I would with any stressful event; this includes perceptions, feelings, and experiences vis-à-vis their view of self and others. These race-related discussions include their parents' experiences of race events and the client's view of others within and outside their race. I have only had positive experiences with this interview. Partners seem to find the attachment and race questions thought-provoking and interesting. This seems to be a safe way to bring racial feelings, thoughts, and experiences into therapy. Of course, there have been a variety of experiences with attachment and race, as well as attachment as a focus of discussion. At the end of the interview, I ask the witnessing partner "What was it like for you to listen to this story?" An overwhelming response of couples and individuals find the in-depth discussions meaningful and useful.

When race-based matters appear foreground in the news, I typically ask: "Given what has been in the news about Blacks, what has it been like for you as a Black couple?" Or, "With so much going on these days, have you been focusing on that at all?" . . . "just wanted to check in with you about that." . . . Of course, after I've conducted the "Attachment and Culture/Race-Related Interview Questions" and know something about racial events or attitudes in their lives, I might say "I'm curious about how the news has been landing on you, and especially since something like that was also in your history?" These gestures communicate that I see that my client(s) is Black and uniquely Black. It is always offered with a reflective question as to whether they have talked to each other about this news. It's also another way to prime them for the integration and interplay of emotions, attachment, and race in interventions.

The Negative Cycle Revisited

The negative cycle is an EFT concept about the repetitive pattern of couple communication that leads to interpersonal disconnection and conflict. Distressed couples get stuck in this negative dance of communication. One of the first mutual goals of the EFT therapist and couples is to carefully track this pattern within each partner and between them. This is a primary focus in stage-one work. The "distress cue" is an important element in beginning to explore this pattern (Johnson). I suggest that there is sometimes a "race distress cue" with African Americans. In this regard, race is similar to the attachment cue in which the Black person's survival is threatened. This is a unique feature of 400 years of race-based assaults.

As a result, there are times when the negative pattern in African American couples involves an interplay of distress attachment cue and distress race cue. This intersection can occur simultaneously with an attachment distress cue (when a Black woman discovers naked pictures of White women on her husband's cell phone, or when a powerful CEO flirts with a married Black woman at a social gathering in front of her husband), or within the escalated cycle of a Black couple (when angry, racially demeaning name-calling occurs). As race is explored in the assessment process and openly discussed throughout therapy, it can become a clinical judgment regarding whether to include race in the negative cycle discussion. That is, the more the therapist knows about how race-related matters have impacted a Black person's view of self, the more they can integrate race into the negative cycle. Of course, sometimes it is more useful only to include the distress attachment cue.

All of the examples that follow are a Black EFT therapist's attempts to integrate the couple's history and race-related matters into their cycle of interactions. Before the therapist gets to these moments, there have been discussions about Blackness, often specifically related to men and women, racial discrimination, and relationships:

****

"As you call for him to have your back, and he's not there, it gets you in touch with feeling that you're on your own. That brings up a painful old feeling from your family, and your busing experiences. . . . 'Black girl on your own' *(responding to the interplay of attachment and race-distress cue)* . . . it's dreadful, lonely, but now as an adult you get in touch with your anger, and you protest and loudly!!" . . . For you, John, you've always been the 'good guy.' You followed the rules, you were not like the Black guys you knew that might 'play women,' so it really hits you hard when Yvette storms off saying you're gaslighting her. It's confusing like she doesn't know you . . . you want her to really see you *(responding to hearing the interplay of race and attachment distress cue)*. You're confused. You don't know what went wrong, or what to do."

****

"Samuel, when she said during sex, 'I'm uncomfortable,' you just stopped. It was jarring *(attachment distress cue and race distress cue)*. The essence of you being a Black man is for you to be a protector, not to harm your wife. You said the emotional connection is important to you *(from prior discussions of race identity in therapy)*. You don't think with your dick, you would rather forgo sex than make her uncomfortable. That's like your essence as a Black man. So you just shut down. For you, Cassandra, you're learning about yourself sexually, you said it was the best way you knew how back then. Your religious upbringing ('what good Black girls do') blocked your feelings, and even talking about it with him was too much. *(Emotion cue and race distress cue)*. So it seems both of you had no models to talk about any of this and so you went without sex, and you felt alone in your distress about that."

****

"The more you got triggered, you just flashed on her, called her a 'bitch,' and accused her of awful stuff *(attachment cue initially, as the escalation develops with 'street' appraisal of Black woman)*, and you fought back to call him a 'weak-ass bitch' *(attachment cue and race distress cue . . . disrespect of Black woman)* and the escalation continued and got worse. As it gets really bad between you, the N-word shows up *(attachment and race distress cues interplay)*. In the end, with all the intensity and name-calling, the hurt is deep, and the recovery is so long."

****

"The more she says something about you smoking weed, you get triggered and say 'stop policing me!!' *(race distress cue)* . . . 'stop vilifying me' *(attachment cue and race distress cue)* 'you need to loosen up.' It felt like it was too much given all you've gone through as a Black man. For you it's triggering too. You react to his loud voice, you're triggered by his intoxication *(attachment distress cue)* but it seems that all you can do is withdraw. Internally you say to yourself 'he doesn't want me, he has another type of Black woman in mind' *(racial distress cue and attachment distress cue, as in. . . 'I'm not Black enough for him')*."

****

Eric: Right. So, I guess my fear is the fact that if you don't have a child, we would not be a complete family. The other fear is adopting a child and adopting the system that comes along with the child. *(Kam nods head in the affirmative.)* (Here the racial distress cue is the system . . . the White foster care system where he experienced racial trauma as a child. And he reacts emotionally to his wife's suggestions that they adopt).

The EFT therapist assembles emotions while pulling together aspects of the person's internal experience. This tracking of their experience, both within and between partners is central to understanding of their emotions, appraisals of distress, and coping behaviors. As the distress cue is more fully articulated, it helps to understand the perspective as to how partners come to their emotionally reactive conclusions. While race is not always a factor, sometimes it is, and often historical race-based macro-circumstances are playing an invisible role (such as housing redlining that negatively impacts Black families and being victims of aggression, crimes, and drugs) or a more explicit role when there are incidences of racial discrimination that impact one or both partners. When these latter circumstances exist, these race-based experiences create greater susceptibility to intense anger, anxiety, and overprotectiveness. Just as American culture often is blind to race-based events, sometimes Black couples, too, do not appreciate the impact racial experiences have on their appraisals of each other, or their needs for greater intimacy. They are aware, however, of their internal appraisals of each other, and frame their responses accordingly. An EFT therapist has to be willing to explore and understand and therefore truly see and hear the macro- and micro-stressors, slowly unpacking first the immediate attachment appraisals, and gently, as needed, also folding in the race relevant experiences.

Brief Examples of the Interplay of Race and Perceptions of Self and Other

The Therapists in these following vinettes are attempting to assemble the emotional experiences with meaning and perceptions:

"As you, Camila, feel him pushing you to be different, it is as if he doesn't see you as a 'together' Black woman, and that's a deep hurt, as if he doesn't like you the way you are, and so you pull away to protect yourself. *(Empathically reflecting with racial distress cue of not being Black enough, and reflecting her withdrawal in the dance).* And for you, Rufus, you want her just to be more flexible to have fun with you, to dance, to drink with you . . . when she says she gets anxious about that, the drinking part, it feels like she is 'going White on you, or worse' *(reflecting attachment longing, and his race-based appraisal self and other)*, like she's saying you're doing something wrong. You get that all the time at work, under the gaze of White people. It doesn't feel right to you. To you, Rufus, you've earned the right . . . in sports and business . . . to relax and play. When she says 'no' it's frustrating . . . so you really push her to join you. *(Reflecting his appraisal of criticism and his felt race-based discrimination at work).* To you, Camila, you want him to like you, to see you, but his pushing hurts, and it's like he's saying you're not Black enough and that hurts, too. This pattern of push and withdrawal leads you both to feel despair about this relationship." *(Empathic reflections with race-based cue and reflecting the despair in their cycle responses).*

****

"When you were growing up at the school you went to, you were the only little Black boy, and had to deal with the White kids all on your own, and you faced harsh punishments. The school didn't treat you fairly. You see your son's aggressive behavior and his mother's tolerance; it scares you. And you want him to learn about being a Black boy, the problems aggression will bring for him, but she interferes . . . it is so frustrating . . . she doesn't get what you're trying to do as a Black father. She interrupts and you feel so disrespected and not seen for what you're doing. So you just go in the bedroom and close the door . . . in pain." *(Empathic reflection with view of self, attachment distress-cue, and racial distress-cue. Empathic reflection of his withdrawal).*

****

"This is really hard, really hard for both of you. You guys have been together since high school. Although you have been romantically connected, you are also each other's only long-term friend. The problem has been that J Lee has never been faithful, and both of you know that. To be real, in J Lee's world, that is what you know. It's sort of hip-hop culture, and otherwise your life hasn't gone well. For A, you're not like that, and you take care of business. You have a degree. Somehow you have a softness for J Lee, and his vibe, his energy; it's street and it's crazy attractive, and you love it! And then you take him back, and he can be so convincing. You want him to be different. Sometimes you think it would be best to move on without him. But you're not sure what that would look like for you. And you guys have been friends, and so you're stuck . . . he's hip-hop and you're romantic rhythm and blues . . . this is so hard it's painful, because you are so different and where is the possibility for a good relationship?" *(Tanisha James, Mary Hinson, and Paul T. Guillory in supervision; developed summary with three similar cases . . . Empathic reflections, attachment dilemma, nonjudgmental approach to Blackness in poor community with lots of trauma). Note: both partners came from extreme poverty and family dysfunction . . . they have been each other's primary social support since early high school when they had no one else. Their couples work is being conducted in a low-fee clinic.*

****

"That's important, Monique. You're saying both of you said some things when you were angry, taken over by the negative cycle, and both were hurt by what was said. Arguments happen between all couples. African American couples can be particularly harsh with name-calling, and sometimes too careful leaning into each other with our hearts. Leading with love. No we can't change people directly, Monique; we can change the way we communicate with each other. When we change the way we communicate . . . like fewer harsh words, name-calling and such, it helps. It helps, too, when we don't quickly create a script and then go after our partner, and Clifton and Monique, we all want to be number one . . . chosen first in love."

****

"So, the fear is that, 'We won't be able to conceive,' right? That 'we won't be able to conceive and that we won't be able to carry the legacy forward through having a child together.' And so there's a fear of potentially a loss, a loss of not being able to have a child together through the connection, through the bond, and the meaning of not being able to bring that into fruition and what that means, that loss of not having that child . . . and continuing the legacy, the family legacy? Yeah. Can you talk about that with Kam? That fear?" *(Family legacy as a way of implicitly talking about importance of Black family, prior discussions about race).*

BLACK LOVE AS SOMETHING THAT IS CELEBRATED

Lyons-Rowe and Rowe (2013) suggest that we should have reverence for and highlight when we see African American love. And as bell hooks (2001a, 2001b) states, Black love is revolutionary, given all the threats to romantic intimacy between African Americans. As a result, when EFT therapists witness the expression of emotional engagement in therapy, it is important to make explicit the wonderful, enduring legacy of love. The implication of conscious and unconscious Black strengths, intelligence, competency, beauty, and creativity suggests that as couples therapists, we must find ways to highlight these aspects. Of course, encouraging the discussion of race early allows for integrating the above strengths into these movements of emotional engagements.

Cassandra: For me, it has been learning that pleasure is good. Pleasure is okay and allowing myself to have it and be responsible for my own pleasure. And being a partner with him for his pleasure. We can do that in uniquely Black ways too. *(Looking at him).* We are in a relationship and your pleasure is important to me, too. This is totally different.

Therapist: It is a new pattern you all are working on for yourselves. Allowing yourselves to have pleasure. And even just connecting to your bodies. And on some level, it requires a grieving process from past difficulties, the lack of models, the right terms and what society and the media taught us about our (Black) bodies. How revolutionary that the two of you are searching to learn from each other. "What's the language for us?" *(Empathic reflections and promoting emotional and sexual engagement with their unique Blackness touch implicit . . . "uniquely Black ways").*

****

"I want to just slow it down for a minute. You're saying you are really seeing John as your advocate. Because you both understand that Black women can die in childbirth, and there can be problems with medications regarding pain. . . . John, what's it like to hear Yvette say that you have inspired so much trust in her? That you've shown up for her and been there for her through some scary times?" *(Evocative reflection, acknowledging Black women face unique dangers in childbirth and health care. Reflection also amplifies the attachment frame, their progress as a couple, and evocatively reflecting on John's sense of self as a Black man).*

****

"There is a beauty in the relationship between the two of you is what I'm talking about. And that after 20 years it can still bring tears to her eyes, and softness to her voice. That's unique. I don't always see that. That's why I want you to just pause and take in the beauty of it, really. If we had a Picasso painting here, I'd like you to sit in front of it and pause and just take in the beauty of it. That's what I just saw, and that's what I want you to do, too. That was a beautiful moment between the two of you." *(Move five. Slowing the process down and reflecting on a soft moment. Heightening a moment when a careful 'strong Black woman' reached for her husband in a vulnerable moment, and he could stay with her . . . both have grown up learning to be allergic to showing weakness).*

****

"There is a lot in all of this, and we will have to come back to this issue of choosing Clifton. It is deeper than just another "pretty Tony." Sometimes, fears of not being good enough come from our earlier relationships and just being a Black man. We learn ways to protect ourselves when we have been hurt. This work tonight has focused on the beautiful and special parts of your relationship. Monique's choosing you, Clifton. We'll have to come back to that, and while you have said some of these things before to Monique, it seems Clifton needs to hear more of this from you. It was beautiful to see how emotional you became. Monique, while talking about your love for Clifton. We'll come back to that too. *(Summarizing a significant moment in therapy. Evocatively reflecting on Clifton being chosen by Monique as an antidote to his own internalized racism).*

INTENTIONALLY RAISING THE BAR HIGH FOR BLACK COUPLES

I am suggesting a renewed commitment to learning about therapy with African American couples. This is more than just being an identified Black therapist or a White therapist with good intentions. The clinical bar for work with Black couples should be high, because the threats to Black love and marriages are great due to discrimination, historical shadow, and current impacts. I suggest that we should involve the informed use and interplay between race, EFT, and the appreciation of the long-standing history of racism-based psychology. This would require a great deal of curiosity, an appreciation of race-based psychology, and an interest in learning about race from a Black perspective. Learning could include reading a variety of books and joining reading groups about African American experiences, focused forums on African American concerns, partnerships with EFT experts and African American therapists, along with infusing Black themes in theatrical plays and musicals. This also could mean EFT trainers engaging with Black colleagues and partnering with them on EFT projects like Hold Me Tights, externships, core skills trainings, and EFT presentations. Moreover, we can explore systematic ways to recruit Black participation in all of these efforts.

Threats to Developing the EFT and Racial Interplay

The effectiveness of EFT is in its experiential essence—in the expressions and acceptance of vulnerability within couples. While the discussion of race-based matters is important, particularly early in therapy, the appropriate interplay of emotions, attachments, and race is an area of scholarship and clinical art. Just acknowledging racial differences and inviting feedback if something offensive is said in the conversation is not enough. The expression of vulnerability in the context of emotional safety is the development of love in action. Race-based distress cues are unique vulnerabilities of African American love that the EFT therapist needs to see, validate, and create a safe space for. When to add a touch or a lot of Black-related experience in the tango moves will vary with each couple, distress moment, and therapist. Not enough can take away from the emotional meaning and potential for emotional engagement, and too much is likely to distract from the attachment emotional expressions so vital for the experience of vulnerability and closeness.

Racial Identity of Couple and EFT Therapist

To skilled EFT therapists, this interplay of cultural race-related experiences that I am suggesting may seem interesting but not necessary for effective couples therapy with African Americans. Black and White therapists may draw on their own experiences of working with African American couples when race did not surface as a significant concern. There are three issues to consider here:

1. EFT is an evidence-based model with consistently positive results as an effective couples therapy, and Black couples are likely to show some benefit.
2. Racial identity development suggests that there are Black couples who avoid dealing altogether with most matters related to race; they may want to work with White EFT therapists for that reason. They may also view White therapists as more competent than Black therapists. Some African Americans are unaware of how race-related matters impact their negative cycle and the appraisals of themselves and their partners. And there can be White EFT therapists who are uncomfortable with race matters, consistent with their White racial identity or those who believe that race is not: (a) necessary to engaging the Black couple in couples therapy; or (b) the therapist is just too afraid that they will make a mistake and say something offensive.
3. There are so few African American EFT therapists in most communities, that Black couples have mainly White therapists as options. Rather than discuss race matters with their White therapists, they are likely to consider discussing these matters with each other outside of therapy.

Racial Humility and EFT

It is a clinical choice as to whether the bar is set at the "do no harm," level and to use the EFT clinical model as historically taught. The alternative is to take the concept of promoting active anti-racist clinical work seriously and encourage setting the bar higher and leaning into excellence. In this regard, understanding the role of race in the negative cycle helps motivate Black couples to fight against the harmful aspects of racism in their patterns of communication. Assembling emotional experiences with an understanding of race-based damaging stereotypes or race-based strengths can enhance the depth of each partner's view of self and the other. Moreover, integrating the beautiful, spiritual, healing, and remarkable aspects of Black love into move five or in the summaries at the end of emotionally engaged moments can be particularly inspiring to the spirit of connection. These emotionally engaged moments have historical and cultural significances that are revolutionary, according to bell hooks (2001a, 2001b).

The EFT working model of love, accessibility, responsiveness, and emotional engagement (A.R.E.) is not well known in the literature on Black couples (see Chapter 4). Yet it is a powerful conceptualization of love, particularly for Black couples. The combination of racial distress cues and promotions of anti-Black propaganda continue to create threats to Black people attempting to enhance their A.R.E. For example, if a partner is emotionally troubled or preoccupied by a troubling situation, there is surely a negative Black stereotype for that. A negative view has been advanced (see Chapters 1 and 2) to appraise oneself as a failed person or a failed partner. Racial priming makes vulnerability more dangerous. This can be where racism is most insidious. The priming of doubt has been promoted for centuries about not measuring up, being a boy, not a true man, about weakness, ugliness, and incompetency, so when we are most vulnerable, we fear accessibility, responsiveness, or being seen . . . let alone making our worst fears known, or responding to this fear from a place of responsive acceptance. Whether the emotion is fear or shame, the impact of racism has been to add a damaging block to emotional engagement. This requires relentless validation and evocative reflections that also include the impact of racism. Racism—external or internalized—creates blocks to accessibility, responsiveness, and emotional engagement. Stage-two of EFT couples therapy should provide many opportunities for processing enactments/encounters of emotional engagement moments for therapists to empathically reflect and summarize the specialness of Black love.

Introducing Race

Black Americans are diverse, and therefore it should not be surprising if bringing up race results in diverse reactions from Black couples. Race can be a sensitive matter, and it may seem risky. This can be true for therapists and Black couples. I do not recommend leading with these discussions, unless the couple does. As a clinician, the presenting problem is central, along with establishing a working alliance. In the first session, I tend to give an overview of the assessment and therapy. Typically, at the end of the first session, I give a brief overview of EFT couples therapy. At that time, I suggest that in a few sessions, I will do a deep dive into their history. This is where I use the "Attachment and Cultural/Race-Related Interview Questions," (Appendix) to help guide and structure the conversation. I explain that the interview questions are associated with the quality of romantic relationships and would be helpful to understand their relationships. Therapists should always be ready to briefly discuss the importance of attachment bonds and the negative impact of discrimination on African Americans love relationships. Engaging in the interview contributes to understanding their attachment histories, racial identities, and other experiences, which can enrich the clinical conversations. During the interview, emotional terms for attachment and race frequently emerge and are explored. The interview questions are a structural guide that are flexible, allowing the curious therapists many to follow-up questions.

Racial matters are viewed and discussed in the context of their other lived experiences and with the same curiosity and exploration as EFT therapists might give attachment histories. Racial stress-related external events or internalized racist thoughts might be explicitly named, accordingly. This could involve the impact of redlining on where they lived as a child or where they went to school or their parents' work experiences. This often reveals the structural racism that impacted one or both of them as part of their experiences and development. This differs from the traditional EFT training suggesting that race matters might be important but unrelated to the universal concepts of attachment and emotions. The implication of that point of view is that EFT therapy with Black people could be effective without discussions of race. I suggest that race is directly intertwined in view-of-self, attachments, and emotions. It manifests in the bodies of African Americans as an increase in baseline stress. To the extent that we avoid addressing racial identity and race-related matters in assessments and integrating them into case formulations, therapists miss opportunities to explore critical emotions and appraisals of self and others. Effectively working with race gives EFT therapists more options to fight against the negative cycle and negative appraisals primed by stereotypes and provides opportunities to mobilize the strength and longing for Black love.

Beyond the incomplete case formulations (i.e., overlooking race matters), not working with race also specifically means that we cannot articulate within the negative cycle racism's negative influence, the depths of despair in withdrawers, or the desperation of pursuer vulnerabilities for personal connection in a socially racist world that leans toward Black social isolation. When African American couples become isolated, this too is also a threat to their secure base of emotional engagement. In this regard, as Black couples become more A.R.E. with each other, it becomes important to have a healthy, positive Black social village surrounding them to enhance their loving connection. This could mean their actively participating with extended family, having a healthy involvement with church family, their participation in interest groups, or social interactions with other Black couples.

Moreover, the joyful features of Black loving relationships also need to be highlighted in EFT therapist move number five, where we "tie a bow" around emotionally engaged attunement. Many Black couples are particularly joyful about their romantic relationships when they become A.R.E engaged, and have "hold me tight conversations." These conversations seems to satisfy a deep longing for African Americans to be lovingly engaged. Together, with love, they have beaten the odds stacked against them and coped with all the racial threats to their connections. The EFT therapists, just as African American couples, have to be reminded of the remarkable healing power of accessible and responsive love and that this "felt sense" of engaged love is a spiritual connection to celebrate.

Appendix Attachment and Culture/Race-Related Interview Questions

I'm going to be asking you questions about your experiences growing up in your family as well as about your current life. These experiences may have affected your adult relationships and will be helpful to this therapy. Relationship research has shown that these topics are important to understand your development, life stressors, and adult relationship satisfaction. So I'd like to start by asking you about your early relationships with your family and explore particular events.

1. Could you start by helping me get oriented to your early family situation and where you live and so on? Could you tell me where you were born, who raised you, and whether you moved around much, and what your family did at various times for a living?
2. I'd like you to describe your relationship with your parents, if you could start from as far back as you can remember.
3. Now I'd like to ask you to choose three adjectives or words that reflect/describe your relationship with your mother, starting from as far back as you can remember . . . as early as you can go. This may take a bit of time . . . then I'd like to ask you why you chose them.
    - Okay, you say the relationship with her was (use his/her phrase); are there any memories or incidents that come to mind with respect to (word)?
4. Now I'd have you do the same for your father.
5. I wonder if you could tell me to which parent did you feel the closest, and why. Why isn't there this feeling with the other parent?
6. When you were upset as a child, what would you do?
    - When you were **upset emotionally**, when you were little, what would you do? Can you think of specific time that happened?
    - Can you remember what would happen when you were **hurt physically**? Again, do any specific incidents (or do any other incidents) come to mind?
    - Were you ever **ill** when you were little? Do you remember what would happen?

7. Did you ever feel rejected as a child? Of course, looking back on it now, you may think differently, but what I'm trying to ask about here is whether you remember ever having been rejected in any way.
   - How old were you when you felt this way, and what did you do?
   - Why do you think your parent/people did those things . . . do you think he/she realized he/she was rejecting you?
8. Were your parents ever threatening to you in any way—maybe for discipline, or even jokingly?
   - What happened?
   - What did you do?
   - How did the situation get resolved?
9. Is there any particular thing that you feel you learned that is important to understand you that comes from your own childhood experiences or life as an adult? I'm thinking here of something you feel you might have gained from the kind of childhood you have had or the life you have lived.
10. In general, how do you think your overall experiences with your parents have affected your adult personality?
    — Are there any aspects to your early experiences that you feel were a setback in your development?
11. Do you strongly identify with a cultural/racial group? If yes, then follow-up answer with curiosity . . . Like "What does that mean to you?" What has been your stance, if any, toward other races/cultures?
12. Has there been any way your race/culture has been a challenge to your view of yourself? Or has it been a challenge to your view of others in your culture/race?
13. Do you think racism or discrimination impacted your parents' lives in any way? Has racism or discrimination impacted your life in any particular way?
14. Given how negative the majority culture can be toward Black Americans, as a Black man/woman, did you get any particular message about Black men/boys growing up?
15. (Same as 14 just shift gender) Did you get any particular message about Black women/girls growing up?
16. Did you strongly identify with any religious faith as a child? What roles has it played in your life? Now?
17. Are you involved in some way in the Black community?

References

Abreu, J. M. (1999). Conscious and nonconscious African American stereotype: Impact on first impression and diagnostic ratings by therapists. *Journal of Consulting and Clinical Psychology, 67*(3), 387–393.

Acharya, A., Blackwell, M., & Sen, M. (2018). *Deep roots: How slavery still shapes southern politics*. Princeton, NJ: Princeton University Press.

Ainsworth, M. D. S. (1995, Fall). On the shaping of attachment theory and research: An interview with Mary Ainsworth. *Monographs of the Society for Research in Child Development, 60* (2–3), 3–24.

Ainsworth, M. D. S., & Bell, S. M. (1970). Attachment, exploration, and separation: Illustrated by the behavior of one-year-olds in a strange situation. *Child Development, 41*, 49–67.

Akbar, N. (1991). Mental disorders among African Americans. In R. L. Jones (Ed.), *Black psychology* (pp. 339–352). Berkeley, CA: Cobb and Henry Publishers.

Alexander, M. (2010). *The new Jim Crow: Mass incarceration in the age of colorblindness*. New York, NY: The New Press.

Alvarez, A. N., Liang, C. T. H., & Neville, H. A. (2016). *The cost of racism for people of color*. Washington, DC: American Psychological Association.

Allen, I. M. (1996). PTSD among African Americans. In A. J. Marsella, M. J. Friedman, E. T. Gerrity, & R. M. Scurfield (Eds.), *Ethnocultural aspects of posttraumatic stress disorder: Issues, research, and clinical applications* (pp. 209–238). Washington, DC: American Psychological Association.

Anderson, R. E., & Stevenson, H. C. (2019). RECASTing racial stress and trauma: Theorizing the healing potential of racial socialization in families. *American Psychologist, 74*(1), 63–75.

Andrews, W. L., & Gates, Jr. H. L. (2000). *Slave narratives*. New York, NY: Literary Classics of the United States.

Aponte, J. F., & Wohl, J. (2000). *Psychological intervention and cultural diversity* (2nd ed.). Boston: Allyn and Bacon.

Bernal, G., & Scharron-del-Rio, M. R. (2001). Are empirically-supported treatments valid for ethnic minorities? Toward an alternative approach for treatment research. *Cultural Diversity and Ethnic Minority Psychology, 7*, 328–342.

Blackman, L., Clayton, O., Glenn, N., Malone-Colon, L., & Roberts, A. (2005). *The consequences of marriage for African Americans: A comprehensive literature review*. New York, NY: Institute for American Values. ISBN#978-1-931764-11-5.

Blackmon, D. A. (2008). *Slavery by another name*. New York, NY: Vantage Books.

Blair, I. V., Judd, C. M., & Fallman, J. L. (2004). *Journal of Personally and Social Psychology, 87*(6), 763–778.

Bowlby, J. (1970). *Loss: Sadness and depression*. New York, NY: Basic Books.
Boyd-Franklin, N. (2003). *Black families in therapy*. New York, NY: The Guilford Press.
Boyd-Franklin, N., & Franklin, A. (1998). African American couples in therapy. In M. McGoldrick (Ed.), *Re-visioning family therapy: Race, culture, and gender in clinical practice* (pp. 268–281). New York, NY: The Guilford Press.
Boyd-Franklin, N., Kelly, S., & Durham, J. (2008). African American couples in therapy. In A. S. Gurman (Ed.), *Clinical handbook of couples therapy*. New York, NY: The Guilford Press.
Brubacher, L. L. (2018). *Stepping into emotionally focused couple therapy: Key ingredients of change*. New York, NY: Routledge.
Bryant, C. M., Wickrama, K. A. S., Bolland, J., Bryant, B. M. Cutrona, C. E. and Stank, C. E. (2010). Race matters, even in marriage: Identifying factors linked to marital outcomes for African Americans. *Journal of Family Theory & Review*, 2, 157–174.
Carter. R. T. (2007). Racism and psychological and emotional injury: Recognizing and assessing race-base traumatic stress. *The Counseling Psychologist*, 35(1), 13–105.
Cassidy, J., & Shaver, P. R. (Ed.). (2008). *Handbook of attachment: Theory, research, and clinical applications*. New York, NY: The Guilford Press.
Chae, D. H., Lincoln, K. D., & Jackson, J. S. (2011). Discrimination, attribution, and racial group identification: Implications for psychological distress among Black Americans in the national survey of American life (2001–2003). *American Journal of Orthopsychiatry*, 81(4), 498–506.
Chou, T., Asnaani, A., & Hofmann, S. G. (2012). Perception of racial discrimination and psychopathology across three U.S. Ethnic minority groups. *Cultural Diversity and Ethnic Minority Psychology*, 18(1), 74–81.
Clark, R., Anderson, N. B., Clark, V. R., & Williams, D. R. (1999). Racism as a stressor for African Americans. *American Psychologist*, 54(10), 805–816.
Comas-Diaz, L., Hall, G. N., Neville, H. A., & Kazak, A. E. (2019). Racial trauma: Theory, research, special issue. Racial trauma: Theory, research, and healing. *American Psychologist*, 74(1), 1–5.
Constantine, M. G. (2002). Predictors of satisfaction with counseling: Racial and ethnic minority clients' attitudes toward counseling and ratings of their counselors' general and multicultural counseling competence. *Journal of Counseling Psychology*, 49(2), 255–263.
Constantine, M. G. (2007). Racial microaggressions against African American clients in cross-racial counseling relationships. *Journal of Counseling Psychology*, 54(1), 1–16.
Cross, W. E., Parham, T. A., & Helms, J. E. (1991). The stages of Black identity development: Nigresence models. In R. L. Jones (Ed.), *Black psychology* (pp. 319–338). Berkeley, CA: Cobb and Henry Publishers.
Cutrona, C. E., Russell, D. W., Abraham, W. T., Gardner, K. A., Melby, J. N., Bryant, C., & Conger, R. D. (2003). Neighborhood context and financial strain as predictors of marital interaction and marital quality in African American couples. *Personal Relationships*, 10. 389–409.
Dance. D. C. (2002). *From my people: 400 years of African American folklore*. New York, NY: W. W. Norton and Company.
DeGruy, J. (2005). *Post traumatic slave syndrome*. Portland, OR: Joy DeGruy Publications. Inc.
DiAngelo R. (2018). *White fragility*. New York, NY: Beacon Press.
Dolezsar, C. M., McGrath, J. J., Herzig, A. J. M., & Miller, S. B. (2014). Perceived racial discrimination and hypertension: A comprehensive systematic review. *Health Psychology*. 33(1), 20–34.

Dunham, S., & Ellis, C. M. (2010). Restoring intimacy with African American couples. In J. Carlson & L. Sperry (Eds.), *Recovering intimacy in love relationships: A clinician's guide* (pp. 295–316). New York, NY: Routledge.

Ester, P. A tourist's view of marriage: Cross-cultural couples-challenges, choices, and implications for therapy. In P. Papp (Ed.), *Couples on the fault line* (pp. 178–204). New York, NY: The Guilford Press.

Fang, C. Y., & Myers, H. F. (2001). The effects of racial stressors and hostility on cardiovascular reactivity in African American and caucasian men. *Health Psychology, 20*(1), 64–70.

Feagin, J., & Bennefield, Z. (2014, February). System racism and U.S. Health care. *Social Science and Medicine, 103,* 7–14.

FitzGerald, C., & Hurst, S. (2017). Implicit bias in healthcare professionals: A systematic review. *BMC Medical Ethics,* 1–18. doi:10.1186/s12910-017-0179-8

Fosha, D. (2003). *The transforming power of affect.* New York, NY: Basic Books.

Fuller-Rowell, T. E., Curtis, D. S., Ryff, C. D. Zgierska, A. E., El-Sheikh, M., & Duke, A. M. (2017). Racial discrimination mediates race differences in sleep problems: A longitudinal analysis. *Cultural Diversity and Ethnic Minority Psychology, 23*(2), 165–173.

Gottman, J. M. (1994). *What predicts divorce?* Hillsdale, NJ: Lawrence Erlbaum Associates, Inc.

Gramham, J. R., West, L. M., Martinez, J., & Roemer, L. (2016). The mediating role of internalized racism in the relationship between racist experiences and anxiety symptoms in a Black American sample. *Cultural Diversity and Ethnic Minority Psychology, 22*(3), 369–376, thank you.

Greer, T. M., Brondolo, E., Amuzu, E., and Kaur, A. (2018). Cognitive behavioral models, measures, and treatments for stress disorders in African Americans. In E. C. Chang, C. A. Downey, I. K. Hirsch, & E. A. Yu (Eds.), *Treating depression, anxiety, and stress in ethnic and racial groups: Cognitive behavioral approaches* (ch. 11). Washington, DC: American Psychological Association.

Guthrie, R. V. (1991). The psychology of African Americans: An historical perspective. In E. L. Jones (Ed.), *Black psychology* (pp. 33–45). Berkeley, CA: Cobb and Henry Publishers.

Hannah-Jones, N. (2019). The 1619 project. *The New York Times Magazine.*

Hardy, K. V., & Awosan, C. I. (2019). Therapy with heterosexual Black couples through a racial lens. In M. McGoldrick & K. V. Hardy (Eds.), *Re-Visioning family therapy: Addressing diversity in clinical practice* (3rd ed.). New York, NY: The Guilford Press.

Helm, K. M., & Carlson, J. (2013). *Love, intimacy, and the African American couple.* New York, NY: Routledge.

Helms, J. E. (1990). *Black and White racial identity: Theory, research and practice.* Westport, CT: Greenwood Press.

Helms, J. E. (1995). An update on Helms's White and people of color racial identity models. In J. G. Ponterotto, J. M. Casas, L. A. Suzuki, & C. M. Alexander (Eds.), *Handbook of multicultural counseling.* Thousand Oaks, CA: Sage.

Hill, L. K., Hoggard, L. S., Richmond, A. S., Gray, D. L., Williams, D. P., & Thayer, J. F. (2017). Examining the association between perceived discrimination and heart rate variability in African Americans. *Cultural Diversity and Ethnic Minority Psychology, 23*(1), 5–14.

Hill, R. (1972). *The strengths of Black families.* New York: Emerson-Hall.

Hill, R (Ed.) (1993). *The research on the African American family: A holistic perspective.* Westport, CT: Auburn House.

Hilsenroth, M. J., Bedics, J., Budge, S. L., Imel, A. E., Marmarosh, C. L., & Owen, J. (Eds.). (2018). American psychologist, special issue: Evidence-based psychotherapy relationships III. *Psychotherapy, 55*(4), 316–537.

References

Hoffman, K. M., Trawalter, S., Axt, J. R., & Oliver, M. N. (2016). Racial bias in pain assessment and treatment recommendations, and false beliefs about biological differences between Blacks and Whites. *Proceedings of the National Academy of Sciences of the United States* doi:10.1073/pnas.1516047113.

hooks, b. (2001a). *Salvation: Black people and love*. New York, NY: HarperCollins.

hooks, b. (2001b). *All about love*. New York, NY: Willian Morrow.

Hook, J. N., Farrell, J. E., Van Tongeren, D. R., Davis, D. E., DeBlaere, C., & Utsey, S. O. (2016). Cultural humility and racial microaggressions in counseling. *Journal of Counseling Psychology*, *63*(3), 369–277.

Hook, J. N., Owen, J., Davis, D. E., Worthington, Jr. E. L., & Utsey, S. O. (2013). Cultural humility: Measuring openness to culturally diverse clients. *Journal of Counseling Psychology*, *60*(3), 353–366.

Hughes, D. A. (2007). *Attachment-focused family therapy*. New York: Norton.

Hunter, L. R., & Schmidt, N. B. (2010). Anxiety psychopathology in African American adults: Literature review and development of an empirically informed social-cultural model. *Psychological Bulletin*, *136*(2), 211–235.

Hurston, Z. N. (2001). *Every tongue got to confess: Negro folk-tales from the gulf states*. New York, NY: Harper-Collins Publishers.

Hurston, Z. N. (2018). *Barrocoon*. New York, NY: HarperCollins Publishers.

Jacobs, H. A. (2012). *Incidents in the life of a slave girl*. New York, NY: Simon and Brown.

Johnson, S. M. (2002). *Emotionally focused couple therapy with trauma survivors: Strengthening attachment bonds*. New York, NY: The Guilford Press.

Johnson, S. M. (2004). *The practice of emotionally focused couple therapy: Creating connection* (2nd ed.). New York, NY: Brunner and Routledge.

Johnson, S. M. (2009). Extravagant emotions: Understanding and transforming love relationships in emotionally focused therapy. In D. Fosha, D. Siegel., & M. Solomon (Eds). *The healing power of emotions: Affective neuroscience, development and clinical practice* (pp. 257–279): New York: Norton.

Johnson, S. M. (2010). *The hold me tight program: Conversation for connection*. New York, NY: Little, Brown and Company.

Johnson, S. M. (2013). *Love sense: The revolutionary new science of romantic relationships*. New York, NY: Little, Brown and Company.

Johnson, S. M. (2019). *Attachment theory in practice: Emotionally focused therapy with individuals, couples, and families*. New York, NY: The Guilford Press.

Johnson, S. M. (2020). *The practice of emotionally focused couple therapy: Creating connection* (3rd ed.). New York, NY: Routledge.

Johnson, S. M., & Sandenfer, K. (2016). *The hold me tight guide for Christian couples*. New York, NY: Little, Brown and Company.

Johnson, S. M., & Whiffen, V. E. (2003). *Attachment processes in couple and family therapy*. New York, NY: The Guilford Press.

Jones, A. C. (1991). Psychological functioning in African Americans: A conceptual guide for use in psychotherapy. In R. L. Jones (Ed.), *Black psychology* (pp. 577–589). Berkeley, CA: Cobb and Henry Publishers.

Jones-Rogers, S. E. (2019). *They were her property*. New Haven: Yale University Press.

Katz, A. D., & Hoyt, W. T. (2014). The influence of multicultural counseling competence and anti-Black prejudice on therapists' outcome expectancies. *Journal of Counseling Psychology*, *61*(2), 299–305.

Kelly, S., & Floyd, F. J. (2001). The effects of negative racial stereotypes and afrocentricity of Black couple relationships. *Journal of Family Psychology*, *15*(1), 110–123.

Kelly, S., & Floyd, F. J. (2006). Impact of racial perspectives and contextual variables on marital trust and adjustment for African American couples. *Journal of Family Psychology*, *20*(1), 79–87.

Kendi, I. X. (2016). *Stamped from the beginning: The definitive history of racist ideas in America*. New York, NY: Nation Books.

Kendi, I. X. (2019). *How to be an antiracist*. New York, NY: One World, Random House.

Kogan, S., Yu, T., & Brown, G. L. (2016, August). Romantic relationship commitment behavior among emerging adult African American men. *Journal of Marriage and Family*, *78*, 996–1012.

Lavner, J. A., Barton, A. W., Bryant, C. M., & Beach, S. R. H. (2018). Racial discrimination and relationship functioning among African American couples. *Journal of Family Psychology*, *32*(5), 686–669.

Lazarus, R. (2006). *Stress and emotion: A new synthesis*. New York, NY: Springer Publishing Company.

Lazarus, R., & Folkman, S. (1984). *Stress, appraisal, and coping*. New York, NY: Springer Publishing Company.

Lee, D. L., & Abn, S. (2013). The relation of racial identity, ethnic identity, and racial socialization to discrimination-distress: A meta-analysis of Black Americans. *Journal of Counseling Psychology*, *60*(1), 1–14.

Levine, B. (2012). *Fall of the House of Dixie*. New York, NY: Random House.

Liu, W. M., Liu, R. Z., Garrison, Y. L., Kim, J. Y. C., Chan, L., Ho, Y. C. S., & Yeung, C. W. (2019). Racial trauma, microaggressions, and becoming racially innocuous: The role of acculturation and White supremacist ideology. *American Psychologist*, *74*(1), 143–155.

Lyons-Rowe, S., & Rowe, D. (2013). Expert interview with Dr. Sanda Lyons-Rowe and Dr. Daryl M. Rowe. In K. M. Helm & J. Carlson (Eds.), *Love, intimacy, and the African American couple*. New York: Routledge.

Magai, C., Cohen, C., Milburn, N., Thorpe, B., McPerson, R., & Peralta, D. (2001). Attachment styles in older European American and African American adults. *Journal of Genecology, Social Sciences*, *56*(1), 528–535.

Main, M., Hesse, E., & Hesse, S. (2011, July). Attachment theory and research: Overview with suggested applications to child custody. *Family Court Review*, *49*(3), 426–463.

Mattis, J. S., Simpson, N. G., Powell, W., Anderson, R. E., Jimbro, L. R., & Mattis, J. H. (2016). Positive psychology in African Americans. In E. C. Chang, C. A. Downey, J. K. Hirsch, & N. J. Lin (Eds.), *Positive psychology in racial and ethnic groups*. Washington, DC: American Psychological Association.

McGuire, D. L. (2010). *At the dark end of the street*. New York, NY: Vintage Books.

Nadal, K. L. (2018). *Microaggressions and traumatic stress: Theory, research, and clinical treatment*. Washington, DC: American Psychological Association.

Nightingale, M., Awosan, C. I., & Stavrianopoulos, K. (2019). Emotionally focused therapy: A culturally sensitive approach for African American heterosexual couples. *Journal of Family Psychotherapy*, *30*(3), 221–244. Poke yes.

Nobles, W. W. (1991). African philosophy: Foundations of Black psychology. In R. L. Jones (Ed.), *Black psychology* (pp. 47–63). Berkeley, CA: Cobb and Henry Publishers.

Oggins, J., Veroff, J., & Leber, D. (1993). Perceptions of marital interaction among Black and White newlyweds. *Journal of Personality and Social Psychology*, *65*(3), 494–511.

Otto, H., & Keller, H. (2014). *Different fades of attachment: Cultural variations on a universal human need*. New York, NY: Cambridge University Press.

Owen, J., Imel, Z. E., Wampold, B. E., & Rodolfa, E. (2014). Addressing racial and ethnic microaggressions in therapy. *Professional Psychology: Research and Practice*, *45*(4), 283–290.

Papp, P. (2000). *Couples on the fault line: New directions for therapists*. New York, NY: The Guilford Press.
Parham, T. A., White, J. L., & Ajamu, A. (2000). *The psychology of blacks: An African centered perspective* (3rd ed.). Upper Saddle River, NJ: Prentice Hall.
Parker, F. S. (2020). *Ella Baker's catalytic leadership: A primer on community engagement and communication for social justice* (vol. 2). Berkeley, CA: University of California Press.
Patton, S. (2017). *Corporal punishment in Black communities: Not an intrinsic cultural tradition but racial trauma*. Washington, DC: American Psychological Association.
Pettit, B. (2012). *Invisible men: Mass incarceration and the myth of Black progress*. New York: Russell Sage Foundation.
Phillips, V. B. (1928). The central theme of southern history. *The Historical Review, 34*(11), 30.
Pieterse, A. L., Neville, H. A., Todd, N. R., & Carter, R. T. (2019). Perceived racism and mental health among Black American adults: A meta-analytic review. *Journal of Counseling Psychology, 59*(1), 1–9.
Pinderhughes, E. (1982). Afro-American families and the victim system. In M. McGoldrick, J. K. Pearce, & J. Giordano (Eds.), *Ethnicity and family therapy*. New York, NY: The Guilford Press.
Pinderhughes, E. (1989). *Understanding race, ethnicity, and power: The key to efficacy in clinical practice*. New York, NY: The Free Press.
Pinderhughes, E. (2002). African American marriage in the 20th century. *Family Process, 41*(2), 269–282.
Pyke, K. D. (2010). What is internalized racial oppression and why don't we study it? Acknowledging racism's hidden injuries. *Sociological Perspectives, 53*(4), 551–572.
Raley, R. K., Sweeney, M. M., & Wondra, D. (2015). The growing racial and ethnic divide in U.S. marriage patterns. *Future Child, 25*(2), 89–109.
Roberts, R. (2017). Addressing occupational stress among African Americans. In T. L. Leong, D. E Eggerth, C.-H. Chang, M. A. Flynn, J. K. Ford, & R. O. Martinez (Eds.), *Occupational health disparities*. Washington, DC: American Psychological Association.
Rothenberg, P. S. (2015). *White privilege*. New York, NY: Worth Publishers.
Rothstein, R. (2017). *The color of law*. New York, NY: Liveright Publishing Corporation.
Saad, L. (2006, July 14). Blacks committed to the idea of marriage. *Gallup News Service*.
Shaver, P. R., & Hazan, C. (1993). Adult romantic attachment: Theory and evidence. In D. Perlman & W. Jones (Eds.), *Advances in personal relationships* (vol. 4, pp. 29–70). London: Jessica Kingsley.
Sibrava, N. J., Bjornsson, A. S., Perez Benitez, A. C. I., Moita, E., Weisberg, R. B., & Keller, M. B. (2019). Posttraumatic stress disorder in African American and Latinx adults: Clinical course and the role of racial and ethnic discrimination. *American Psychologist, 74*(1), 101–116.
Smith, T. C. (2005). *The relationship between racial identity attitudes and relationship satisfaction in middle-class African American couples* (Unpublished doctoral dissertation). John F. Kennedy University, Pleasant Hill, CA.
Speight, S. L. (2007). Internalized racism: One more piece of the puzzle. *The Counseling Psychologist, 35*(1), 126–134.
Some', S. (1999). *The spirit of intimacy*. New York, NY: Harper.
Stockett, K. (2009). *The help*. New York, NY: Penguin Books.
Sue, D. W. (1990). Culture-specific strategies in counseling: A conceptual framework. *Professional Psychology Research and Practice, 21*(6), 424–433.

Sue, D. W., Nadal K. L., Capodilupo, C. M., Lin A. I., Torino G. C., & Rivera D. P. (2008). Racial microaggressions against Black Americans: Implications for counseling. *Journal of Counseling and Development, 86.*

Sue, D. W., Alsaidi, S., Awad, M. N., Glaeser, E., Calle, C. A., & Mendez, N. (2019). Disarming racial microaggressions: Microintervention strategies for targets, White allies, and bystanders. *American Psychologist, 74*(1), 128–142.

Sue, S., & Zane, N. (2009). The role of culture and cultural techniques in psychotherapy: A critique and reformulation. *Asian American Journal of Psychology, S*(1), 3–14.

Szanton, S. L., Gill, J. M., & Allen, J. K. (2005, July). Allostatic load: A mechanism of socioeconomic health disparities? John Hopkins university school of nursing, 525 N Wolfe street, Baltimore, MD 21205. *Biot Reserch Nursing, 7*(1), 7–15.

Thomas, K. S., Bardwell, W. A., Ancoli-Israel, S., & Dimsdale, J. E. (2006). The toll of ethnic discrimination on sleep architecture and fatigue. *Health Psychology, 25*(5), 635–642.

Troxel, W. M., Matthews, K. A., Bromberger, J. T., & Sutton-Tyrrell, K. S. (2003). Chronic stress burden, discrimination, and subclinical carotid artery disease in African American and Caucasian women. *Health Psychology, 22*(3), 300–309.

Upchurch, D. M., Stein, J., Greendale, G. A., Chyu, L., Tseng, C-H., Huang, M. H., . . . Seeman, T. (2015, May). A longitudinal investigation of race, socioeconomic status, and psychosocial mediators of allostratic load in midlife women: Findings from the study of women's health across the nation. *Psychosocial Medicine, 77*(4), 402–412.

Valk, A., & Brown, L. (2011). *Living with Jim Crow: African American women and memories of the segregated south.* New York, NY: Palgrave Macmillan.

Wilkins, E. J., Whiting, J. B., & Watson, M. F. (2013). Residual effects of slavery: What clinicians need to know. *Contemptary Family Therapy, 35,* 14–28.

Yeh, C. J., Trimble, J. E., & Parham, T. A. (2012). *Culturally adaptive counseling skills: Demonstrations of evidence-based practices.* Thousand Oaks, CA: Sage.

Yetman, N. R. (2000). *Voices from slavery: 100 authentic slave narratives.* Mineola, NY: Dover Publications, Inc.

Index

"1619 Project, The" 5, 22, 63, 189

abandonment 98, 120, 135, 140–142, 162, 173
acceptance 44–46, 62, 70–71, 93, 109, 137, 142–143, 148–150, 152, 159, 161, 189, 200–201
accessibility 61–62, 66, 72, 84, 91, 113, 140, 161, 172, 190–191; *see also* accessibility, responsiveness, and emotional engagement (A.R.E.)
accessibility, responsiveness, and emotional engagement (A.R.E.) 12–13, 28, 40, 43, 46, 58, 60, 63, 65–67, 69, 71, 91–92, 94, 113–114, 135, 154, 156, 158, 201–203
acculturation 18, 30, 35, 54
adaptability 23, 26
adoption 141, 144–145, 151, 155
"Adult Attachment Interview and Racial Identity Questionnaire" 68, 193
affairs 68, 81, 186
affirmation 173, 177
African American community(ies) 24, 29, 35, 62, 81, 85, 92, 96, 98, 112, 156, 169, 192; *see also* Black community(ies)
African American couples 6–7, 9, 11–12, 16–19, 22, 29, 33, 36, 38, 55, 58, 60, 63, 69, 74, 79, 86, 140, 155, 161–162, 172, 178, 187–190, 192, 194, 197, 199–200, 202–203
African American divorce rates 6
African American love 6, 29, 38, 184, 198, 200
African American music 3, 5, 29–30, 199
African Americans 1, 4–8, 10–12, 16–19, 23, 29–32, 34–37, 41, 45, 52–53, 57–58, 60, 62–65, 74, 85, 93–94, 98, 111, 134, 172, 178, 181, 185–186, 188–190, 194, 198, 200, 202–203; stress and 23–28; *see also* African American community(ies); African American couples; Blacks

Afrocentricity 18
Afrocentrism 25
agency 10–11, 23, 47, 192
alcohol abuse 80, 143
Americanized Africans 3–4, 6, 57, 60
anger 19, 23, 27, 36–37, 70, 76–77, 79, 82–84, 91–92, 98, 113, 139, 141–142, 147, 162, 167, 169, 172, 177, 194, 196; *see also* anger reactivity
anger reactivity 48, 112
anti-Black laws/codes 1, 3, 10, 24, 184, 191; *see also* Jim Crow laws
anti-Blackness 162
anti-Black racism 5, 46, 155
anxiety 2, 16–18, 20–21, 25–26, 39, 41, 55, 62, 74, 83–84, 101, 105, 108–109, 112, 121, 126, 132, 136, 143, 162, 168, 174, 176, 178–179, 196; *see also* attachment anxiety
Anxious pursuing 69
Arbery, Ahmaud 54
Armstrong, Louis 29
assaultive behavior 5, 16, 24
assessment 24, 32–33, 38, 40, 45, 55, 67–72, 192, 194, 201–202
attachment anxiety 168
attachment base 58, 148
attachment-based bonding *see* attachment bonds
attachment-based therapy 1
attachment bonds 1, 6, 10, 15, 23, 26, 28–29, 34–35, 47, 57–60, 85, 134–135, 148, 150, 152–153, 184, 191, 202
attachment cue 194–195
attachment disconnections 27, 36–37, 46, 62, 65
attachment distress 27, 42, 67
attachment distress cues 141–142, 194–195
attachment emotions 35, 37, 96, 107, 142, 145, 148, 161–162, 169, 172
attachment fear 93, 130

Index

attachment feelings 70, 79, 84, 91, 106, 142
attachment figure 57–59, 136
attachment focus 69, 77, 149
attachment-infused conversations 67
attachment injury 48, 99, 162–163, 171, 176
attachment insecurity 38, 84
attachment lens 1, 6, 15, 36, 60, 66, 159, 184
attachment longing 70–71, 94, 107, 114, 150, 161, 179, 188, 196
attachment love 15, 36, 176
attachment needs 71, 85, 96, 103, 105, 107, 114, 142, 150, 152–153, 161–163, 166, 169, 172, 188
attachment-reactive emotions 58
attachment reframes 143–144, 154
attachment science 184
attachment significance 68, 70–71, 151, 166–168
attachment strategies 20, 58–59, 68, 98
attachment style 20, 57, 59, 64, 121, 141–142, 162, 191
attachment theory 10, 33, 58–60
attachment threats 38
attachment trauma 10, 96, 99, 140, 161
attachment vulnerability 37, 149
attachment wounds 149
attack-attack pattern 98
attunement 71, 155–156, 161–162, 202; mis- 41, 64, 174, 176
aversive racism 30
avoidance attachment 170
avoidant attachment style 59, 64
Avoidant withdrawing 69

Baldwin, James 29
baseline stress 11, 24–25, 126, 185–186, 188, 202; *see also* stressors
"Beale Street Blues" 29
Bell, Mary A. 15, 51
belonging 12, 46, 135, 142, 151
betrayal 74–75, 78, 82; *see also* affairs; infidelity
bewilderment 162, 168
bipolar disorder 119
Black church 170; *see also* church family
Black community(ies) 52, 54–55, 75, 84–85, 98, 109, 112, 143, 155
Black consciousness 54
Black couples 11–14, 16, 29, 34–35, 38, 54–55, 63, 68, 75, 94, 184, 186–187, 190, 192, 196, 199–202; *see also* African American couples
Black culture 12, 75, 118, 171, 188, 192
Black feminism (womanist) 143

Black identity 180
Black inferiority 4, 8, 25, 45, 185
Black LGBTQ experiences 54
Black love 30, 62, 68, 85, 184–185, 198–199, 201–202
Black marriages 6–8, 185
Black men 6–8, 22, 26, 29, 33, 46–49, 53, 65, 74, 84, 112, 116, 119, 125–126, 155, 157, 186, 190
Blackness 4, 10–11, 25, 46, 115–116, 134, 155, 180, 187, 194, 197–198; anti- 162
Black protest 48
Black romantic relationships 11, 24, 55, 118; *see also* Black love
Blacks 3–4, 10, 31, 46, 188, 192–193
Black self-identity 108; *see also* Black identity
Black socialization 55
Black women 7–8, 18, 22–23, 26, 43, 45, 47–48, 65, 119, 131, 135, 150, 161, 172, 187, 191, 198
blamer 183
blamer softening 183
blaming 21, 182–183; self- 20; victim- 163
Bland, Sandra 54
body image 143
Bowlby, John 1, 33, 58, 191
Brown, Michael 54
bullying 26, 97
burned-out pursuer 96, 98, 118
burnout 121

call-and-response patterns 59–61, 68, 72
Canada 39, 53, 158
Castile, Philando 54
church family 58, 202
civil rights 18, 34
Civil Rights Act 7–8
civil rights movement 11, 155
Civil War 3, 15
Clark, Stephon 54
co-affect regulation 12
collective, the 33, 36, 57, 65, 191–192; slave community 57; spirit of 192; tribal community 1
collective community 33, 57, 65; *see also* African American communities; Black community(ies)
colorism 155
communication consultant 67–68
communication problems 97, 186
community violence 134

compassion 132, 179
Confederacy 3
confused withdrawer 163
control 3–4, 30, 59, 62, 64, 67, 91, 108–109, 112–113, 116, 119, 122, 125, 150, 176
coping 5, 16, 20, 22–24, 26, 51, 59, 63, 96, 107, 115, 123–124, 133, 141, 179, 195; avoidance style of 133; *see also* coping strategies
coping strategies 16, 22, 24, 84, 96, 142, 150
counseling *see* couples therapy; EFT couples therapy
couple disconnection 36, 66, 96, 107, 192
couples therapy 1, 9–10, 12–13, 27, 29, 35, 37, 39, 62–63, 65, 67–70, 75–76, 79, 82, 90, 96–97, 107, 118–119, 128, 132, 134–136, 140–141, 145, 150, 156, 159, 161–162, 168, 179, 182, 184–188, 190, 192, 200; with African Americans 1, 186–187, 200; challenges to 11–12; emotionally focused 12–13; *see also* EFT couples therapy
COVID-19 pandemic 13, 24, 96, 101, 107
crack cocaine 155; epidemic 155
criminality 11
critical pursuer 14, 92, 163
critical withdrawer 96, 98
criticism 51, 63–65, 72, 98, 106, 108–109, 141–143, 173, 196
cultural emersion 54
cultural humility 12–13; and couples therapy 29–56; EFT with 184–203; interplay with EFT consultation 48–51
cultural self-awareness 54

Darwin 4, 58
de-escalation phase 13, 37, 70
de-escalation/stabilization 37, 67, 72, 79, 94, 96, 107, 110, 114, 139, 161; *see also* de-escalation phase
defensiveness 64, 173, 179
demeaning language 74; racialized 80
depression 13, 16–17, 121–122, 128, 133, 136, 143, 162, 190
despair 64, 107, 141, 155, 162, 176, 196, 202
developmental trauma 169
disconnection 9, 13, 24, 27–28, 32, 36–38, 40–41, 43, 46, 48, 58–60, 62, 64–69, 74, 83, 85, 94, 96, 98, 101–104, 106–107, 115, 119, 128, 136, 140–142, 145, 163–164, 174, 176, 182, 186, 192–194; cycle of 13, 37, 102, 163; emotional 64; pattern of 96, 106–107, 140, 193

discrimination 1, 4–5, 7–8, 10, 12, 16, 18–19, 24, 26–27, 29, 52, 54–55, 63, 71, 74, 84, 94, 134, 155–156, 170, 185, 199, 202, 205; employment 26, 186; housing 26; structural discrimination 10; *see also* discriminatory harassment; racial discrimination
discriminatory harassment 17
disposable income 187
dissociation 121
distress cues 26, 76–77, 79–80, 82–83, 163, 166, 168, 192, 194–195; adaptive 24; *see also* attachment distress cues; race distress cues; racial distress cues
distress tolerance 133
divorce 6–7, 64, 74, 80–81, 143, 169, 178
Douglass, Frederick 9–10
Dred Scott decision 5
drug abuse 142–143; *see also* substance abuse
dyads 1, 33, 36, 57

economic disadvantage 7
EFT couples therapy 20, 35–36, 38, 68, 96, 107, 111, 118, 140, 190, 201; cultural humility and 29–56; stages of 13–14, 72–73, 92–93, 114, 145–146, 179, 201; *see also* emotionally focused therapy (EFT); EFT therapist
EFT therapist 12–13, 27, 29, 37–38, 40, 42, 44, 48, 53, 60, 64–65, 67–69, 71, 75, 79, 93–94, 107, 136, 138, 146, 161, 173, 178, 182, 187–190, 192–196, 198, 200, 202–203
emotional alarm 58, 66, 186; race-based 186
emotional availability 140
emotional communication 107
emotional dysregulation 133
emotional engagement 12–13, 26, 28, 36, 38, 40, 43, 46, 52, 58, 60–63, 65–69, 71–73, 86, 90–93, 114, 121, 128, 132–135, 137, 154, 158, 161, 169, 172, 176, 178, 191, 198, 200–202
emotional flash point 116
emotional intimacy 12, 132, 186
emotionally focused therapy (EFT) 1, 9, 35–38, 66–67, 184; in-session communication processing (macro-moves) 69–71; experiential interventions 71; micro-interventions 69, 71–72; stages of 13–14, 72–73, 92–93, 114, 145–146, 179, 201; systemic interventions 72; *see also* assessment; RISSSC; tango moves
emotional pain 96, 166

emotional regulation 108
emotional responsiveness 7, 140
emotional safety 12, 36, 38, 46, 58–62, 64, 67, 69–70, 79, 91–93, 96, 107, 114–115, 128, 134, 157, 161, 178, 192–193, 200
emotional signals 36, 58–59
emotional vulnerability 12, 61, 84, 91, 103, 110, 128, 145
emotional weakness 186
emotional withdrawal 109, 161
emotions 16, 20, 25, 27, 33, 36–38, 40, 42, 48–49, 52, 55, 58–59, 62, 64, 66–67, 69–72, 77, 80, 83, 87, 90, 93–94, 96, 100, 105, 108, 110, 112–113, 116–117, 118, 120, 124, 128, 133–134, 136, 138–143, 145, 150, 154–157, 162–163, 165, 171–172, 178, 182, 190–191, 193, 195, 200, 202; *see also* attachment emotions; reactive emotions
empathetic conjecture 147, 151–154
empathic reflection/reflecting 28, 39, 46, 67, 69, 70–72, 78–80, 86, 89, 92–94, 101–107, 109, 111, 123–124, 126–127, 129–132, 134, 136, 143, 145, 147–150, 153–154, 156–157, 164–168, 176–179, 188, 190–191, 196–199
empathy 71, 79, 92–94, 107–109, 114–115, 129, 136, 142, 154, 179, 189
empowerment 7, 141
enactment 28, 140, 144–148, 152–154, 169, 172–180, 201
engagement 20, 25, 38, 54–55, 62, 64–65, 67, 72, 81, 85, 96, 132, 140, 145, 150, 152, 159, 161, 169, 198; *see also* accessibility, responsiveness, and emotional engagement (A.R.E.); emotional engagement; response engagement; withdrawer re-engagement (WRE)
England 39; *see also* Great Britain
ethnic cleansing 112
ethnic diversity 34
ethnic identity 20, 35
ethnicity 20–21, 30–31, 118, 134, 186
Europe 2, 4, 7, 96, 100, 112; Eastern 96, 111, 191
Evers, Medgar 54
evocative questioning 78, 80, 86, 88, 90, 110–111, 122–123, 127, 129–130, 146–147, 151, 164–165, 174–175, 177, 179
evocative reflection 72, 77, 86, 88, 104, 127, 168, 198, 201

evocative responding 56, 62, 66, 71, 86, 88, 136, 147–148, 153–154, 177, 194, 201; *see also* responsiveness
experiential therapy 12
extended family 57, 63, 118–119, 124, 126, 178, 202

family: arrangements 7; bonds 23; connections 118; of creation 120–121, 133; dynamic 118, 120; dysfunction 8, 197; histories 14, 114, 133; home 98; income/finances 80, 99; legacy 14, 151, 198; members 8, 23, 65, 119, 124, 133, 178, 192; migration 135; multigenerational 135; nurturance 111; of origin 65, 120–121, 141, 168, 174, 178; relationships 24, 124, 172; role expectations 119; support 107; structures 178; trauma 107, 191; units 58; *see also* extended family
farming attachment model 57
fear 1–5, 13–14, 20–21, 23, 25–26, 36–37, 60–63, 65, 70, 85, 89–91, 93–94, 98, 100–107, 109–116, 125–126, 128–131, 140–142, 144–148, 150–152, 154, 156, 162, 174, 176–178, 183, 186, 190, 195, 197–199, 201; *see also* attachment fear
fertility 140, 146, 154
fight or flight 178, 180
flash points 94, 115–116, 138, 180
Floyd, George 53–54
folktales 1, 3
forgiveness 120, 175
foster care system 141–143, 149–150, 154–155, 158, 190, 195; compared to slavery 155
frustration 33, 36, 42, 70, 97, 99, 113, 137, 141, 143, 162–164, 169

Galton, Sir Francis 4
gaslighting 163–165, 167, 194
gender roles 187
GI Bill 7
great American migration 10, 57, 63, 184
Great Britain 53
Great Depression 7

Hall, G. Stanley 5
Handy, W.C. 29
happiness 47; marital 7; global 6–7
hate crimes 30
health insurance 187

heightening 71, 111, 145–154, 175, 180, 190, 199
historically Black college 171–172
"hold me tight conversations" 183, 189, 203
hooks, bell 30, 198, 201
hopelessness 141, 152, 162, 179
Hughes, Langston 184
Hurston, Zora Neale 29, 73
hurt 27, 36–37, 42–43, 50–51, 62, 64–65, 70, 74, 76–77, 79–80, 83–84, 87–88, 90, 93–95, 97, 108, 120, 125, 127, 135, 142, 151–152, 162, 166–168, 195–197, 199

identity 46, 51, 62, 150, 155; *see also* Black identity; Black self-identity; ethnic identity; race identity; racial identity; White identity; White racial identity
implicit bias 11, 29–32, 42, 52–54, 161, 185
inequality: structural inequalities 10
infant mortality 34, 57
infertility 140
infidelity 82, 84; *see also* affairs
internalized devaluation 8, 33
internalized racism 13, 17–18, 22, 25, 43–46, 54, 199
interracial couples 13, 40, 94, 96, 108, 112
isolation 58, 74, 102, 109, 121, 147, 202; emotional 59; physical 59; social 61, 63, 99, 112, 202

Jacobs, Harriet 34, 38–39
Jim Crow era 10, 19, 22–23, 34, 47, 184; post-traumatic Jim Crow syndrome 11
Jim Crow laws/codes 3, 8, 10, 16, 22, 24, 57
John Henryism 26
Johnson, Sue 1, 38, 64, 66–68, 79, 93–95, 115–117, 136–139, 156–160, 180–183

kayaking tango 133
King, Martin Luther, Jr. 54
kinship bonds 34

legacy 5, 33, 64, 149, 151, 158, 172, 188, 197–198; family 14, 151, 198; of slavery 11, 24, 47, 63, 65, 187, 189
loneliness 42, 61, 66, 70, 112, 121, 147, 150, 154, 162, 178, 194
love 4, 5, 9–10, 12–13, 28, 29, 33, 35, 37–38, 41, 44, 46–47, 50–51, 57–64, 70, 73, 78–79, 82, 85–87, 89–94, 100, 106–108, 114, 117, 119–120, 125–126, 131, 133–134, 137, 142–144, 147–150, 153, 156, 158–160, 162, 172–173, 175, 178, 184–185, 189, 191, 197–203; principles of 60–61; relationships 10–11, 34–35, 59, 157, 202; romantic 11, 34, 60, 119; unconditional 49, 175; *see also* African American love; attachment love; Black love; love bond
love bond 58, 73, 114

majority culture 8, 18, 20–21, 25–26, 30, 32, 35, 53, 58, 60, 63, 68, 205
marital dissatisfaction 119, 121
marriage 6–8, 30, 34, 36, 43, 46–47, 57, 84–85, 100, 118–119, 121, 123–124, 130–134, 137, 139, 159, 169, 172, 177–178, 190, 199; *see also* Black marriages; marriage counseling
marriage counseling 6; *see also* couples therapy
Martin, Trayvon 54
mass incarceration 8, 155, 158
McDougall, William 4
Mendelian genetics 4
mental illnesses 99, 118, 134; *see also* serious and persistent mental illness (SPMI)
meta-reflection 21, 26, 52
microaggressions 13, 19–20, 26, 28, 31–32, 37, 40, 42–43, 48, 51, 68, 71, 187
middle class 10, 18, 29
Middle Passage 10
minority culture 19–20, 53
Moore, Fannie 22–23
Morrison, Toni 29

name-calling 64–65, 78–79, 85, 94, 194–195, 197
negative cycle 13–14, 37–40, 42, 46, 48, 67, 69, 71–72, 74–75, 79–80, 84–85, 92, 101, 104–106, 108, 110–111, 113–114, 116, 118, 121, 128, 131, 136, 144–145, 161–163, 168–169, 171–173, 175–180, 187–192, 194, 197, 200–202; *see also* negative dance; negative interactional cycle; negative pattern
negative dance 94, 104–105, 107, 109, 115, 194
negative interactional cycle 156
negative pattern 41, 43, 47, 54, 63–64, 67–68, 70, 72, 74–76, 79, 82–83, 94, 96, 98, 104, 107, 109, 111, 123–124, 126, 130, 140, 169, 176, 194
New Deal 7
Nigeria 118, 120, 134–135

non-Black therapist 29; *see also* White therapist
norms 118; cultural 118, 120; religious 119; White 20
North, the 23, 58

oppression 5, 19, 172, 185
optimism 38, 143, 179–180
oral tradition 1

panic 122, 125, 141, 176–177
parenting 63, 108–109, 112–113, 115–116, 119, 121, 133, 172; co- 50
partner violence 68
patience 76, 82, 92–93, 161, 172, 175, 181; im- 93–94, 190
people of color 16, 19–21, 25, 31–32, 35, 37, 49, 52, 68, 191–192; *see also* persons of color
personhood 34
persons of color 16, 20–21
physical intimacy 118, 130, 132, 168
physical pain 96, 98, 108, 110, 113
point/counterpoint patterns 82
police brutality 134
policing 8, 195; over- 74, 185; unresponsive 74, 185; *see also* police brutality
porn addiction 168, 174, 179
positive cycle 114, 132, 136, 175–176; *see also* positive pattern
positive pattern 61
"Post-Traumatic Slave Syndrome" 11, 19, 24, 53
poverty 98, 169, 178, 197
power 4, 10, 20, 22, 32, 35, 46, 65, 136, 187, 203; -lessness 141
pre-marital counseling 162
premarital sex 7
psychotherapy 6, 24, 29, 32, 34–35, 136, 187; evidence-based 35
PTSD 16, 24, 54, 159; *see also* "Post-Traumatic Slave Syndrome"
pursuer 14, 39, 72, 96, 98, 103, 118, 141, 154, 158, 161, 163, 172, 179–180, 183, 191, 202; critical 14, 92, 163; *see also* burned-out pursuer; pursuer softening; pursue-withdraw cycle; pursuit
pursuer softening 14, 92, 161, 169, 183
pursue-withdraw cycle 121–128, 141, 188
pursuit 62, 69, 74, 98, 128, 133, 177, 182, 188

race 4–5, 12, 17, 21, 25–26, 30, 32–33, 37, 39–43, 46, 48, 54–55, 68, 94, 96, 100, 134–136, 140, 155–156, 158, 170, 172, 185, 188, 191–196, 198–202; definitions 9–10; influences of 84–86, 98; priming 25
race-based alarm triggers 24
race-based appraisal 192, 196
race-based distress 41, 48, 51–52; cues 11, 39, 189, 200; *see also* race distress cues
race-based events/incidents 17, 20–21, 24–28, 29, 40–43, 48, 55, 187–189, 196
race-based murders 54
race-based stress 16–18, 20, 26, 38, 58, 186; *see also* racial stress
race-based trauma 5, 16–17, 20, 48, 185; *see also* racial trauma
race-based triggers 39, 41–42, 46, 48; *see also* race-based alarm triggers
race distress cues 13, 24, 42, 54, 194–195; *see also* racial distress cues
race identity 54, 195
race matters 21, 32, 45, 47, 53, 65, 68, 71, 102, 110–113, 161, 171–172, 188, 200, 202
race-stress cue 188
racial assaults 11, 40, 186, 189; external 13
racial-based alarm signals 24; *see also* race-based triggers
racial discrimination 5, 10, 16–17, 30, 36, 156, 185, 194, 196
racial distress cues 24–25, 40, 50, 55, 108–109, 141, 188, 195–196, 201
racial group membership 60
racial harassment 17, 37
racial identity 11, 20, 25–28, 30, 35, 40–41, 44–46, 54–55, 60, 68, 71, 135, 162, 186, 188–189, 192, 200, 202; development 13, 32, 52–53, 63, 161–162, 172, 188, 200; stress 37; stages of 19–22; threats 26, 37; *see also* racial-identity stress
racial-identity stress 37; *see also* racial stress
racial priming 25, 201
racial stereotypes 18, 29–30, 45, 172
racial stress 27, 63, 202
racial trauma 11, 16, 27, 33, 36, 39, 53, 65, 150–151, 155, 186, 195
racism 4, 7–8, 10, 16–17, 21, 24, 28, 30, 32–33, 40, 43, 51, 53, 101, 158, 161, 172, 201–202; anti- 12; structural 185, 202; *see also* anti-Black racism; aversive racism; internalized racism; structural racism; systemic anti-Black racism
racism-based psychology 199
racist jokes 26

Index 219

racist stereotypes 4, 8; *see also* racial stereotypes
rageful violence 178
reactive cycle 70, 106, 118
reactive emotions 37–38, 58, 66, 70, 72, 79, 101, 103, 105–107, 113, 118, 141–142, 163
Reconstruction 3
redlined communities 46, 74; *see also* redlining
redlining 63, 155, 187, 196, 202
re-engagement *see* withdrawer re-engagement (WRE)
reflecting/reflection *see* empathic reflection/reflecting
refugee experience 100, 105–106, 110–112
rejection 112, 130–132, 140
relationship bonds 6, 36, 65, 67, 162
relationship disappointments 168
relationship distress 8, 69, 160, 161, 191
relationship therapy 63; *see also* couples therapy
religious minority 111–112
resentment 121
resilience 133, 179
"respectability" politics 170
responding *see* evocative responding
response engagement 161
responsiveness 12–13, 17, 28, 31, 36, 39–41, 43, 58–63, 65–67, 69, 71–72, 74, 90–92, 113, 135, 140, 147, 150, 158, 173, 190–191, 201; un- 46
Rice, Tamir 54
RISSSC 72, 77–78, 102, 116, 127, 143, 146, 154, 157, 164, 167, 175
romantic relationships 6, 35–36, 48, 55, 78, 82, 85, 91, 118, 184, 202–203; stress and threats to 15–28; *see also* Black romantic relationship

sadness 36, 70, 83, 113, 133, 142, 144–148, 150, 152, 154, 179
safe haven 36, 58–62, 71, 102, 154
safe space 162, 168–169, 173–174, 200
secure base 25–26, 36, 59–62, 147, 152, 202
segregated communities 187
segregated housing 7, 155, 185
segregated schools 7, 74, 185
segregation 36, 52, 74, 155
self, sense of 5, 8, 16, 33, 63, 74, 106, 150, 155, 159, 198; *see also* self-acceptance; self-esteem; self-judgment; self-preservation; self-worth
self-acceptance 143

self-esteem 120–121, 155, 170
self-judgment 128, 134
self-preservation 131
self-worth 11, 16, 19–20, 25–26, 43, 46, 51, 63–64, 85, 129, 131, 133, 142
serious and persistent mental illness (SPMI) 118, 134
sexism 143
sexual desire 129–130
shame 21, 25, 39, 128, 134, 142, 158, 201
shaming 163
sibling relationship 143
skin color 29, 65, 155
slave labor camps 3, 10, 19, 29, 34, 57, 184, 189, 191–192
slave narratives 9, 15, 34, 36, 38, 51
slavery 1, 3–6, 8, 10–11, 15–16, 19, 22–24, 34, 36, 47, 57, 63, 65, 189; legacy (residual) of 11, 24, 47, 63, 65, 187, 189
slaves 2–4, 15, 22–23, 34, 57
slave stories 16
social bonding 58
social class 8, 30, 55, 65
social conditioning 30
social justice 134
South, the 3, 19, 57–58, 135, 162, 170–171
South Africa 53
spirituality 18, 22–23, 34, 36, 55, 119, 133
stereotypes 4–5, 8, 20–21, 30–31, 37, 54, 63, 96, 172, 185–186, 201–202; internalized 32, 188; negative 20–21, 54, 172, 188; *see also* racial stereotypes
stonewalling 64–66
street mentality 55
stressors 11–12, 17, 63, 110, 113, 115, 185, 188; macro- 188, 196; micro- 188, 196
Strong Black Women 26, 150, 172, 191
structural racism 185, 202
structured interview 68, 193
substance abuse 17, 68, 99, 169, 178
suicidality/suicidal ideations 121
Supreme Court 5
survival of the fittest 4
survival strategy 156, 178
systemic anti-Black racism 155

tango moves 48, 52, 69, 71, 137, 146, 155, 189, 200; *see also* kayaking tango
Taylor, Breonna 54
therapeutic alliance 107, 124, 128, 134; *see also* working alliance
therapists of color 28, 32, 68
Till, Emmett 54

tracking the cycle 77, 107, 121–128, 147, 154; *see also* negative dance
transatlantic slave labor trade 2–3, 9
transformational moment 183
trauma 38–39, 41, 49, 51, 59, 63–64, 91–92, 96, 98, 105, 108, 112, 134, 137–138, 140, 142–143, 150–151, 154, 156, 158–160, 178–179, 181, 185, 189, 191, 197; backgrounds 158; childhood 13, 179, 185; developmental 169; emotional 91, 128, 134; historical 64, 108, 110; history 13, 24, 36, 38, 66, 109, 159, 161, 178; intergenerational transmission of 19; psychological 3; survivors 36; *see also* attachment trauma; developmental trauma; family; Jim Crow era; "Post-Traumatic Slave Syndrome"; PTSD; race-based trauma; racial trauma
tribal community 1, 57
triggering events 192; *see also* race-based alarm triggers; race-based triggers; triggers
triggers 24, 28, 42–43, 46, 82, 94, 109, 132, 141, 178, 189; *see also* race-based alarm triggers; race-based triggers
trust 18, 37, 60, 74, 78, 88, 93–94, 107, 129–130, 137, 152, 167, 175, 177, 179–180, 182, 187, 190, 198; dis- 25, 92, 156; mis- 155, 174; relationship 18, 187; in therapy 37
"tying the bow" 46, 154, 175, 177

United States 3–7, 29–30, 53, 57–58, 63, 96, 101, 108, 112, 118, 120, 135, 155, 188
U.S. civil rights movement *see* civil rights movement

validation/validating 27–28, 36, 39, 67, 69–72, 77–78, 80, 86, 89–91, 93–94, 103–107, 109, 122, 124, 126–128, 131, 133–134, 136, 138, 143–144, 146–148, 154, 156–158, 160, 161, 163–166, 168–169, 188, 190–191, 201; in- 31, 165, 172
victim-blaming 163
victim system 18, 48, 65
victim values 65
voiceless-ness 8, 33, 49

vulnerability 20–21, 25, 37, 58–59, 61–63, 72, 83, 90–94, 101, 111, 113–114, 129, 137, 139, 142–143, 147–148, 156–157, 160, 161, 173–174, 178, 181, 183, 186, 190, 192, 200–201; in therapy 37; *see also* attachment vulnerability; emotional vulnerability

war on drugs 155, 158
wealth disparities 8
"we-ness" 3, 6, 18, 35–36
West Africa 3, 6, 22–23, 33–34, 36, 57, 60, 191
West Africans 36, 57, 60
Western society 22, 33, 57
White American culture 185; *see also* majority culture; White culture
White backlash 48
White culture 21, 53, 170
White fragility 47, 53, 189
White identity 47–48, 53; arrogance 48; development 42, 189; *see also* White racial identity
White privilege 47, 53, 189
White racial identity 25, 46, 188–189, 200
White social power 46
White social workers 150, 156, 158
White superiority 4
White therapist 29, 37, 52–53, 68, 151, 154–155, 192, 199–200
withdrawal 65, 69, 83, 98, 102, 108, 116, 123–124, 128, 139, 142, 145, 162, 168, 173–174, 188, 196–197; *see also* emotional withdrawal; pursue-withdraw cycle; withdrawer
withdrawal behaviors 128, 142
withdrawer 14, 39, 66, 72, 96, 98, 103, 115, 118, 146, 154, 156, 158–159, 161, 169, 172, 174, 179, 183, 202; critical 96, 98; *see also* confused withdrawer; withdrawer re-engagement (WRE)
withdrawer re-engagement (WRE) 13–14, 92, 140, 145–146, 155, 161
working alliance 31–32, 37, 54, 69, 71, 77, 79, 85, 107, 134, 145, 161, 185–186, 193, 201
working model of self and others 17, 38, 59–60, 71
World War II 7

Printed in the United States
by Baker & Taylor Publisher Services